Listening & Notetaking Skills

With Audioscripts

Phyllis L. Lim and William Smalzer

With

Lynn Bonesteel
Christine Salica Seal

Australia • Brazil • Japan • Korea • Mexico • Singapore • Spain • United Kingdom • United States

Listening and Notetaking Skills 2 With Audioscripts: Intermediate Listening Comprehension, Fourth Edition

Phyllis L. Lim and William Smalzer

Publisher: Sherrise Roehr

Executive Editor: Laura Le Dréan

Director of Global Marketing: Ian Martin

International Marketing Manager: Caitlin Thomas

Product Manager: Emily Stewart

Director, Content and Media Production: Michael Burggren

Content Project Manager: Andrea Bobotas

Print Buyer: Mary Beth Hennebury

Cover Designers: Christopher Roy and Michael Rosenquest

Cover Image: Paul Chesley/National Geographic Image Collection

Compositor: Page Designs International

Student Book With Audioscripts ISBN: 978-1-133-95060-8

National Geographic Learning
20 Channel Center Street
Boston, MA 02210
USA

Cengage Learning is a leading provider of customized learning solutions with office locations around the globe, including Singapore, the United Kingdom, Australia, Mexico, Brazil and Japan.

Cengage Learning products are represented in Canada by Nelson Education, Ltd.

Visit National Geographic Learning online at **ngl.cengage.com**

Visit our corporate website at **www.cengage.com**

Printed in the United States of America
4 5 6 7 8 20 19 18

CONTENTS

SCOPE AND SEQUENCE

Notetaking Preparation	Expansion	Unit Video
• Number Notation	**Reading:** Crowding Our Planet	
• Recording Dates • Names of Countries and Peoples	**Reading:** Climate Change Creating Millions of "Eco Refugees," UN Warns	
• Using Symbols and Abbreviations 1	**Reading:** Boomtowns: China's Instant Cities	
• Listening for Key Content Words	**Reading:** Female Empowerment in Brazil and its Effect on the Fertility Rate	
• Using Indentation to Organize Notes 1	**Reading:** The Geography of Religion	
• Using Symbols and Abbreviations 2	**Reading:** African Marriage Rituals	
• Transition Words and Phrases	**Reading:** Marseille's Melting Pot	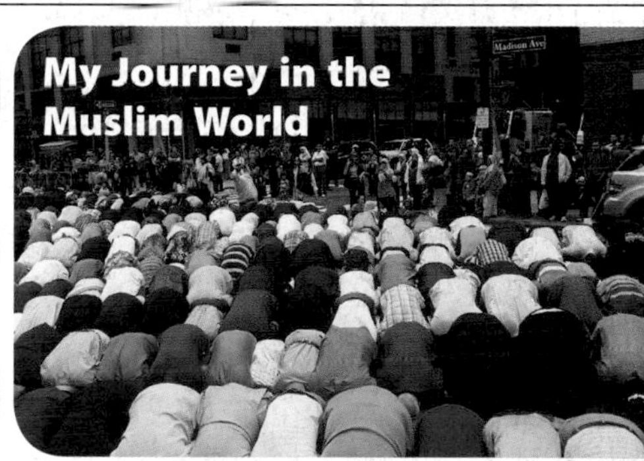
• Using Indentation to Organize Notes 2	**Reading:** The Singapore Solution	
• Acronyms and Abbreviations 1	**Reading:** Can China Go Green?	
• Using Outline Form with Letters and Numbers	**Reading:** China's Sudden Prosperity Brings New Freedoms and Anxieties	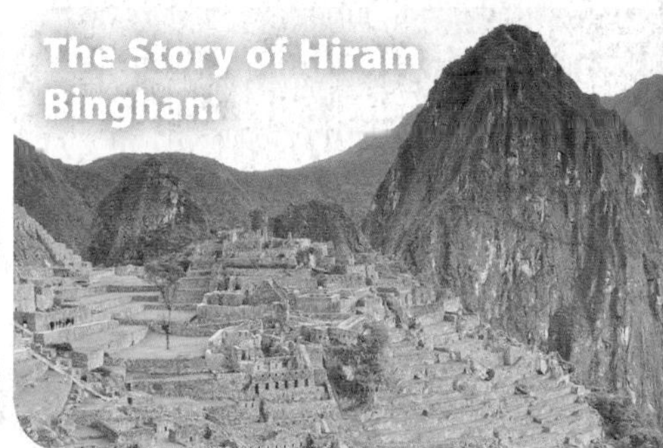
• Acronyms and Abbreviations 2	**Reading:** International Ranking of Systems of Higher Education	
• Reviewing Basic Notetaking Skills	**Reading:** Rising Numbers of Americans Study Abroad	
• Preparing for the Lecture by Reading	**Reading:** Bhutan's Enlightened Experiment	
• Pre-Lecture Reading and Key Words	**Reading:** The World According to Rome	
• Pre-Lecture Reading and Abbreviations and Symbols	**Reading:** Experimenting with the Jury System	

New to This Edition

- Authentic **National Geographic videos** provide a meaningful context for discussion and application of essential listening, notetaking, and vocabulary skills.
- New and updated **academic lectures** offer compelling, cross-curricular content that simulate authentic scenarios for maximum academic readiness.
- Every unit introduces a focused aspect of **notetaking** and provides varied opportunities for practice and application of the skill.

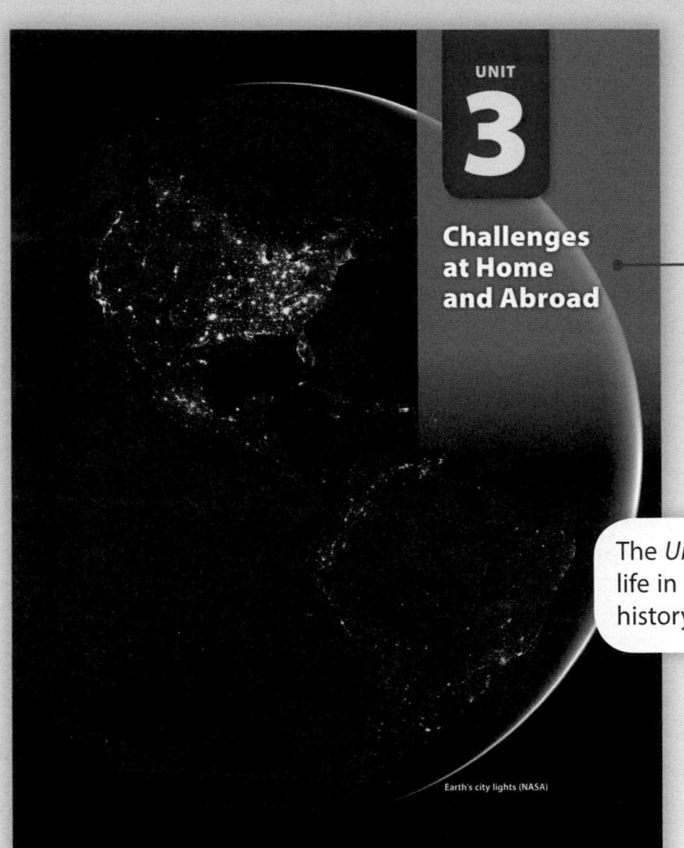
UNIT
3
Challenges at Home and Abroad

Earth's city lights (NASA)

The *Unit Theme* focuses on different aspects of life in the United States through lectures on history, politics, and the educational system.

Before Listening activities prepare students for success by activating background knowledge and providing the language and skills necessary for comprehension.

CHAPTER
9

The United States and the World

TOPIC PREVIEW

Discuss the following questions with a partner or your classmates.

1. Ten years from now, which country, or countries, do you think will be the most powerful in the world?
2. What kinds of responsibilities, if any, do powerful countries have to other countries?
3. Rank these three kinds of power in order from most to least important: (a) military, (b) economic, (c) political. Explain your reasons.

Coke bottle design contest held in Nanjing, China.

80 Unit 3 • Challenges at Home and Abroad

BEFORE LISTENING

VOCABULARY PREVIEW

CD 1, TR 11

A **Read through the sentences below, which are missing vocabulary from the lecture. As you read, try to imagine which words would fit in the blanks. Then listen to the sentences and write the missing words in the blanks.**

1. Some experts are ________________ that China will become the new global leader because of its size as well as its economic and military strength.
2. It seems very likely that the United States will remain very important globally, at least for the ________________ future.
3. The United States can also help maintain financial ________________ in the world because of the size of its economy.
4. I'm describing hard power—that is, the ________________ or use of force.
5. This force can be economic, which would include ________________ against trading with a country.
6. For better or for worse, the United States has taken on the role of keeping a certain ________________ of power in many parts of the world.
7. The United States is also a member of NATO, an organization of mostly European nations ________________ to keeping peace in the world.
8. ASEAN countries like Indonesia and Malaysia engage in massive trade with China and may at times feel a little ________________ by China's size and power.
9. Soft power does not come from economic or military threat, but from how attractive or ________________ a country's culture, political ideals, and policies are.
10. The United States is still a ________________ to immigrants for both political and economic reasons.
11. My goal today was to give you a ________________ for understanding some of what you learn in the media about the U.S. economic, military, and political influence in the world today.

B **Check the spelling of the vocabulary words with your teacher. Discuss the meanings of these words and any other unfamiliar words in the sentences.**

PREDICTIONS

Think about the questions in the Topic Preview on page 80 and the sentences you heard in the Vocabulary Preview. Write three questions that you think will be answered in the lecture. Share your questions with your classmates.

Chapter 9 • The United States and the World 81

The *Notetaking Preparation* section presents a variety of effective notetaking techniques. Using content from the unit, students practice these techniques in authentic academic situations.

NOTETAKING PREPARATION

Acronyms and Abbreviations 1

Acronyms are formed from the first letter of each word in a group or name. They are pronounced as words. For example, BRIC, which stands for Brazil, Russia, India, and China, is pronounced /brɪk/.

Abbreviations, like UN (United Nations), are different from acronyms and are pronounced letter by letter. Two common abbreviations usually used only in written language come from Latin: *e.g.*, used for "for example," and *i.e.*, used for "that is."

A **Practice saying these acronyms and abbreviations with a partner.**

1. NATO (North Atlantic Treaty Organization /ˈneɪ.t̬oʊ/)
2. ASEAN (Association of Southeast Asian Nations /əˈziː.ən/),
3. UNESCO (United Nations Educational, Social, and Cultural Organization /juːˈnes.koʊ/)
4. EU (European Union)

CD 3, TR 14 **B** **Listen and complete the following sentences using acronyms and abbreviations.**

1. Many countries have better economies, ______, ______.
2. ______ is an important arm of the ______.
3. France is a member of ______.
4. Some ______ countries are small, ______, Cambodia.
5. Some people think the ______ countries should become a federation, ______, have a political structure that is similar to the ______.

C **Discourse Cues** **Number the following excerpts from the lecture from 1 to 5 in the order that you think you will probably hear them. Discuss with a partner or as a class the discourse cues that helped you figure out the order.**

____ First, let me give you some of the economic reasons Yetiv gives for why the United States will probably continue to be an important player globally.

____ Now let's move on to the United States' use of what I'm describing today as hard power—that is, the threat or use of force.

____ Professor Steve Yetiv of Old Dominion University in Virginia wrote three articles in which he gave a number of reasons why believes the United States will remain a global leader.

____ Today I'd like to discuss the role of the United States in the world.

____ Soft power does not come from economic or military threat, but from how attractive or persuasive a country's culture, political ideals, and policies are.

82 Unit 3 • Challenges at Home and Abroad

Notetaking Skills

Throughout the *Listening & Notetaking Skills* series, learners develop a wide variety of notetaking strategies necessary for academic success. Learners are taught the essential principles of notetaking and encouraged to personalize the strategies for maximum results.

Listening sections introduce the academic lecture. Learners listen to the lecture three times, focusing on a different listening and notetaking skill with each repetition.

LISTENING

FIRST LISTENING

CD 3, TR 15

Listen to the lecture and take notes. Look at the lecturer's visual aids as you listen. These may help you understand parts of the lecture.

Introduction

The U.S. and the World
- Introduction
- The U.S. economy
- U.S. hard power
- U.S. soft power

Subtopic 1: ______

Economic Reasons
- Ability to help others in crisis
- Ability to maintain financial stability
- U.S. dollar = global currency

Subtopic 2: ______

Hard Power
- Middle East
- NATO
- ASEAN

Chapter 9 • The United States and the World 83

Subtopic 3: ______

Soft Power
- Democracy
- Economic competitiveness
- Education

SECOND LISTENING

CD 3, TR 16

Listen to the lecture again and make your notes as complete as possible.

THIRD LISTENING

CD 3, TR 17 **A** **You will hear part of the lecture again. Listen and complete the notes by adding the information from the box.**

ASEAN	econ	force	Mid	NATO	wrld	&

Hard Power = threat or use of ______
- *______*
  sanctions
- *mil*
  US role = bal of power in ______
  - *______ East (free flow of oil)*
  - *Europe – ______ (organ of Eur ntns keep peace in wrld)*
  - *Asia – bal bet. ASEAN ______ China*
    ______ incld e.g. Indonesia, Malaysia

B **Compare your answers with a partner. Then compare the notes in A with the notes you took for this part of the lecture.**

84 Unit 3 • Challenges at Home and Abroad

After Listening sections provide learners with opportunities to test their knowledge of the lecture and to discuss its content through pair and group activities.

AFTER LISTENING

ACCURACY CHECK

CD 1, TR 18

A Listen to the following questions, and write short answers. Use your notes. You will hear each question one time only.

1. ______
2. ______
3. ______
4. ______
5. ______
6. ______
7. ______
8. ______
9. ______
10. ______

B Check your answers with your teacher. If your score is less than 70 percent, you may need to listen to the lecture again and rewrite some of your notes.

The *Oral Summary* asks learners to use their notes to reconstruct the content of the lecture.

ORAL SUMMARY

Use your notes to create an oral summary of the lecture with your partner. As you work together, add details to your notes that your partner included but you had missed.

Through guided prompts, *Discussion* activities provide opportunities for learners to hone communicative and critical thinking skills.

DISCUSSION

Discuss the following questions with a classmate or in a small group.

1. Which of the four BRIC nations, besides China, is most likely to be the next superpower?
2. Would the world be a safer place if the United States were less powerful?
3. In what ways are economic sanctions preferable to military force?
4. What are the advantages of having more than one superpower in the world? What are the disadvantages?

Chapter 9 • **The United States and the World** **85**

An *Expansion* section in each chapter includes high-interest National Geographic articles that present information related to the unit theme.

EXPANSION

PRE-READING

The following Reading is about China's rapid economic growth. Before you read, answer the following questions. Share your answers with a classmate.

1. Look at the title of the article. What do you think "Go Green" means?
2. Scan the article for sentences that mention the United States. What comparisons does the writer make between the United States and China?

READING

Now read the article.

Can China Go Green?

Rizhao, in Shandong Province, is one of the hundreds of Chinese cities beginning to really grow. The road into town is eight-lanes wide, even though at the moment there's not much traffic. But the port is very busy. A big sign tells the residents to "build a civilized city and be a civilized citizen."

Rizhao is the kind of place that has scientists around the world deeply worried—China's rapid growth and new wealth are pushing carbon emissions higher and higher. It's the kind of growth that has led China to pass the United States to become the world's largest source of global warming gases.

And yet, after lunch at the Guangdian Hotel, the city's chief engineer, Yu Haibo, led me to the roof of the restaurant for another view. First we climbed over the hotel's solar-thermal system, a system that takes the sun's energy and turns it into all the hot water the kitchen and 102 rooms can possibly use. Then, from the edge of the roof, we looked at the view of the spreading skyline. On top of every single building a similar solar system could be seen. Solar is in at least 95 percent of all the buildings, Yu said proudly. "Some people say 99 percent, but I'm shy to say that."

Whatever the percentage, it's impressive—outside Honolulu, no city in the United States even comes close. China now leads the planet in energy produced by renewable solar and wind energy sources.

So, which is true? Is China the world's largest producer of global warming gases? Or is it the world's largest producer of renewable energy? The truth is, it's both.

Here's what we know: China is growing faster than any other big country has ever grown before, and that growth is opening real opportunities for environmental progress. Because it's putting up so many new buildings and power plants, the country can incorporate the latest technology more easily than countries with more mature economies. It's not just solar and wind energy. Some 25 Chinese cities are putting in subway systems or adding to existing ones. High-speed rail tracks are spreading in every direction. But all that growth takes lots of steel and cement, and as a result pours carbon into the air, which overwhelms the environmental progress. According to many energy experts, China's carbon emissions will continue to rise until at least 2030. This means that environmental progress in China will probably come too late to prevent more dramatic global warming, which could lead to environmental disasters such as the melting of the Himalayan glaciers and the rise of the seas.

It's a dark picture. Changing it in any real way will require change beyond China—most important, some kind of international agreement involving economies that use the most carbon—including of course the United States. At the moment China is taking steps that make sense for both the environment and its economy. "Why would they want to waste energy?" Deborah Seligsohn of the World Resources Institute asked, adding that "if the U.S. changed the game in a fundamental way—if it really committed to dramatic reductions—then China would look beyond its domestic interests and perhaps go much further." But for the moment, China's growth will continue, a roaring fire that throws off green sparks but burns with dangerous heat.

86 Unit 3 • **Challenges at Home and Abroad**

DISCUSSION

Discuss these questions with a classmate.

1. How is the focus of the lecture different from the focus of the article? Are there topics in the reading that are not mentioned in the lecture? Are there topics in the lecture that are not mentioned in the reading?
2. Do you think the author of the article would agree with the lecturer's view of the importance of the United States as a global power? Why or why not?
3. Do you think the lecturer would agree with the author of the article about the importance of China as a global power? Why or why not?

PURSUING THE TOPIC

Explore the topic of this chapter further by doing the following.

Watch a short YouTube video in which Professor Joseph Nye from Harvard's Kennedy School of Government speaks to Knoowii TV about the use of hard power, soft power, and smart power in international relations. Be prepared to discuss the ideas in the video with your classmates.

www.youtube.com/watch?v=cH9hn3_Q4qQ

Chapter 9 • **The United States and the World** **87**

In *Pursuing the Topic*, students are encouraged to go online or watch a movie to explore further the topic of the lecture.

Unit Video

Each unit ends with an authentic **National Geographic** video that is related to the unit theme. Most of the videos are in a lecture format, giving students a further opportunity to practice notetaking skills.

UNIT 3 VIDEO

My Journey in the Muslim World

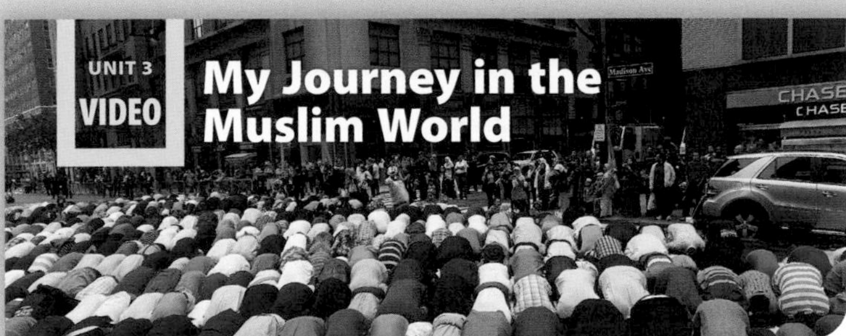

BEFORE VIEWING

TOPIC PREVIEW

Alexandra Avakian is a photojournalist. She was asked to take photographs of Muslims living in the United States. Answer the following questions with a partner.

1. What images or scenes would you expect to see in her photographs?
2. What different types of people would you expect to see in her photographs?
3. Do you think that Muslims in America have more or fewer difficulties than other immigrants living in the United States? Why or why not?

VOCABULARY PREVIEW

A **Read the definitions of these key words and phrases that you will hear during the video.**

engaged in actively involved in or part of something
an expert a person having a lot of knowledge about a particular topic
post 9/11 after the September 11, 2001, attack on the United States
fled left an area quickly in order to escape danger
reflected shown on a surface such as a mirror; seen in a person's expression
mainstream average; usual for the typical people in a group
are converting to are changing from one belief system, such as a religion, to a new one
maximum-security prison a prison where the most dangerous criminals are kept
protective keeping someone or something safe from harm

B **Work with a partner and write in the blank the word from the box that completes the sentence.**

artistic	civil war	pressure	security
Catholics	granddaughter	relatives	village

1. The ________________ she was under was **reflected** in her face.
2. The man was not an **expert** photographer, but his photos were very ________________.
3. The ________________ were very **protective** of their young ________________.
3. **Post 9/11**, there has been increased ________________ at U.S. airports.
4. There are **mainstream** ________________ who **are converting to** Islam.
5. The whole ________________ was very **engaged in** preparations for the fair.
6. Some people **fled** during the ________________; others were placed in a **maximum-security prison**.

VIEWING

FIRST VIEWING

Watch the video, and then compare your first impressions with a partner. Talk about what you remember, what surprised you, and what interested you.

SECOND VIEWING

Watch the video again. Listen for the missing words and write them in the blanks.

1. I hope to ________________ a wider view of a group of people much misunderstood, especially ________________ 9/11.
2. And these are Ryazan ________________, and they're an alternative, Islamic alternative to Barbie.
3. And you know Muslim Americans, like all Americans, have fled civil war, dictatorship, ________________ hardship.
4. These are Persian Americans, Iranian Americans, and they jump over ________________ on their New Year to cast off the bad luck of the previous year, you know, for good luck in the ________________ year.

Islamic Center, Dearborn, Michigan

88 Unit 3 • Challenges at Home and Abroad

Unit 3 • Video Lesson 89

Listening and Notetaking Skills Series Components

The Audio CDs provide all the lectures and listening activities contained in the Student Book.

The Video DVD contains five authentic **National Geographic** videos relating to the units in the book.

UNIT

1

The Face of the People

CHAPTER

1

The Population

TOPIC PREVIEW

Answer the following questions with a partner or your classmates.

1. Do the people you see in the picture here match your idea of the kinds of people who live in the United States? In what ways?
2. Do you think there are more old people or more young people in the United States?
3. Would you guess that the U.S. population has increased or decreased since the census in 2010? Why?

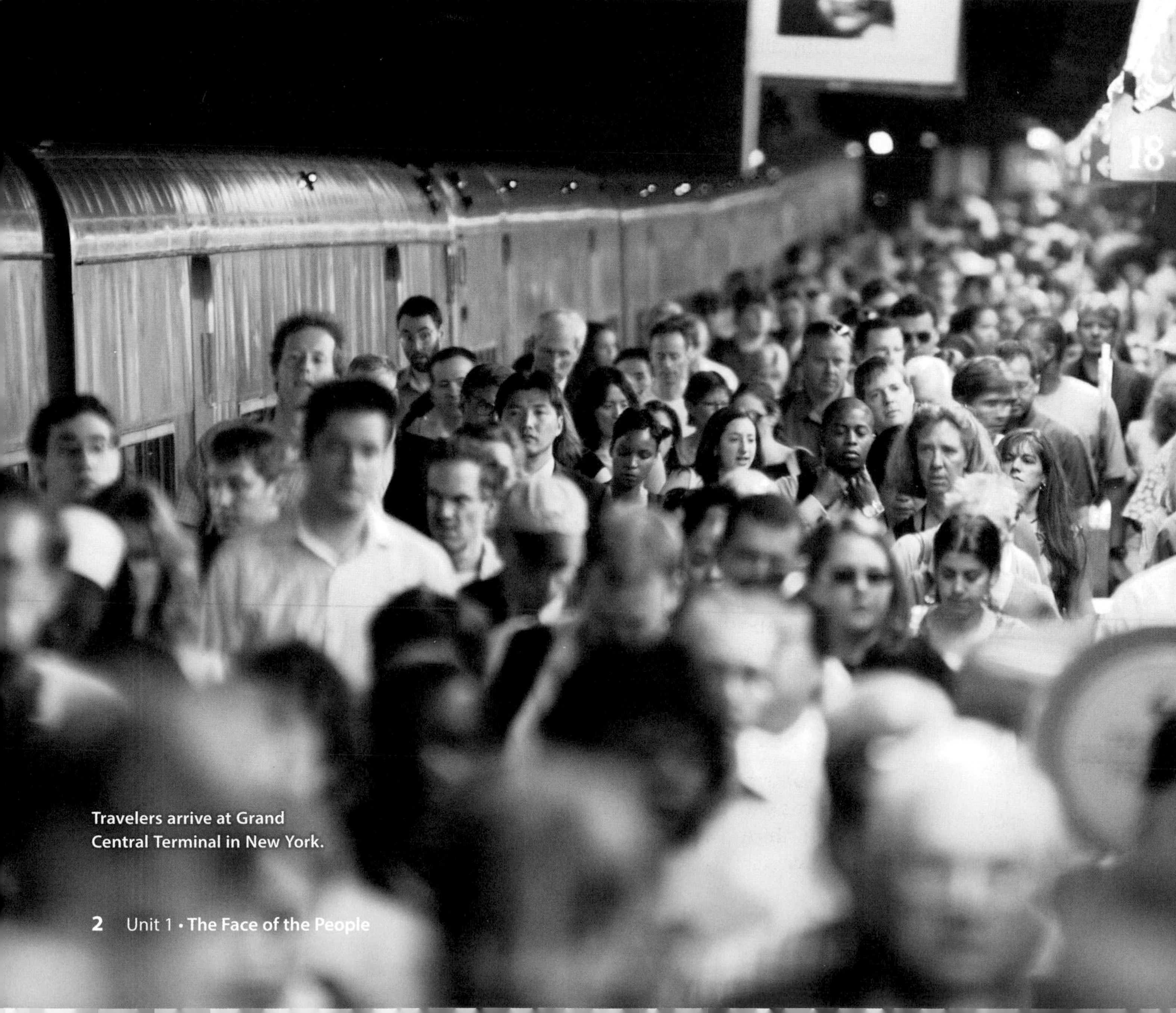

Travelers arrive at Grand Central Terminal in New York.

BEFORE LISTENING

VOCABULARY PREVIEW

CD 1, TR 1

A **Read through the sentences below, which are missing vocabulary from the lecture. As you read, try to imagine which words would fit in the blanks. Then listen to the sentences and write the missing words in the blanks.**

1. Most countries take a ____________ every 10 years or so in order to count the people and to know where they are living.
2. A country with a growing population is a country that is becoming more ____________.
3. A person's ____________ is partly determined by skin color and type of hair as well as other physical characteristics.
4. The majority of the U.S. population is of European ____________.
5. The ____________ distribution of a country's population gives information about where the people are living.

6. Many different kinds of people ____________ the total U.S. population. In other words, people of different races and ages ____________ up the population.
7. The median age of the U.S. population, which is a ____________ large one, has been getting ____________ higher recently.
8. ____________ areas are more ____________ populated than rural areas. That is, they have more people per square mile.
9. I want to discuss the distribution of the U.S. population in terms of age and ____________.
10. In fact, ____________, women generally live longer than men worldwide.
11. A country whose ____________ rate is higher than its death rate will have an ____________ population.
12. On the average, women have a higher life ____________ than men do.

B **Check the spelling of the vocabulary words with your teacher. Discuss the meanings of these words and any other unfamiliar words in the sentences.**

PREDICTIONS

Think about the questions in the Topic Preview on page 2 and the sentences you heard in the Vocabulary Preview. Write three questions that you think will be answered in the lecture. Share your questions with your classmates.

NOTETAKING PREPARATION

Number Notation

During a lecture, you will sometimes need to write down many numbers. They may be expressed as whole numbers, percentages, fractions, or ratios. Here are some ways to write them as numerals when you are taking notes.

Whole numbers:	thirty-seven million	37 mill. or 37M
	four hundred ninety-five thousand	495,000 or 495 thou or 495K
Fractions:	three-fourths, three-quarters	3/4
	two-thirds	2/3
	one and a half	1 1/2
Percentages:	thirteen point four percent	13.4%
	zero point nine percent	0.9%
Ratios:	two out of ten	2:10

CD 1, TR 2

A You will hear ten numbers. As you listen, write them in notetaking form in the spaces below.

1. ______________ 6. ______________
2. ______________ 7. ______________
3. ______________ 8. ______________
4. ______________ 9. ______________
5. ______________ 10. ______________

Discourse Cues A discourse cue is a word, phrase, or sentence that a lecturer uses to help you follow the flow of ideas in a lecture. It often lets you know that a new subtopic or point is being introduced.

B Number the following excerpts from the lecture from 1 to 5 in the order that you think you will probably hear them. Discuss with a partner or as a class the discourse cues that helped you figure out the order.

_____ Another way of looking at the population is by geographical distribution.

_____ Today we're going to talk about population in the United States.

_____ First of all, let's take a look at the population by race and origin.

_____ Now, to finish up this section on geographical distribution, consider that about 83 percent of the people live in metropolitan areas,

_____ Before we finish today, I want to discuss the distribution of the U.S. population in terms of age and gender.

FIRST LISTENING

CD 1, TR 3

A **Listen to the beginning of the lecture. Circle the set of notes below that best records the information you hear.**

a.

Pop of US
2010, 309M (27M more since 2000)
US 3rd most pop in wrld
most PRCh, 2nd India, 4 Indonesia, 5 Brazil, 6 Pakistan
US pop – look at 3 ways
Race & origin – % wht/blk/etc; where fr
Geog. distrib – where live
Age & gender

b.

US gov't census 2010
US pop = 309M – 27M more 2000
US 3rd most pop in wrld
1st China
2nd India
4th 5th 6th – Indonesia Brazil Pakistan
In notes – 1st pop by race and origin, 2nd by geographical distribution, last by age and gender

CD 1, TR 4

B **Now listen to the whole lecture and take notes. Look at the lecturer's visual aids as you listen. These may help you understand parts of the lecture.**

Subtopic 1: Population by Race and Origin

US Population by Race and Origin

Percentage: 0, 20, 40, 60, 80

White, Black, Asian, Mixed, American Indian, Native Hawaiian and Pacific Islander, Other

Subtopic 2: Population by Geographical Distribution

Subtopic 3: Population by Age and Gender

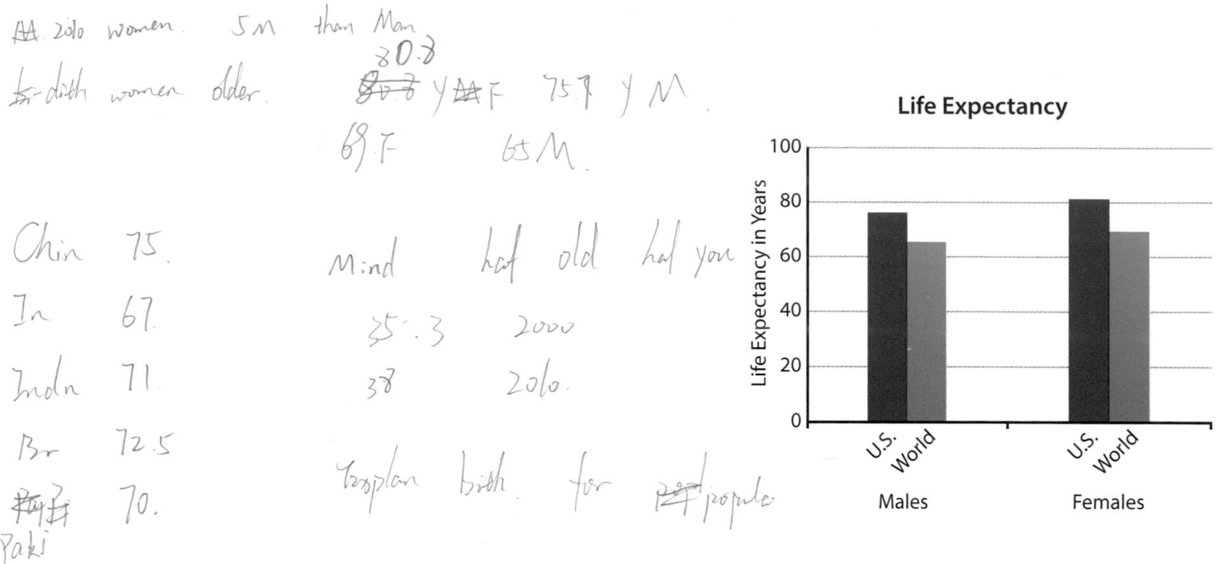

SECOND LISTENING

CD 1, TR 5

Listen to the lecture again and make your notes as complete as possible.

THIRD LISTENING

CD 1, TR 6

A **You will hear part of the lecture again. Listen and complete the notes by adding the information from the box.**

19M–	2:10	pop	metro	TEX	W.

5 most pop states:
CA 37M+; __________ 25M+; NY 19M+; FL __________; ILL 13M
- 50%+ pop in S. & __________
But E = more dense __________
- 83% in __________ areas (LA, NY, Chicago, Houston)
< __________ in rural areas

B **Compare your answers with a partner. Then compare the notes in A with the notes you took for this part of the lecture.**

ACCURACY CHECK

CD 1, TR 7

A **Listen to the following questions, and write short answers. Use your notes. You will hear each question one time only.**

1. ? pop M for China India.
2. ? lage pop than U.S.? U.S pop in 2010? 309M.
3. ~~U.S pop in 2010~~ Black or Hispan wich bigger? Hisp.
4. Popluer FL TEX.? TEX.
5. ? Pagen Count most US Live? SW
6. rasio Pop live in rural areas.? 21%.
7. ~~How~~ How many W than M in U.S pop? 5M
8. How many year longer W than M in U.S? 5Y
9. Mind age incares in 2000 to 2010 35.3 2000 to 38. 2010.
10. ? Facta in cares in Mide Mind age? Pergera life expetiay.

B **Check your answers with your teacher. If your score is less than 70 percent, you may need to listen to the lecture again and rewrite some of your notes.**

ORAL SUMMARY

Use your notes to create an oral summary of the lecture with your partner. As you work together, add details to your notes that your partner included but you had missed.

DISCUSSION

Discuss the following questions with a classmate or in a small group.

1. What points in the lecture surprised you? Why?
2. In what ways do you think the U.S. population will change in the future?
3. What population problems do other countries you know about face, for example, in terms of origins, age, or number of males and females?
4. What population issues might become more important as the world moves toward a population of 8 billion people?

PRE-READING

The following Reading is about population trends. Before you read, answer the following questions. Share your answers with a classmate.

1. The lecture was about the U.S. population. Look at the title of the article. What population will it be about? How do you think the author sees that population changing?
2. In what ways do you think worldwide population trends might be similar to U.S. population trends? In what ways might they differ?

READING

Now read the article.

Crowding Our Planet

As of 2009, there were 6.8 billion people in the world. This is twice the number of the population in 1960, and four times as much as 100 years ago. As a result, more and more places on the globe are incredibly crowded. This is especially true of cities along the coasts, where more and more people are settling. Yet a full city today can mean an empty village or town across the country, or on the other side of the world. Our growth has taken place in surprising ways.

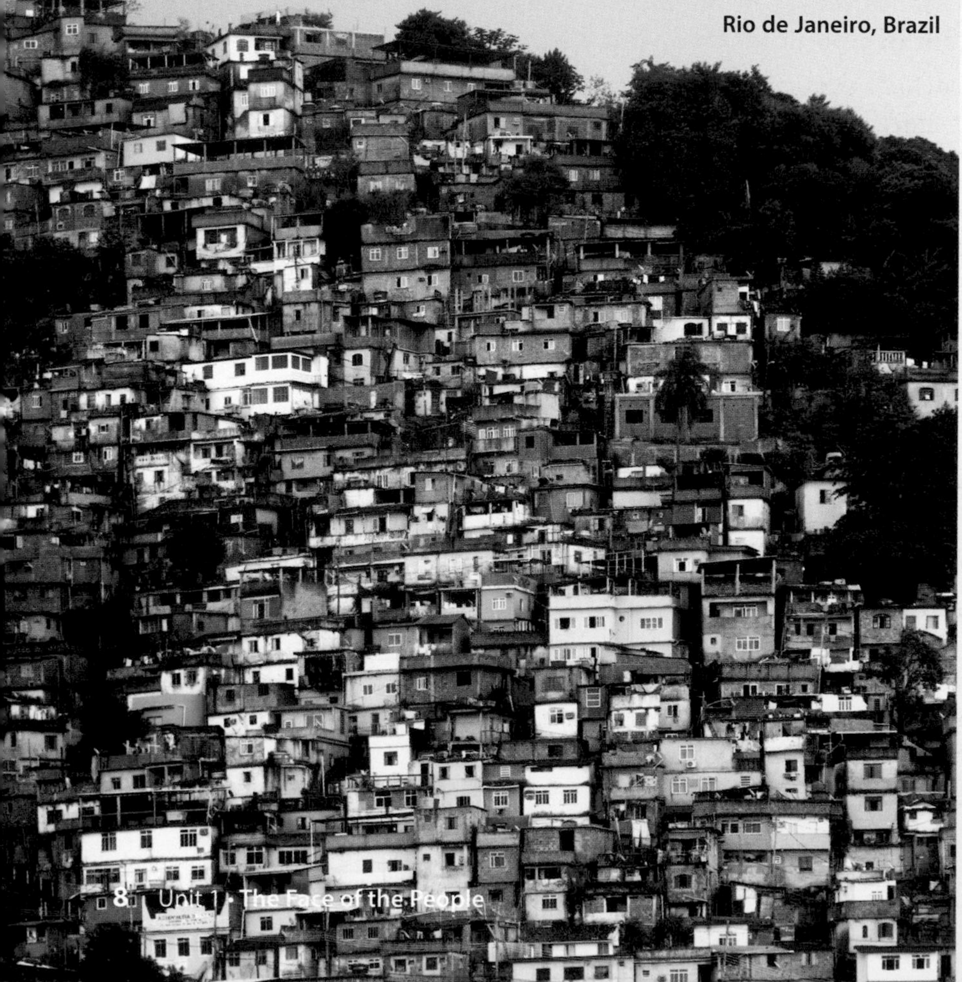
Rio de Janeiro, Brazil

The human population continues to expand by more than 200,000 people every day. There are more than 1 billion teenagers in the world today who will soon be having children. As a result, we can expect the boom in births to continue for a long time. The UN estimates that the global population will reach 9.2 billion by the middle of this century. Even that enormous number may be too small, however, since it is based on the theory that family sizes will drop throughout developing regions—a theory that may not turn out to be true.

From the crowded streets of Lagos and Mumbai (Bombay), to the suburbs of the United States, to disappearing tropical forests around the world, the harmful effects of more people than the planet can comfortably support are obvious almost anywhere we look.

Not all countries grow the same, of course. Almost all of the expected population increase in the near future will come in developing countries. In the advanced economies in much of Europe, however, where rapid growth started with the industrial revolution two centuries ago, and in Korea, Japan, and elsewhere, national populations are stable or, in some cases, are even getting smaller. This brings challenges of its own, as newer generations struggle to care for and support their elders.

Humanity is also on the move as never before. More than 3 percent of the global population—more than 200 million people—live outside their country of birth. Many millions more have moved, or been moved, within their home borders.

Our numbers and our mobility, together with improved communication, all make Earth seem smaller, even as our impact on it grows larger every day. If we are to preserve the biological wealth of our planet and increase the well-being of its people, we must first understand how and why our own population is changing.

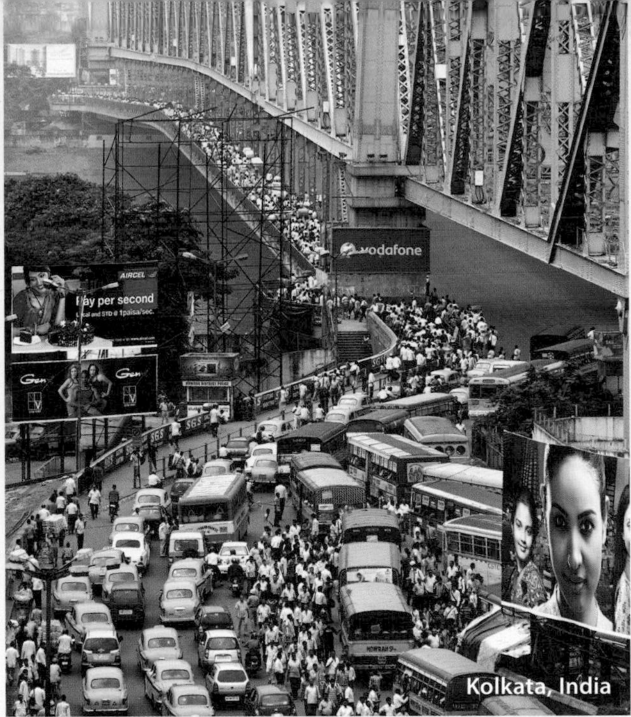

Kolkata, India

DISCUSSION

Discuss these questions with a classmate.

1. Based on what you know, which countries or regions mentioned in the article have populations that are most similar to the population of the United States? Which are the least similar?
2. Which of the U.S. population trends mentioned in the lecture are also true for the world population? Discuss race and origin, geographic distribution, and age and gender.
3. What problems related to population are mentioned in the article? Which of these problems apply to the United States?

PURSUING THE TOPIC

Explore the topic of this chapter further by doing the following.

Individually or with a partner, research population trends—racial composition, geographic distribution, age, and gender—for a country that interests you. Write down the details for a short presentation to the class. You can use the Web site listed below, consult a contemporary encyclopedia, or find another source by doing a Web search for the specific country in which you are interested.

www.cia.gov/library/publications/the-world-factbook/

CHAPTER

2

Immigration

TOPIC PREVIEW

Answer the following questions with a partner or your classmates.

1. What reasons might a person have for immigrating to a new country?
2. What challenges might immigrants face adjusting to a new culture? What personal qualities might people need to start life in a new culture?
3. Can immigration help the country from which the immigrants came? How?

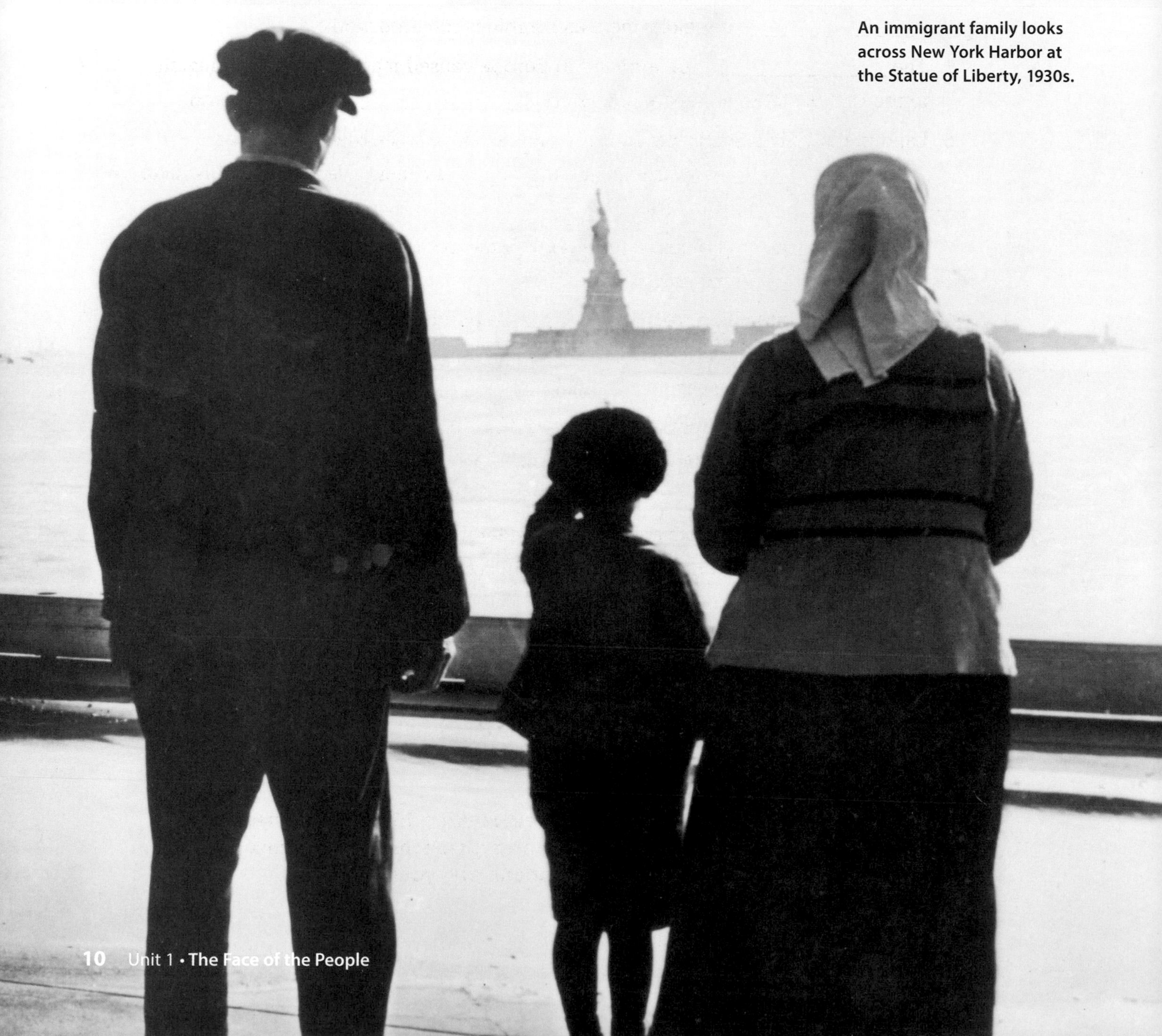

An immigrant family looks across New York Harbor at the Statue of Liberty, 1930s.

VOCABULARY PREVIEW

CD 1, TR 8

A Read through the sentences below, which are missing vocabulary from the lecture. As you read, try to imagine which words would fit in the blanks. Then listen to the sentences and write the missing words in the blanks.

1. Sometimes people immigrate to a new country to escape political or religious ________________.
2. Rather than immigrants, the early ________________ from Great Britain considered themselves ________________; they had left home to settle new land for the mother country.
3. The so-called Great Immigration, which can be divided into three ________________, or time periods, began about 1830 and lasted till about 1930.
4. The Industrial Revolution, which began in the nineteenth century, caused ________________ unemployment as machines replaced workers.
5. The ________________ of farmland in Europe caused many people to immigrate to the United States, where there was an ________________ of available land.
6. Land in the United States was plentiful and available when the country was ________________ westward. In fact, the U.S. government offered free public land to ________________ in 1862.
7. The failure of the Irish potato crop in the middle of the nineteenth century caused ________________ starvation.
8. The first law that limited the number of immigrants coming from a certain part of the world was the Chinese Exclusion Act of 1882, but in 1965 strict ________________ based on nationality were ________________.
9. This is the largest number of immigrants in history, although the ________________ of the total population, 12.8 percent, has been larger in the past.
10. Strict anti-immigration laws at the state or federal level and ________________ against employers who hire illegal immigrants could lead to a ________________ in immigration to the United States.

B Check the spelling of the vocabulary words with your teacher. Discuss the meanings of these words and any other unfamiliar words in the sentences.

PREDICTIONS

Think about the questions in the Topic Preview on page 10 and the sentences you heard in the Vocabulary Preview. Write three questions that you think will be answered in the lecture. Share your questions with your classmates.

NOTETAKING PREPARATION

Recording Dates

Hearing dates accurately and writing them down in your notes correctly are very important, but sometimes it can be difficult because we usually say dates two numbers at a time. For example, 1776 is said as *seventeen seventy-six*, and 2010 is often said as *twenty ten*. A whole decade is given as a plural: the 1940s / the nineteen forties.

Another difficulty is that it is easy to confuse *teens* and *tens*. For *teens*, both syllables are stressed—FIF TEEN—with slightly more stress on the second syllable. For *tens*, only the first syllable is stressed—FIF ty.

CD 1, TR 9

A **You will hear ten dates and phrases. As you listen, write each date or phrase in notetaking form in the spaces below.**

1. ______________
2. ______________
3. ______________
4. ______________
5. ______________
6. ______________
7. ______________
8. ______________
9. ______________
10. ______________

Names of Countries and Peoples

Greece or Greek? To take accurate notes of a lecture that includes many names of countries and peoples, you must know the terms used for each of them. The following few guidelines may help you.

- The plural for most nationalities is formed by adding -*s*: *a Mexican, Mexicans*.
- Nationalities ending in -*ese* can be singular or plural: *a Vietnamese, the Vietnamese*.
- When a nationality adjective ends in -*sh* or -*ch*, add *the* to mean the people of those countries: *the French*; *the British*.

CD 1, TR 10

B **Below is a list of countries and peoples that will be mentioned in the lecture. Fill in the missing words, then listen as the list is read and check your answers. Check the spelling with your teacher.**

	Country	People
1.	France	the French
2.	Germany	______________
3.	______________	Scots or the Scottish
4.	Ireland	______________

5. ______________________ the British or Britons

6. ______________________ Danes

7. ______________________ Norwegians

8. ______________________ Swedes

9. the Netherlands or Holland ______________________

10. Greece ______________________

11. ______________________ Italians

12. ______________________ the Spanish or Spaniards

13. ______________________ the Portuguese

14. China ______________________

15. ______________________ Filipinos

16. ______________________ Mexicans

17. India ______________________

18. ______________________ Russians

19. ______________________ Poles

20. Vietnam ______________________

C Answer the following questions with a partner or your classmates.

1. Which of the countries in the list in Exercise B are Scandinavian?
2. Which of the countries in the list in Exercise B are Southern European?
3. Which of the countries in the list in Exercise B are Eastern European countries?

D Discourse Cues Number the following excerpts from the lecture from 1 to 5 in the order that you think you will probably hear them. Discuss with a partner or as a class the discourse cues that helped you figure out the order.

_____ Now that we've talked about the historical situation, let's discuss the current situation with respect to immigration.

_____ Now that we know something about the numbers and origins of immigrants who came to the States during the Great Immigration, let's consider the reasons.

_____ Immigration declined somewhat after the Great Immigration.

_____ We'll begin our discussion today with the period of history called the Great Immigration.

_____ Last, it might be interesting to speculate on immigration in the future.

FIRST LISTENING

CD 1, TR 11

A **Listen to the beginning of the lecture. Circle the set of notes below that best records the information you hear.**

a.

Immigration
Early Britons
Settlers—no immig, mother country
  Dutch, French, Ger, Scot, Irish, Afr
  40% live in US spk Eng 1776
  Colonial period
  Immigration great in 1830
    1930 – reasons why great
    Decrease 1940
    1970 – US today

b.

Americans see nation of immigrants
Colonial peri
  Britons – settlers/colonists, not immig
    settle land for Gr Brit
  Dutch, French, Ger, Scot-Irish settlers
  African slaves
  independ from Gr Brit 1776
    40% not Brit, but maj. speak Eng
Great Immig 1830–1930
Reasons for Gr Immig
Decreased immig 1940–1970
Immig in US today

CD 1, TR 12

B **Now listen to the whole lecture and take notes. Look at the lecturer's visual aids as you listen. These may help you understand parts of the lecture.**

Subtopic 1: ______________________________

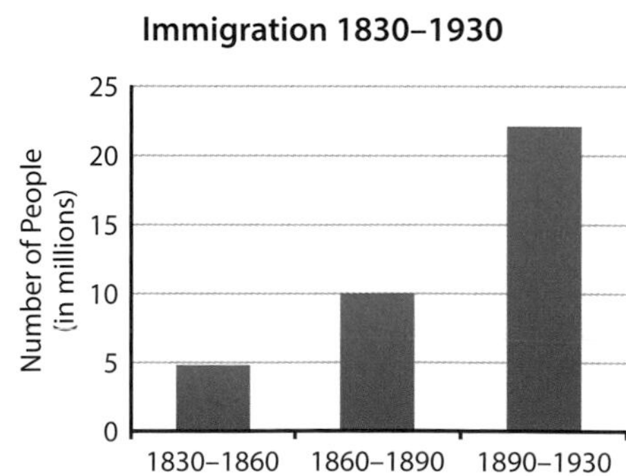

Subtopic 2: ______________________________

Causes

1. Doubling of European population 1750–1850
2. Industrial Revolution—Unemployment
3. Land scarcity in Europe
4. Religious and political persecution
5. Natural disasters

Subtopic 3: ______________________________

Decline

- Chinese Exclusion Act of 1882
- Great Depression of 1929
- World War II (1937–1945)

Subtopic 4: ___

Top Countries of Origin 2000–2010

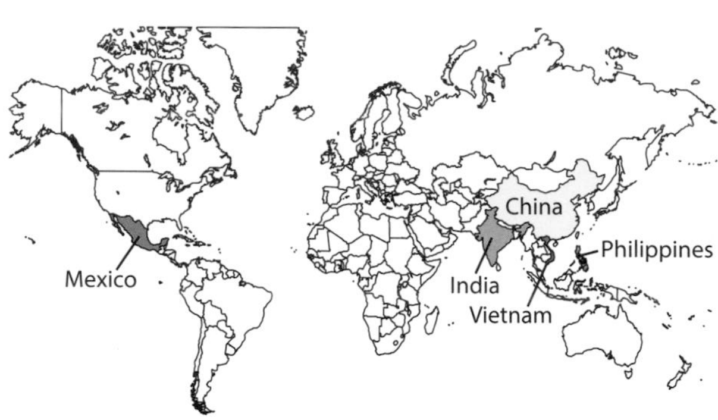

CD 1, TR 13

SECOND LISTENING

Listen to the lecture again and make your notes as complete as possible.

THIRD LISTENING

CD 1, TR 14

A **You will hear part of the lecture again. Listen and complete the notes by adding the information from the box.**

↑	1965	2000	12.8	3/4	Eur	VN

Immigr. ___ –Nat. quotas elim & ___ imm. since then

- 2010 40M imm (___ % ttl pop)
  ___ legal
- lgst # in histry
- NOT ___; 58% Lat Am (___ –2010)
  1. Mex 12M
  2. China
  3. India
  4. Phili.
  5. ___

B **Compare your answers with a partner. Then compare the notes in A with the notes you took for this part of the lecture.**

ACCURACY CHECK

CD 1, TR 15

A **Listen to the following questions, and write short answers. Use your notes. You will hear each question one time only.**

1. ______________________________
2. ______________________________
3. ______________________________
4. ______________________________
5. ______________________________
6. ______________________________
7. ______________________________
8. ______________________________
9. ______________________________
10. ______________________________

B **Check your answers with your teacher. If your score is less than 70 percent, you may need to listen to the lecture again and rewrite some of your notes.**

ORAL SUMMARY

Use your notes to create an oral summary of the lecture with your partner. As you work together, add details to your notes that your partner included but you had missed.

DISCUSSION

Discuss the following questions with a classmate or in a small group.

1. How different would the United States culture, economy, or its politics be today if there had been no immigration after the year 1900?
2. When discussing the history of immigration in the United States, do you think it is right to use the term *immigrants* for black Africans brought to the United States as slaves? Why or why not?
3. What are some of the benefits of having immigrants in a country? What are some of the disadvantages? Give specific examples.

PRE-READING

The following Reading is about environmental refugees. Before you read, answer the following questions. Share your answers with a classmate.

1. Look up the word *refugee* in a dictionary. What is the difference between an immigrant and a refugee? Which of the immigrants in the lecture could be described as refugees?
2. What do you think the term *environmental refugee* means? What kinds of environmental problems could cause people to leave their home countries?

READING

Now read the article.

Climate Change Creating Millions of "Eco Refugees," UN Warns

Environmental problems around the world are creating a new category of people known as "environmental refugees," says the United Nations University—Institute for Environment and Human Security (UNU-EHS). What's more, the number of these refugees is growing rapidly. There are at least 20 million environmental refugees worldwide, the group says.

UNU-EHS predicts that by 2010 the number of environmental refugees could grow to 50 million. According to other estimates, there could be as many as 150 million by 2050. That's why nations and aid groups need to immediately recognize and help this new category of refugee, UNU-EHS says. But helping them first requires a clear definition of an environmental refugee. "How you define somebody can be an issue of life and death for them," said Anthony Oliver-Smith, a University of Florida anthropologist who is a member of the UN group.

Global Warming Refugees?

Environmental disasters like Hurricane Katrina in New Orleans can destroy the homes of millions of people in a moment. But many other people are displaced by gradual environmental changes. And these changes may be linked to climate change.

In China, the Gobi desert expands more than 10,000 square miles each year, forcing many farmers there to leave, the UNU-EHS reports. Thousands of miles away in Alaska about 200 villages are in serious danger due to rising sea levels. The entire Inupiat village of Shishmaref is planning to move 13.5 miles inland in the next four years to avoid rising waters.

"Human migrations are expected to increase as average global temperatures continue to rise and we experience rising sea levels, more severe weather disasters, and other impacts as a result," said Janet Sawin, a climate change expert.

Gobi desert, Central Asia

Shishmaref, Alaska

Long-term drought, or lack of rain, another possible effect of global warming, could also force people to leave increasingly dry lands. Some people, who in the past would leave during the dry season and then come back after it rained, may decide never to return.

Because many environmental changes are ultimately caused by humans, some experts say the term *environmental refugee* is misleading. "It tends to suggest that nature is at fault, when in fact humans are deeply implicated in the environmental changes that make life impossible in certain circumstances," Oliver-Smith said.

What's In a Name?

While victims of political conflict are entitled to food and shelter through government and aid groups, environmental refugees are not yet recognized by international law. Some have pointed out that environmental change may be just one of many factors that cause people to leave their homes. But Oliver-Smith disagrees. "An environmental issue may not be the only thing driving people away, but it may be the big one," he said.

The UN university experts are now working to establish terms to define people who have been displaced by environmental change. Once this new class of refugee is defined, the UN experts say, work can begin on providing them with aid. "Despite the seriousness of these trends, the issue of environmental refugees has received scant attention at the highest level," said Rhoda Margesson, foreign affairs analyst with the U.S. Congressional Research Service in Washington, D.C.

DISCUSSION

Discuss these questions with a classmate.

1. Make a list of the reasons for immigration described in the lecture and those described in the article. Are any of these reasons the same? In what ways?
2. How are today's environmental refugees different from the immigrants who came to the United States in the nineteenth and twentieth centuries?
3. Based on what you learned in the lecture and the article, do you think the number of immigrants to the United States will increase or decrease in the next 50 years? Why?

PURSUING THE TOPIC

Explore the topic of this chapter further by doing the following.

Watch the documentary *The Other Side of Immigration*, directed by Roy Germano, available online at the Web page below. Be prepared to discuss it with your classmates.

www.theothersideofimmigration.com/HOME.html

CHAPTER 3

Work in America

TOPIC PREVIEW

Discuss the following questions with a partner or your classmates.

1. What type of work do you do now or hope to do in the future?
2. In what types of jobs do workers provide a service rather than produce something?
3. In which country do you think a larger percentage of the workforce is engaged in agriculture, the United States or China? Why do you think so?

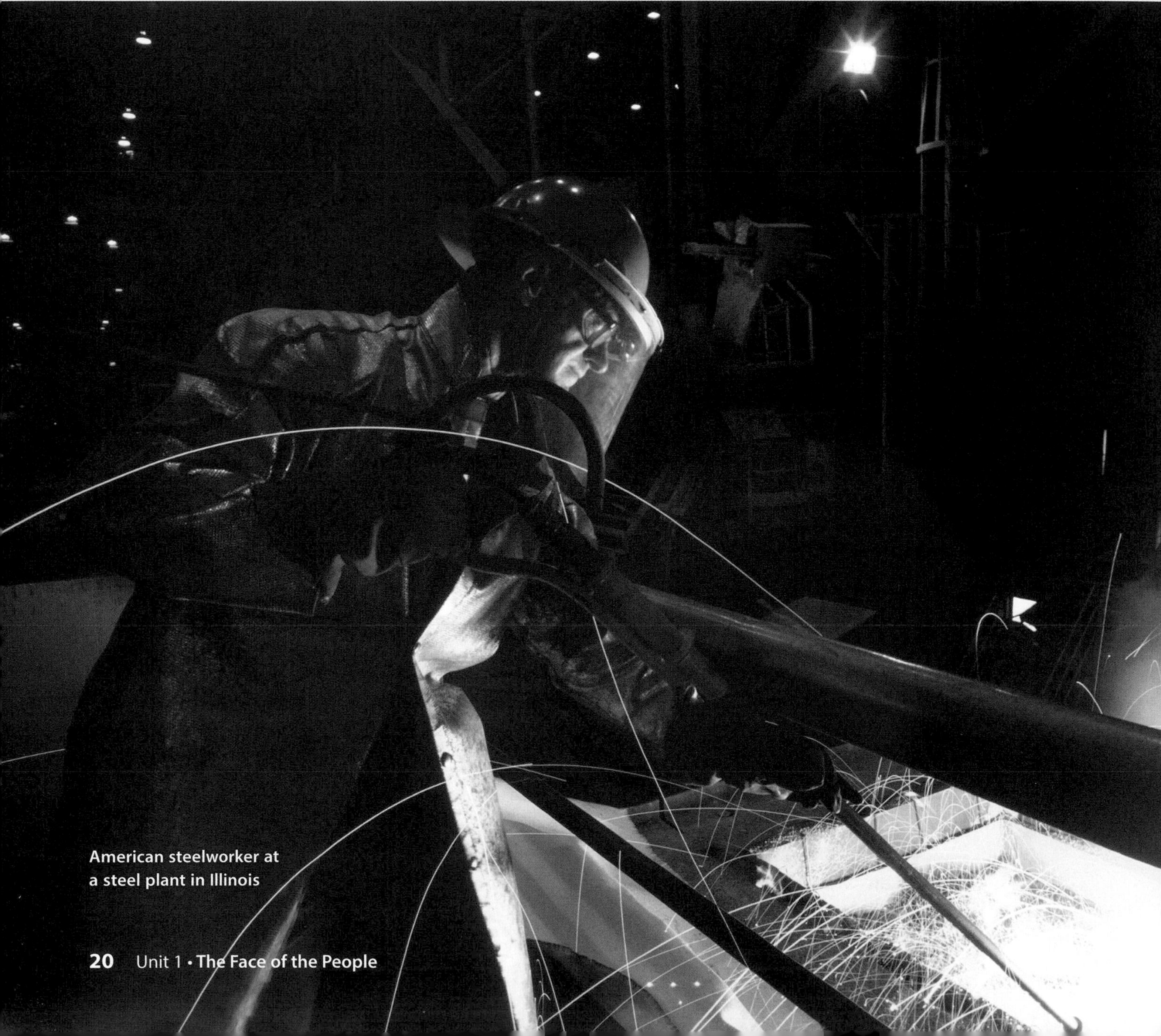

American steelworker at a steel plant in Illinois

VOCABULARY PREVIEW

CD 1, TR 16

A Read through the sentences below, which are missing vocabulary from the lecture. As you read, try to imagine which words would fit in the blanks. Then listen to the sentences and write the missing words in the blanks.

1. There was also a large ________________ in the number of people working in ________________, that is, in making, or manufacturing, things in factories.
2. While the number of people in agriculture and manufacturing industries went ________________, the number of people in the services went ________________ dramatically.
3. Over the years, child labor laws became much ________________ and by 1999, it was ________________ for anyone under 16 to work full-time in any of the 50 states.
4. In 1900, only 19 percent of women were ________________; in 2010, almost 73 percent of women were holding ________________ jobs.
5. For much of the twentieth century, U.S. workers saw rising ________________, increased benefits like Social ________________ and health insurance, and better working conditions.
6. While the productivity of the U.S. ________________ has continued to increase since the 1970s, wages for the working class have not increased.
7. Let me give you some statistics that may help you understand the impact of ________________ wages and high ________________.
8. Labor ________________, which protect workers' rights, have become weaker in the past decades.
9. Lack of regulation of financial institutions has led to very ________________ investments, which have led to loss of jobs, lost ________________, and loss of homes.
10. "Cautious ________________" about the U.S. economy seems to be the watchword of the day in newspapers and magazine articles about the economy at this time.

B Check the spelling of the vocabulary words with your teacher. Discuss the meanings of these words and any other unfamiliar words in the sentences.

PREDICTIONS

Think about the questions in the Topic Preview on page 20 and the sentences you heard in the Vocabulary Preview. Write three questions that you think will be answered in the lecture. Share your questions with your classmates.

NOTETAKING PREPARATION

Using Symbols and Abbreviations 1

When you take notes on a lecture, you will not have time to write down all the important information. That is why good notetakers use symbols and abbreviations. Try these tips.

Use conventional symbols

& or +	and
=	equals; is the same as
≠	not; not the same as
>;<	more than; less than
@	at
↑	go up; increase
↓	go down; decrease
"	ditto (the same as above)

Use conventional abbreviations

cent.	century
ex	example
info	information
intro	introduction
max	maximum
min	minimum
psych	psychology; psychological
stats	statistics

Use the first syllable or the first syllable + the first letter of the second syllable

educ	education
lect	lecture
pres	president
subj	subject
transp	transportation subject

Make up your own abbreviations

Lectures will usually include words for which you cannot use conventional symbols and abbreviations. Most lectures will also have words that are unique to the topic of the lecture. In such cases, make up your own abbreviations. Just be sure to create abbreviations that will help you remember the complete words when you go back and read your notes.

CD 1, TR 17

A **Listen to the statements from the lecture. Circle the notes that best use symbols and abbreviations to record what you hear.**

1. a. *large peop work in industry*
   b. *# of people in indus ↓ a lot*
   c. *many people lost jobs*
2. a. *> 16: illeg to wk full time*
   b. *< 60 illegal to work in 50 sts*
   c. *in 50 sts: >16 illegal to work.*
3. a. *end of 20th C.: 3% on farms*
   b. *end cent.: 3% wkd on farms*
   c. *end of century: 30% of workers on farms*

B **Write abbreviations for the following terms used in the lecture. Use abbreviations that you will understand when you read your notes a few days or a few weeks later.**

Term	Abbreviation
1. agriculture	______________
2. the service sector	______________
3. child labor	______________
4. stagnant wages and high unemployment	______________
5. health insurance	______________
6. income	______________
7. outsourcing and advanced technology	______________
8. lower wages and loss of jobs	______________
9. lack of regulation	______________
10. conservative	______________
11. liberal	______________
12. polarized	______________

C **Cover the terms on the left. With a partner, take turns saying the terms that your abbreviations stand for.**

D **Discourse Cues** **Number the following excerpts from the lecture from 1 to 5 in the order that you think you will probably hear them. Discuss with a partner or as a class the discourse cues that helped you figure out the order.**

_____ Finally, let's take a look at some of the possible reasons for the current situation.

_____ OK, now let's take a look at how the U.S. workforce is doing today.

_____ First, we'll take a historical look at work in America.

_____ We're going to take a look at work in the United States today in different ways.

_____ Let's get back to the changes in the U.S. workforce in the last century or so before we move on to the current situation.

CD 1, TR 18

FIRST LISTENING

Listen to the lecture and take notes. Look at the lecturer's visual aids as you listen. These may help you understand parts of the lecture.

Introduction

Work in America

Introduction

Changes – 1900 to 2010
U.S. workers today
The current economic situation
The role of the government

Subtopic 1: ______________________________

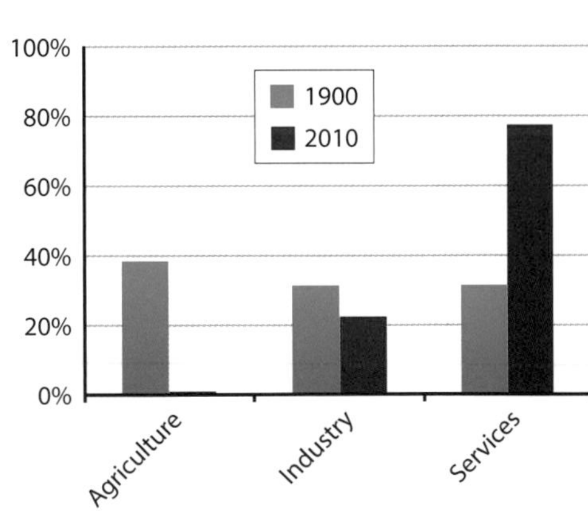

Subtopic 2: ______________________________

U.S. Workers Today

Most of Twentieth Century
- Rising wages
- Increased benefits
- Better working conditions

Today
- Productivity up, but not wages
- High unemployment

Subtopic 3: ______________________________

Current Economic Situation

Reasons
- Agriculture mechanized
- Outsourcing
- Advances in technology
- Weaker labor unions

Subtopic 4: ______________________

Role of the Government

Government Policy

- Tax cuts vs. tax increases
- More regulation of business vs. less regulation
- Liberals and conservatives are polarized

CD 1, TR 19

SECOND LISTENING

Listen to the lecture again and make your notes as complete as possible.

THIRD LISTENING

CD 1, TR 20

A **You will hear part of the lecture again. Listen and complete the notes by adding the information from the box.**

"	↑	+	mid	Stats	WWII	33%

U.S. wrkfrce today

______ Produc since 1970, but wrking cl wages same

______ Unempl

______

After ______: poor child 50% ______ class as adult

1980: ______ child 40% " " " "

2012: " " ______ " " " "

B **Compare your answers with a partner. Then compare the notes in A with the notes you took for this part of the lecture.**

AFTER LISTENING

ACCURACY CHECK

CD 1, TR 21

A **Listen to the following questions, and write short answers. Use your notes. You will hear each question one time only.**

1. ______________________________
2. ______________________________
3. ______________________________
4. ______________________________
5. ______________________________
6. ______________________________
7. ______________________________
8. ______________________________
9. ______________________________
10. ______________________________

B **Check your answers with your teacher. If your score is less than 70 percent, you may need to listen to the lecture again and rewrite some of your notes.**

ORAL SUMMARY

Use your notes to create an oral summary of the lecture with your partner. As you work together, add details to your notes that your partner included but you had missed.

DISCUSSION

Discuss the following questions with a classmate or in a small group.

1. The lecture doesn't discuss solutions to problems in the economy. What solutions can you offer?
2. How do you think the American economy might change in the next 10 years?
3. What advantages and disadvantages are there in globalization, where the world's economies are interconnected through outsourcing and global markets?

EXPANSION

PRE-READING

The following Reading is about Zhejiang Province in China. Before you read, answer the following questions. Share your answers with a classmate.

1. What sector of the economy do you think employs the largest percentage of workers in China?
2. Look at the title of the article. What is a *boomtown*? What do you think an *instant city* is?

READING

Now read the article.

Boomtowns: China's Instant Cities

For the past 30 years, China's economy has averaged nearly 10 percent growth per year. This rapid growth rate is at least partially the result of one of the largest population movements in history: An estimated 140 million rural Chinese have already left their homes, and another 45 million are expected to join the urban workforce in the next five years. Most have gone to factory towns along the coast. However, in recent years more have moved to cities in the middle of the country, where there's less competition for jobs.

One of these cities is Wenzhou. The Wenzhou airport bookstore sells a book titled *Actually, You Don't Understand the Wenzhou People.* It shares a shelf with *The Collected Secrets of How Wenzhou People Make Money*. For the Chinese, this part of Zhejiang Province has become a source of fascination. Recently, Wenzhou's *Fortune Weekly* conducted a study of local millionaires. One question was: If forced to choose between your business and your family, which would it be? Sixty percent chose business.

Throughout history, difficult circumstances helped create the Wenzhou business tradition. The region is dry and not easy to farm, and the mountains make travel challenging. With few options, Wenzhou natives turned to the sea. By the end of the seventeenth century, they had developed a strong trading culture. But in 1949, the communists came to power and cut off overseas trade, as well as most private business. Even in the early 1980s, when China introduced free-market reforms, Wenzhou started with definite disadvantages. The people from Wenzhou did not have the education of people in Beijing, and they didn't attract the foreign investment of Shanghai.

But Wenzhou had something very valuable: native instinct. Families opened small workshops, often with fewer than a dozen workers, and they produced simple goods. Over time, workshops grew into factories, and Wenzhou began to dominate certain low-tech industries. Today, one-quarter of all shoes bought in China come from Wenzhou. The city makes 70 percent of the world's cigarette lighters.

The Wenzhou Model spread throughout southern Zhejiang Province, where an amazing range of products is manufactured. In the city of Qiaotou, population 64,000, 380 local factories produce more than 70 percent of the buttons for clothes made in China. The region also produces one-third of the world's socks and 40 percent of the world's neckties.

Everything is sold in a town in Zhejiang Province called Yiwu. Yiwu is in the middle of nowhere, a hundred miles from the coast, but traders come from all over the world to buy. The China Yiwu International Trade City, a local mall, has more than 30,000 shops—if you spend one minute at each one, eight hours a day, you'll leave two months later.

One of the 30,000 shops in Yiwu market

Although nearly 80 percent of all Zhejiang business owners have a formal education of only eight years or fewer, the province has become the richest in China by most measures. The incomes for both rural and urban residents are the highest of any Chinese province (this excludes specially administered cities such as Shanghai and Beijing). Zhejiang reflects China's economic miracle: a poor, mostly rural nation that has somehow become the world's most productive factory center.

DISCUSSION

Discuss these questions with a classmate.

1. What information from the lecture was exemplified in the article?
2. Based on the article and what you learned from the lecture, what are the similarities between China today and the United States in 1900?
3. Compare the economic situation in China as explained in the article to the economic situation in the United States today as explained in the lecture. Which economy do you think is likely to do better over the long term? Why?

PURSUING THE TOPIC

Explore the topic of this chapter further by doing the following.

The Web site for the U.S. Bureau of Labor Statistics has a large amount of current information about all aspects of employment in the United States. Individually or with a partner, choose a topic that interests you and read about it. Write up the details for a short presentation to the class.

www.bls.gov

UNIT 1 VIDEO Cowboys in North America

BEFORE VIEWING

TOPIC PREVIEW

Answer the following questions with a partner.

1. What do you know about the history of the American cowboy?
2. What do you think the working life of a cowboy is or was like?
3. Do you think there are many cowboys in America today? Why or why not?

VOCABULARY PREVIEW

A Read the definitions of these key words and phrases that you will hear during the video.

hold on to their culture keep their traditions and lifestyle

ranches large areas of land where cows and horses are raised and where the owner, workers, and their families live

exposed to forced to experience, usually something bad like bad weather

gear equipment; clothes and tools needed for a particular job, sport, or activity

the outdoors places outside and away from the house; in the natural world

50 below an outside temperature of 50 degrees below zero Fahrenheit (-50°F)

don't mind are not bothered by or not worried about

child-bearing age between approximately age 13 and 50, when a woman is able to have a baby

duties responsibilities

a vanishing breed types or groups of people who are starting to disappear

B **Work with a partner and write vocabulary from A in the blanks in the sentences.**

1. Families living on these __________________ really __________________ the difficulties of this lifestyle.
2. Sometimes women work as cowboys, especially when they are past __________________.
3. To work as a cowboy, one has to love __________________.
4. Even the children have many __________________ around the ranch.
5. These men and women can be __________________ temperatures as low as __________________.
6. Cowboys have been able to __________________ and not become __________________.
7. A cowboy's __________________ includes a big hat, pointed boots, and a rope, among other things.

VIEWING

FIRST VIEWING

Watch the video, and then compare your first impressions with a partner. Talk about what you remember, what surprised you, and what interested you.

SECOND VIEWING

Watch the video again. Listen for the missing words and write them in the blanks.

1. The cowboy basically breaks into __________________ different types.
2. These people have been able to hold on to their culture because they love the __________________.
3. So, you know a typical __________________ guy at one of these ranches makes anywhere from eight to twelve hundred dollars a __________________.
4. So, when you do the __________________ on it, it's, you know, three to four dollars an hour.
5. I mean, what it takes to cowboy is good __________________ skills, skill with a rope, and a real understanding on how to work __________________ on a horse.
6. But still, the cheapest way to raise cattle is by __________________ them grass, and you're not going to do that on a four-wheeler on 1.3 __________________ acres.

THIRD VIEWING

Complete these notes as you watch the video. Write only important words, not full sentences, and abbreviate common words.

1) ________________ types of cb

2) hold on to ________________
   - love their ________________
   - earn ________________
   - get housing and ________________
   - work ________________ hrs a ________________

3) Gear and skills
   - understand ________________
   - love ________________
   but cold – sometimes = 50 ________________

4) Women as cbs – not ________________
   - usu young or ________________
   - kids ________________

5) Ppl predict cbs a ________________
   - but still cheapest way ________________

AFTER VIEWING

ORAL SUMMARY

Use your notes to create an oral summary of the video with your partner. As you work together, add details to your notes that your partner included but you had missed.

DISCUSSION

Discuss the following questions with a classmate or in a small group.

1. Based on what you learned about a cowboy's working life in America today, would you like to be a cowboy? Why or why not?
2. According to the speaker, the cowboy has been around for over 150 years in America but is not a "vanishing breed." What are some cultures and jobs that have vanished in that time period and why?
3. Do you think there will always be a need for cowboys in the United States? Why or why not?

UNIT 2

The American Character

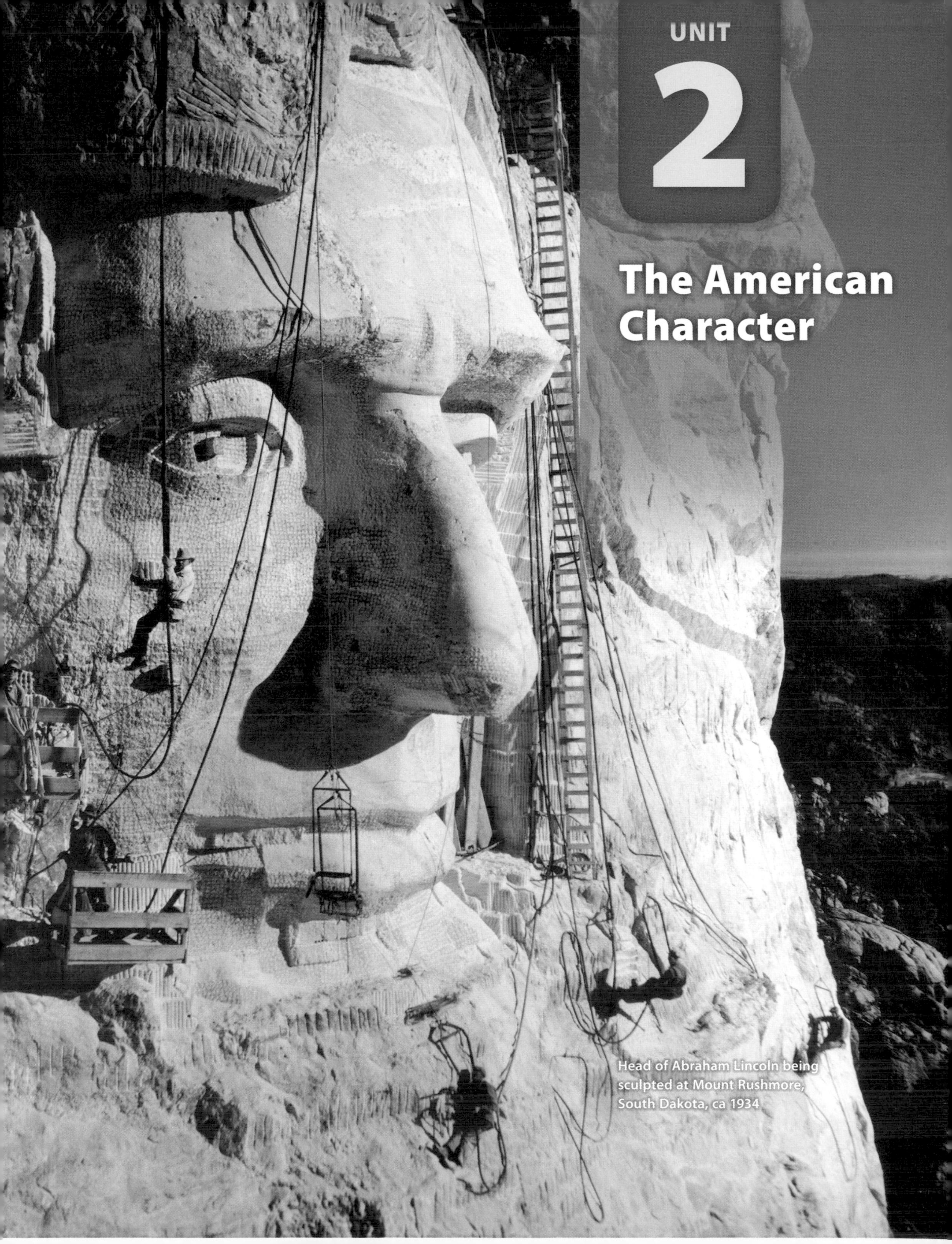

Head of Abraham Lincoln being sculpted at Mount Rushmore, South Dakota, ca 1934

CHAPTER

4

Family in the United States

TOPIC PREVIEW

Discuss the following questions with a partner or your classmates.

1. How would you describe a typical U.S. family?
2. Are single-parent families common in your culture?
3. Is it common for parents in your culture to leave children in day care while they are away at work?

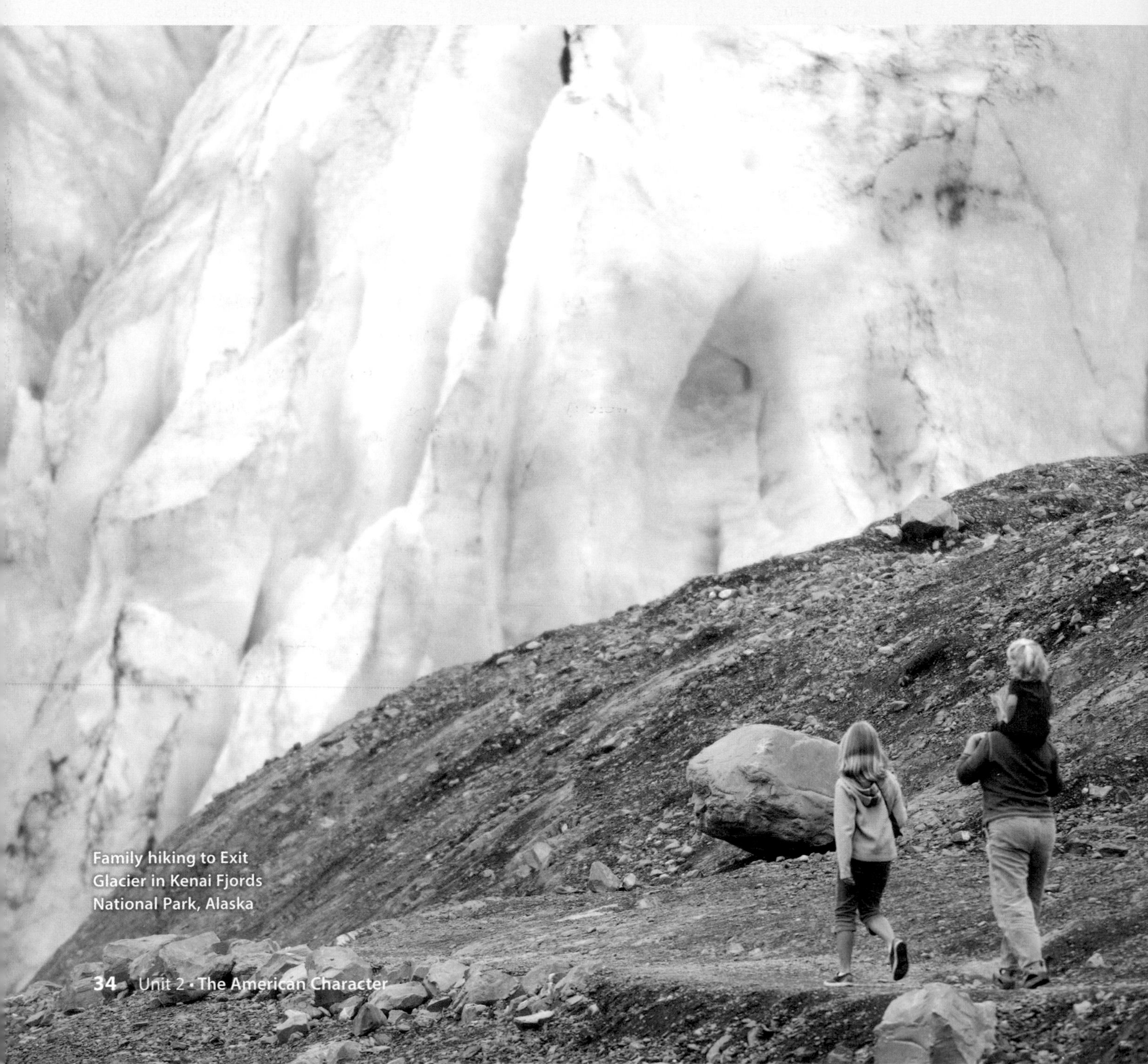

Family hiking to Exit Glacier in Kenai Fjords National Park, Alaska

VOCABULARY PREVIEW

CD 2, TR 1

A **Read through the sentences below, which are missing vocabulary from the lecture. As you read, try to imagine which words would fit in the blanks. Then listen to the sentences and write the missing words in the blanks.**

1. Although many social scientists are concerned about the decrease in marriage and its possible negative effects on the family, others say it is wrong to assume that marriage in the United States is "on the ________."
2. In any society, economic and cultural elements ________ with each other and bring ________ change.
3. This was the period after World War II, a period ________ by a very strong economy, a rising ________ of living, and a growing middle class.
4. The typical ________ of the family in these years was the traditional one: a married couple with children.
5. Culturally, three characteristics stand out in this period: ________ to social norms, greater male domination of the family than in the later periods, and very clear gender roles.
6. The women's liberation movement was an ________ of the struggle for civil rights.
7. Women's liberation challenged ________ against women in the home, in the work place, and in society in general.
8. Three movements—the sexual revolution, women's liberation, and the antiwar movement—were typical of the ________ nature of these decades.
9. With more women having careers and making money, there was less economic pressure for them to stay in an ________ marriage.
10. Many experts ________ that children have paid a high price for the social changes that took place in the second period.

B **Check the spelling of the vocabulary words with your teacher. Discuss the meanings of these words and any other unfamiliar words in the sentences.**

PREDICTIONS

Think about the questions in the Topic Preview on page 34 and the sentences you heard in the Vocabulary Preview. Write three questions that you think will be answered in the lecture. Share your questions with your classmates.

NOTETAKING PREPARATION

Listening for Key Content Words

Use key words to write down the essential information in a lecture. It is neither possible nor necessary to write every word you hear. Here are some tips for choosing key words.

- Concentrate on content words: nouns, verbs, adjectives, and adverbs.
- Choose the most important words to convey the meaning in the fewest words possible. For example, you hear

  Culturally, three characteristics stand out in this period: conformity to social norms, greater male domination of the family than in the later periods, and very clear gender roles, that is, clear and separate roles for men and women at home and at work.

  You write

  3 characteristics: social conformity, male domination & clear gender roles @ home & work

- You may also choose to put some information in your own words. For example, instead of writing conformity to social norms, you might write social conformity.

CD 2, TR 2

A **Practice reducing information to key words as you listen to sentences from the lecture. Then compare what you wrote with a classmate.**

1. ______________________________
2. ______________________________
3. ______________________________

B **Discourse Cues** **Number the following excerpts from the lecture from 1 to 5 in the order that you think you will probably hear them. Discuss with a partner or as a class the discourse cues that helped you figure out the order.**

_____ The third period is harder to see because we are living in this period now.

_____ So, let's begin with the first period, the mid-1940s to the mid-1960s.

_____ In addition to the cultural changes during this period of individualism, there were also economic changes that affected families.

_____ The second period that I want to talk about today, the period of individualism, lasted from the mid-1960s to the mid-1980s.

_____ Let me begin today's lecture by saying that many people today are concerned about the decline in the number of people who are married in the United States.

FIRST LISTENING

CD 2, TR 3

A **Listen to the beginning of the lecture. Circle the set of notes below that best records the information you hear.**

a.

Fewer peopl married in US

	1960	today
whts	74%	55%
hisp.	72%	48%
blks	61%	31%
18–24	45%	9%

Cult. changes – diff. ideas marr & fam
- econ + cult = change
- views ch over time

3 time peri. (soc. Barbra Dafoe Whitehead)
1. mid-40s to mid-60s: trad. fam
2. mid-60s to mid-80s: individualism
3. present: new fam

b.

↓ marriage in US
- 55–74% whts
- 48–72% hisp
- 31–61% blks
- 45–9% young

Neg. impact on fam?
Diff. ideas about marr & fam?
Change happening in US
- Way Am see fam
- How views have changed
  - ex: tradt fam, individ, new fam

CD 2, TR 4

B **Now listen to the whole lecture and take notes. Look at the lecturer's visual aids as you listen. These may help you understand parts of the lecture.**

Subtopic 1: 1940s–1960s: Traditional Family

Traditional Family
- Conformity to social roles
- Male domination
- Clear gender roles

Subtopic 2: 1960s–1980s: Individualism

Individualism

Cultural developments
- Focus on career and work
- Self-expression/fulfillment

Economic changes
- Women work outside the home

Subtopic 3: Present: The New Family

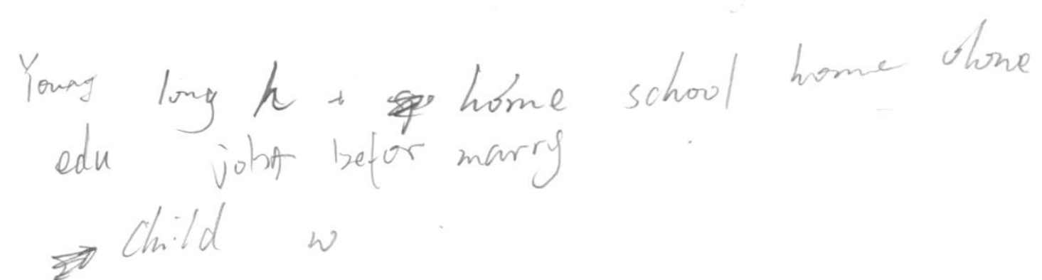

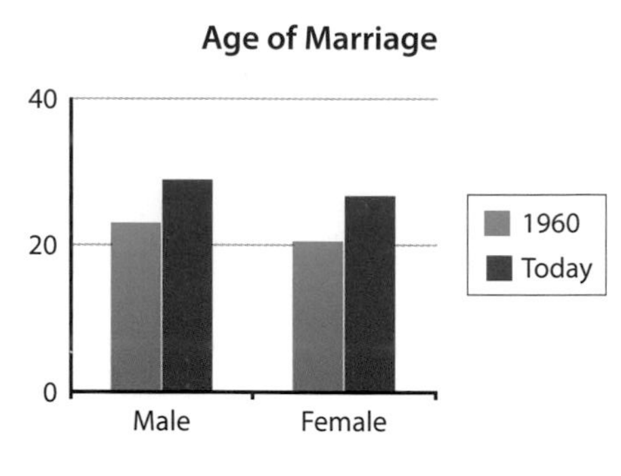

SECOND LISTENING

CD 2, TR 5

Listen to the lecture again and make your notes as complete as possible.

THIRD LISTENING

CD 2, TR 6

A **You will hear part of the lecture again. Listen and complete the notes by adding the information from the box.**

charac	div	mid	soc	WWII	+	@

mid 1940s – mid 1960s = Tradtl Fam
After ________ + Econ
↑ standard of liv, ↑ ________ class
• Fam = marr couple + child: husb work, wife ________ home
• low ________ rate, + birth rate
• 3 cult ________
1. ________ conformity
2. ________ male domination of fam
3. Clear gender roles

B **Compare your answers with a partner. Then compare the notes in A with the notes you took for this part of the lecture.**

ACCURACY CHECK

CD 2, TR 7

A **Listen to the following questions, and write short answers. Use your notes. You will hear each question one time only.**

1. 18-24
2. married childre. worcing father mother stay home
3. uncome
4. Picture
5. Creer & work secter revelotion wemens revlouthion inoration
6. storge foces Prie for salt
7. econeme, famliy
8. secend
9.
10. No they doesn't

B **Check your answers with your teacher. If your score is less than 70 percent, you may need to listen to the lecture again and rewrite some of your notes.**

ORAL SUMMARY

Use your notes to create an oral summary of the lecture with your partner. As you work together, add details to your notes that your partner included but you had missed.

DISCUSSION

Discuss the following statements with a classmate or in a small group.

1. What similarities are there between what you've learned about typical U.S. families and families in your culture?
2. What effects have economic and cultural changes in the last 20 years or so had on the family in your culture?
3. Is divorce always a bad idea? Can it ever have positive consequences for the family?

PRE-READING

The following Reading is about changes in family size in Brazil. Before you read, answer the following questions. Share your answers with a classmate.

1. Was there a women's movement in your country? If so, how was that movement similar to the women's movement in the 1970s in the United States?
2. Look at the title of the article. What does "female empowerment" mean? How do you think changes in family size might be related to female empowerment?

READING

Now read the article.

Female Empowerment in Brazil and its Effect on the Fertility Rate

Eighty-eight-year-old Brazilian Dona Maria Ribeiro de Carvalho had just finished telling me about her 16 pregnancies. Then she looked at José Alberto, her oldest son, who had come for a Sunday visit. "With the number of children I had," Dona Maria said, "I should have more than a hundred grandchildren right now."

Dona Maria's son José Alberto Carvalho, one of the most important Brazilian demographers of the past 50 years, smiled. He knew the total number of grandchildren, of course: 26. For much of his working life, he has been studying the remarkable Brazilian demographic phenomenon that is illustrated by his own family, which within two generations had crashed its fertility rate to 2.36 children per family, close to the national average of 1.9.

That new Brazilian fertility rate is below replacement level—the level at which a population replaces itself. It is lower than the two-children-per-woman fertility rate in the United States. And it's not simply wealthy and professional women who have stopped having multiple children in Brazil—every class and region of Brazil has experienced a drop.

This sudden fertility drop is not just a Brazilian phenomenon. Close to half the world's population lives in countries where the fertility rates have fallen to below replacement rate, just over two children per family. However, what has happened in Brazil since the 1960s provides a fascinating case study.

"What took 120 years in England took 40 years here," Carvalho told me one day. "Something *happened*." At that moment he was talking about what happened in São Vicente de Minas, the town of his childhood, where nobody under 45 has large families anymore. But he could have been describing the entire female population of Brazil. For although there are many reasons Brazil's fertility rate has dropped so far and so fast, central to them all are Brazil's women.

Brazilian women's overall position in society was deeply affected by the women's movement of the 1970s and '80s. Today, Brazil is led by its first female president, Dilma Rousseff; during the campaign, one of Rousseff's strongest competitors was a female senator. Brazil has high-ranking female military officers, special police stations run by and for women, and the world's most famous female soccer player, the one-name-only Marta.

Aníbal Faúndes, a Chilean professor who immigrated years ago to Brazil and has helped lead national studies of reproductive health, explains what he regards as a primary reason for the changes in birthrate in his adopted country. "The fertility rate dropped because women decided they didn't

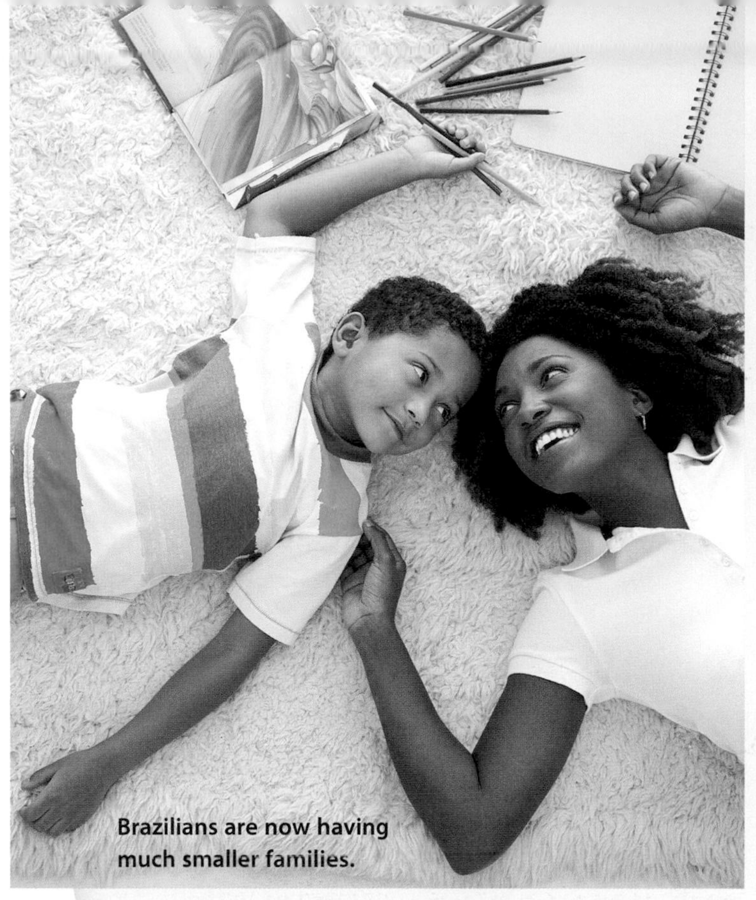
Brazilians are now having much smaller families.

want more children," he said. "Brazilian women are tremendously strong."

Keeping the family small is what Brazilian women of all ages now seem to expect of themselves—and what contemporary Brazil, in turn, appears to expect from them. "Look at the apartments," said a 31-year-old Rio de Janeiro marketing executive named Andiara Petterle. "They're designed for a maximum of four people. Two bedrooms. In the supermarkets, even the labels on frozen foods—always for four people."

The company Petterle founded specializes in sales research on Brazilian women, whose buying habits and life priorities seem to have changed completely in the years since Petterle was born. It wasn't until 1977, she reminded me, that the nation legalized divorce. "We've changed so fast," she said. "We've found that for many young women, their first priority now is their education. The second is their profession. And the third is children and a stable relationship."

DISCUSSION

Discuss these questions with a classmate.

1. What are some of the similarities in how Brazilian and American attitudes toward the family have changed over time?
2. How did the women's movement of the 1970s and 1980s affect Brazilian society? Compare its impact to the impact of the women's movement on American culture described in the lecture.
3. In what ways are Brazilian families today similar to American families? How are they different?

PURSUING THE TOPIC

Explore the topic of this chapter further by doing the following.

The Web site for the United States Census Bureau has a large amount of information about American families. Individually or with a partner, research the most recent statistical information available on family size, relationships, and living arrangements. Write up the details for a short presentation to the class.

www.census.gov/hhes/families/

CHAPTER 5

Religion

TOPIC PREVIEW

Discuss the following questions with a partner or your classmates.

1. What do you think the expression "freedom of religion" means?
2. Do people in your culture practice many different religions in your culture?
3. In what country other than the United States do you think you might find all of these religions: Hinduism, Islam, Sikhism, Christianity, Judaism, Jainism, Zoroastrianism, and Buddhism?

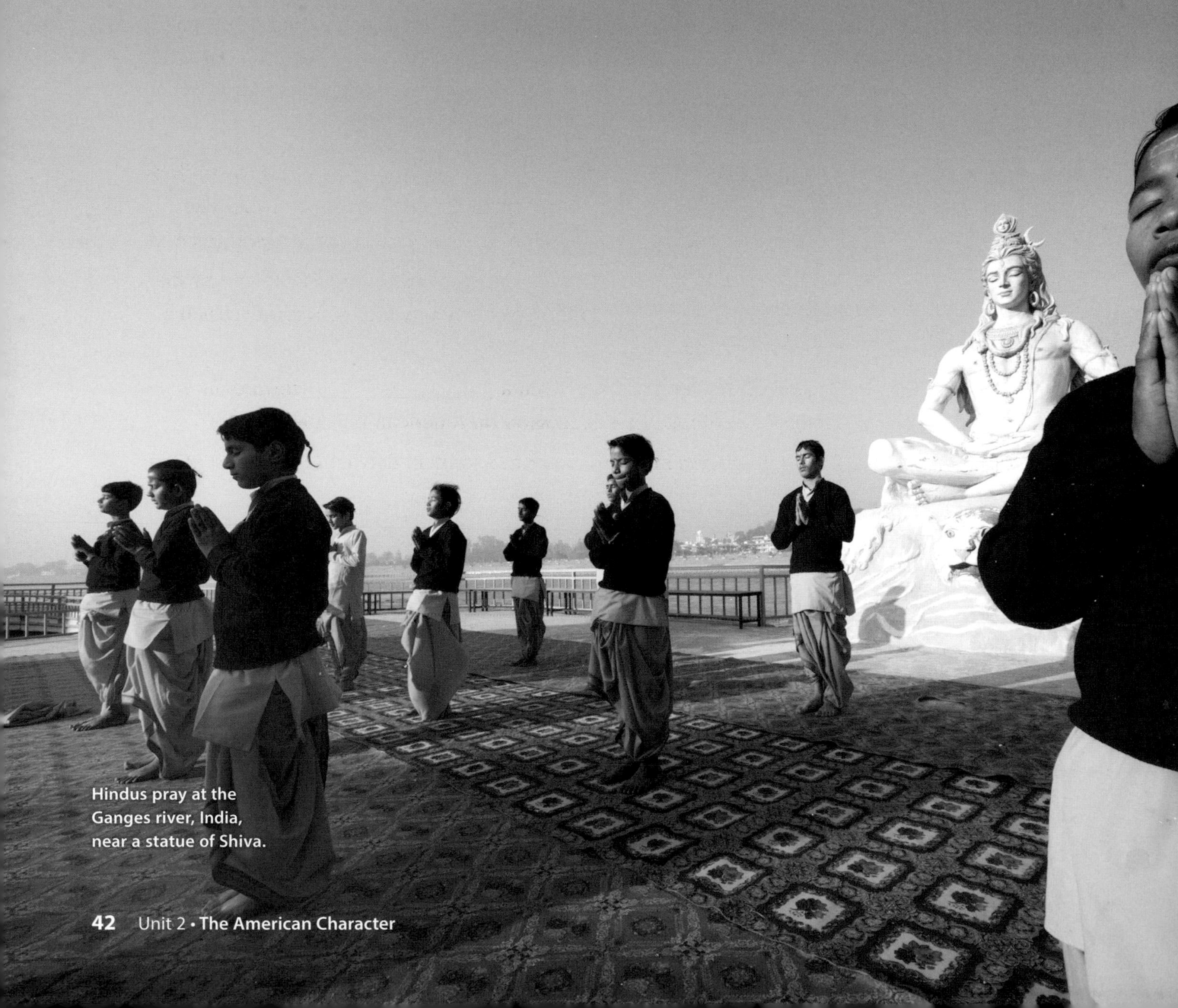

Hindus pray at the Ganges river, India, near a statue of Shiva.

VOCABULARY PREVIEW

CD 2, TR 8

A **Read through the sentences below, which are missing vocabulary from the lecture. As you read, try to imagine which words would fit in the blanks. Then listen to the sentences and write the missing words in the blanks.**

1. These churches generally represent the two major Christian traditions, Catholic and Protestant, but often include several different Protestant ____________.
2. Larger towns and big cities will also have other places of ____________ including synagogues, mosques, and temples representing other religious traditions.
3. The U.S. government cannot ask for information on religious ____________ in any official capacity, for example, on the census.
4. Statistical information must be gathered from ____________ of the population done by nongovernmental agencies or from organizational reports from religious groups themselves.
5. A 2009 Gallup ____________ asked, "Is religion an important part of your life?"
6. Most writers and scholars agree that Europeans are generally more ____________ than Americans.
7. They may believe in God, but they ____________ to stay away from religious ____________ except on certain formal occasions like weddings, baptisms, and funerals and a few very important religious days.
8. It's important to remember that freedom of worship is guaranteed by the First ____________ to the Constitution, which also establishes the separation of church and state.
9. Recently, however, there has been a ____________ toward an increase in the influence of religion on American political life.
10. Although religion in America seemed to be in decline during most of the last century, in the 1970s, there was a religious ____________ that surprised many people.

B **Check the spelling of the vocabulary words with your teacher. Discuss the meanings of these words and any other unfamiliar words in the sentences.**

PREDICTIONS

Think about the questions in the Topic Preview on page 42 and the sentences you heard in the Vocabulary Preview. Write three questions that you think will be answered in the lecture. Share your questions with your classmates.

NOTETAKING PREPARATION

Using Indentation to Organize Notes 1

Organizing your notes in a visual pattern will help you understand the relationship between the main ideas and the details or examples that support those ideas.

One way to organize your notes visually is by writing a main idea and then indenting the details and indicating them with bullets. Here are two examples.

Estimating people in diff. religions difficult
- U.S. govt can't ask for rel affiliation
- Statistics come from nongov surveys and reports

2007 survey gives % by rel
- 78% Christian
    - 51% Cath
    - 24% . . .
- 1.7% . . .
- 0.7% Budd
- 0.6% . . .
- 0.4% Hindu

A **The following are lines of notes from a lecture titled "Effective Notetaking." Find three main ideas and circle them.**

Do assigned rdg in prep

Fix notes as necess

Use symbols & abbrevs

After lecture

Put a ? for missed info

Bring ntbook & sharp pencils or pens

While notetaking

Ask prof ?s if nec

Before class

Be on time & find good seat

Review notes asap

Chk notes with classmate

B **Now find three supporting details for each main idea. Draw lines from the details to the main idea they support.**

C **Using your ideas from A, write an outline of the lecture "Effective Notetaking." Use indentation and bullets for the supporting details.**

Effective Notetaking

D **Discourse Cues** **Number the following excerpts from the lecture from 1 to 5 in the order that you think you will probably hear them. Discuss with a partner or as a class the discourse cues that helped you figure out the order.**

__2__ Now let's look at two major ways that religion in the United States differs from religion in other modernized Western nations.

__1__ Let's start today with facts and figures.

__3__ One major survey conducted in 2007 reported that 78 percent of Americans identified themselves as Christians.

__5__ Finally, I'd like to briefly focus on religious diversity in the States.

__4__ To sum up, then, the importance of religion and belonging to a church or religious organization seem greater to Americans than to Europeans.

FIRST LISTENING

CD 2, TR 9

A **Listen to the beginning of the lecture. Circle the set of notes below that best records the information you hear.**

a.

Relig in US complic
- not understood by peop other count.
  - know Am cult fr TV, film, video
    - don't show imp of relig in US
- sm towns many dif churches
  - Chrisian: Cath & Protest (sev. dif)
- lg towns & cities also synag., mosques, temples =other rel trad
- people dif count. & relig immigr to US
  - lg numb. dif relig

1 Facts & figures var relig groups in US
2 Comp US w other mod W nations
3 Imp of rel esp ↑ relig US polit recent yrs
4 Incr diversity of relig in US

b.

Religion in U.S.
- Compl topic misunderst bec other cults exposed to Am cult thru TV, film video on Internet
- Internt visit to sm towns surprised bec Cath & Protest church (diff denom) & lg towns synag., mosque, temples
- Peopl many diff countries & rel backg immig not surprised many dif rel US
- Talk about today: 1st Facts and fig. var rel groups, 2nd comp US-modern West nat, 3rd import of rel increase in US polit, final increase diver rel in US

CD 2, TR 10

B **Now listen to the whole lecture and take notes. Look at the lecturer's visual aids as you listen. These may help you understand parts of the lecture.**

Subtopic 1: ______________________________

Americans' Religious Affiliation, 2007

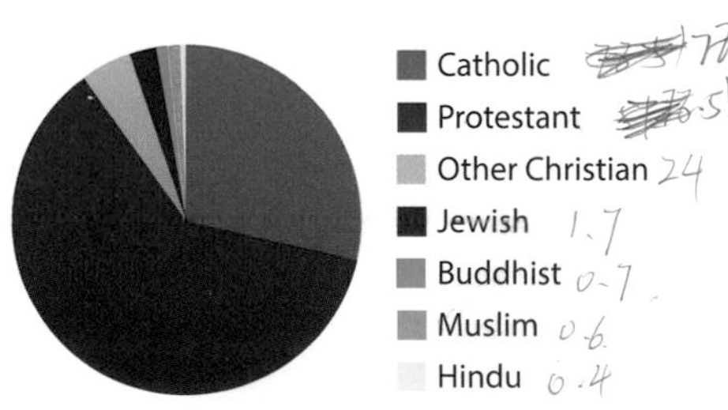

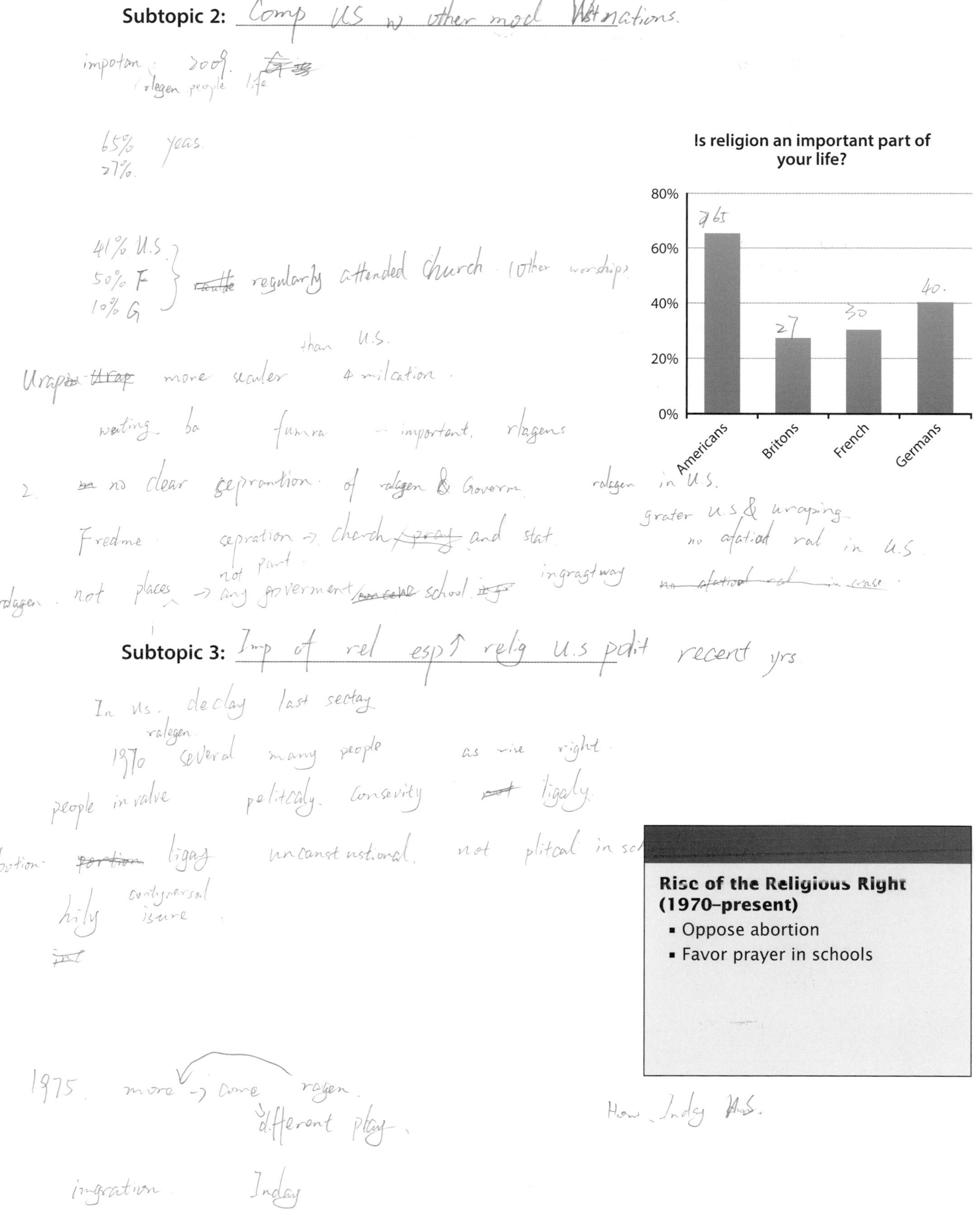
Subtopic 2:
Is religion an important part of your life?
80%
60%
40%
20%
0%
Americans
Britons
French
Germans
Subtopic 3:
Rise of the Religious Right (1970–present)
▪ Oppose abortion
▪ Favor prayer in schools

Subtopic 4: ____________________

Religious Diversity

- 1965: Immigration quotas eliminated
  - More religious diversity
- Work of Harvard professor Diana Eck

The Future

SECOND LISTENING

CD 2, TR 11

Listen to the lecture again and make your notes as complete as possible.

THIRD LISTENING

CD 2, TR 12

A **You will hear part of the lecture again. Listen and complete the notes by adding the information from the box.**

Eur	free	indirect	influ	sep	&	ex.

Modrn, __________ nat.
  no sep of rel __________ govt.
US
  __________ of rel – 1st Amend to Const.
    __________ of church & state
  __________ rel not part of govt or pub schools
  Rel. beliefs, values __________ pol & ed,
    but __________ influ

B **Compare your answers with a partner. Then compare the notes in A with the notes you took for this part of the lecture.**

ACCURACY CHECK

CD 2, TR 13

A **Listen to the following questions, and write short answers. Use your notes. You will hear each question one time only.**

1. ______________________________
2. ______________________________
3. ______________________________
4. ______________________________
5. ______________________________
6. ______________________________
7. ______________________________
8. ______________________________
9. ______________________________
10. ______________________________

B **Check your answers with your teacher. If your score is less than 70 percent, you may need to listen to the lecture again and rewrite some of your notes.**

ORAL SUMMARY

Use your notes to create an oral summary of the lecture with your partner. As you work together, add details to your notes that your partner included but you had missed.

DISCUSSION

Discuss the following statements with a classmate or in a small group.

1. Do you believe that religious freedom is always a good thing? Why?
2. Should religion and government be totally separate? Why or why not?
3. Why might it be good for people learn about other people's religions?

PRE-READING

The following Reading is about religious beliefs around the world. Before you read, answer the following questions. Share your answers with a classmate.

1. What are the major religions in your country of origin? Are most people in your country religious?
2. Which areas of the world do you think have the highest number of people who are nonreligious or do not believe in God? Do you think there is a difference between someone who is nonreligious and an atheist who does not believe in God?

READING

Now read the article.

The Geography of Religion

The meaning of *religious belief* varies in different places, among different people. In general, *religion* refers to a set of beliefs and practices about what is sacred or spiritual—beliefs and practices held in common by a group. Religion usually involves beliefs about the origin and meaning of the world and of human life as well as guidelines for moral behavior.

Counting Adherents

There are many ways to approach the geography of religion, the simplest being to count numbers of believers by location. The data here came from the World Christian Database (WCD), which, despite its name, tracks data on hundreds of world religions in 238 political entities.

An *atheist* is someone who actively claims disbelief in the existence of God or any other deity. *Nonreligious* is a broader category that includes people who do not have a religion and also includes those who aren't opposed to religion, but who aren't interested in the question. Not surprisingly, the only country with no atheists or nonreligious citizens at all is Vatican City—home of the Roman Catholic Church. Afghanistan is next with a 99 percent Muslim population and a 99.99 percent religious-believer rate. Some other countries with at least a 99.90 percent religious-believer rate are: Bhutan (Buddhism); Bangladesh, Chad, Pakistan, and Somalia (Islam); Botswana, Burundi, and Kenya (Christianity).

There are very few countries in which more than 10 percent of the population claims to be atheist. They include North Korea (15.6 percent) and Sweden (11.7 percent). When you add the nonreligious and atheist populations together, however,

The holy Kaaba in Mecca, Saudi Arabia

the list of countries with significant percentages of nonbelievers grows. Here is a sampling of countries by region with nonbeliever populations of over 15 percent:

The Far East
North Korea (71.3%)
Mainland China (49.8%)

Central Asia
Mongolia (39.1%)
Kazakhstan (35.7%)
Kyrgyzstan (27.4%)

Eastern Europe
Czech Republic (35.6%)
Estonia (34.4%)
Russia (32.1%)

South America and the Caribbean
Uruguay (32.8%)
Cuba (24.5%)

Western Europe
Sweden (29.8%)
Netherlands (20.8%)
Germany (20.4%)

Australasia
New Zealand (21.4%)
Australia (16.9%)

The Problem of Numbers

The vast majority of the world's people—almost 86 percent, according to the WCD—hold some sort of religious belief. However, exact information about religious belief is among the hardest sociological data to collect. Religions count their members in a variety of ways, making comparisons difficult. Some include only those who regularly attend religious services; others count all known members, whether they attend services or not. Some count children from birth; others require some sort of ceremony before counting people as members. Polls, such as those collected by the Association of Religious Data Archives or the Pew Forum on Religion & Public Life, are frequently used to count believers, but results can vary widely.

Other approaches to understanding religion through geography include looking at sacred places and examining why some points on a map are considered so special to one or more religions that they become destinations for pilgrims. Another approach is to ask what direct physical impact a religion has had on a particular place: for example, cathedrals in Europe or the use of less-modern technology in Amish farming practices in North America.

DISCUSSION

Discuss these questions with a classmate.

1. What ideas presented in the lecture are given some support by information in the article?
2. Why is it difficult to collect exact data on people's religious beliefs, according to the lecture and the article? Make a list.
3. Look at the list of countries by region in the article. Using information from the lecture and your own ideas, can you think of reasons why these particular places might have so many nonbelievers?

PURSUING THE TOPIC

Explore the topic of this chapter further by doing the following.

Read an online interview with Professor Diana Eck in which she discusses her book, *A New Religious America: How a Christian Country Has Become the World's Most Religiously Diverse Nation*. Take notes and be prepared to discuss what you learned with your classmates.

www.pbs.org/wnet/religionandethics/episodes/april-26-2002/diana-eck-extended-interview/11617/

CHAPTER 6

Birth, Marriage, and Death

TOPIC PREVIEW

Discuss the following questions with a partner or your classmates.

1. Have you been to a big American wedding? What was it like? Are weddings in your culture similar?
2. How do you think a couple in the United States would celebrate the birth of their baby?
3. What are some rituals people might carry out after the death of a loved one?

Wedding on a glacier! Tongass National Forest, Alaska

VOCABULARY PREVIEW

CD 2, TR 14

A **Read through the sentences below, which are missing vocabulary from the lecture. As you read, try to imagine which words would fit in the blanks. Then listen to the sentences and write the missing words in the blanks.**

1. Customs vary so much from culture to culture that it's often ________________ for someone trying to understand the traditions and customs of a new place.
2. The birth of a baby is a ________________ occasion in most families and is celebrated in some way or another.
3. Traditionally, Christian babies are ________________ in a ceremony involving washing the baby's head with water.
4. The traditional reception that follows the ceremony can be as simple as cookies and punch in the house of worship where the ceremony took place or as ________________ as a large sit-down dinner at a local hotel.
5. Traditionally, most wedding ceremonies have been ________________ in houses of worship.
6. All traditions and religions have to cope with one basic issue: how to deal with the body of the ________________ person.
7. Some religions such as Judaism and Islam require that the body be very quickly ________________, or put into the ground.
8. This event, sometimes called a ________________, usually takes place at a funeral home for a day or two before the funeral ceremony.
9. At the ________________, it is customary for a religious leader to speak some words of comfort to the friends and family of the deceased. In addition, a ________________ is usually given by someone close to the deceased person.
10. If the body is ________________, the ashes are placed in a special jar, called an urn.

B **Check the spelling of the vocabulary words with your teacher. Discuss the meanings of these words and any other unfamiliar words in the sentences.**

PREDICTIONS

Think about the questions in the Topic Preview on page 52 and the sentences you heard in the Vocabulary Preview. Write three questions that you think will be answered in the lecture. Share your questions with your classmates.

NOTETAKING PREPARATION

Using Symbols and Abbreviations 2

Here are some additional tips to save writing time when you take notes.

Use as few vowels as possible

bewildering	*bewldrng*
ceremony	*cermny*
cremated	*cremtd*
reassured	*reassrd*

Omit the final letters of the word

elaborate	*elab*
reception	*recep*
significance	*signif*

Use these abbreviations

someone	*s/o*
something	*s/t*
with	*w/*
without	*w/o*

Use other conventional symbols

→	causes, leads to
←	is the result of

CD 2, TR 15

A **Listen to the sentences. As you listen, write the sentences in notetaking form below. Use symbols and abbreviations. Then use your notes to read the sentences to a classmate.**

1. often bewildrng for s/o undstan the trad & costms New stays.
2. The bride shod be werng s/t old, s/t New s/t brode s/t blue
3. The wedng cermny can be very smpl one, with only few familymembers & ~~doth~~ close friends present, or can very elab.
4. As for actual wedng cermny & related celbrations, tradi is bride's family who pays for these expenses.

B **Discourse Cues** **Number the following excerpts from the lecture from 1 to 5 in the order that you think you will probably hear them. Discuss with a partner or as a class the discourse cues that helped you figure out the order.**

3 After the baby is born, most families participate in some kind of spiritual ceremony...

1 Today I want to talk about customs in the United States, not all customs of course, but customs surrounding certain important events in almost everyone's life.

5 The last passage I'm going to talk about today is the passage from life to death.

4 As I said before, in a society so large and diverse as the United States, customs can vary greatly.

2 Today let's look at some widely accepted customs and traditions of most Americans concerning three of life's most important events, or passages: birth, marriage, and death.

FIRST LISTENING

CD 2, TR 16

Listen to the lecture and take notes. Look at the lecturer's visual aids as you listen. These may help you understand parts of the lecture.

Introduction customs in U.S customs surrounding certain importa event in life.
customs bewildering → s/o tr undstan → tradition & customs
difrnt → more bewildrng ~~to day~~
~~Birth → most family & celebrated momentons~~
~~given → baby is due shower → new baby~~
most impotant events / passages

Conterning

Customs and Traditions

Introduction
Birth
Marriage
Death

Subtopic 1: Bithy of baby is momentons in most fimily
in most families & is celebrated in some way or another.
one way. U.S baby shower befor baby born → shower
shower is due giftes with new baby.
gift very emtional expression for good wishes.

After baby born.
Traditionally Christian babies washing head.
they all involve celebration of bith baby

Birth

- Baby shower before
- Spiritual ceremony after

Subtopic 2: Marriage

is customs & traditions
much among differ people
some customs often observed.
young man to ask permission for woman's family.
have some young people want parent's approval
give ~~person~~ diamond ring
traditionally is bride's family pay
can few family / hundreds of people
can cookies & punch after traditiond reception
gifts to help her set up new household
applinces, sheets, towels, pots & pans & so forth
man can no see dres befor

Marriage

- Engagement
- Shower
- Wedding ceremony

houses of worship
nonreligions.
home, officials office or park.

Subtopic 3: Death memorial

body be very quickly buried or put into the ground

'visit' and say good-bye to their friend

wake. takes place a funeral home for a day/two

befor funeral ceremony → eulogy

family/friend ~~speak~~ speak

flower card

Death

- The deceased
- Funeral service / religious ceremony
- Memorial service

SECOND LISTENING

CD 2, TR 17

Listen to the lecture again and make your notes as complete as possible.

THIRD LISTENING

CD 2, TR 18

A **You will hear part of the lecture again. Listen and complete the notes by adding the information from the box.**

cermny	fath's	ppl	@	=	w/	100s

Marr. ++custm & tradi, esp for weddg

- Not nec for man to ask fath's permiss.
  - mst yng ppl. want parnts' approv
- Tradi ~~w/~~ = man gives diamnd engagmnt ring
- Weddng
  - Bride's fam pays
  - Cermny
    - simple w/ few frnds & fam OR
    - elabrt w/ 100s. of ppl
  - Recept. follows ceremony
    - simple: cookies OR
    - elab: dinnr @ hotl w/mus & dancng

B **Compare your answers with a partner. Then compare the notes in A with the notes you took for this part of the lecture.**

ACCURACY CHECK

CD 2, TR 19

A **Listen to the following questions, and write short answers. Use your notes. You will hear each question one time only.**

1. When are baby shower usually given?
2. What are the reason change cencerng the cersten of baby showers?
3. what do we call the crestiorlge series hald after a baby is bornd?
4. How tradital pay for U.S weeding?
5. Do must U.S. caups have sarca sermony or raleges sermony when thy marryed?
6. what 4 things tradition says abrond shoud have her weeding?
7. Who should not saw in weeding dress befor weeding sermony?
8. Under what secrmstens is mermny severs heald in stand of funral?
9. 2 Just out family ofter famly of dissed.
10. what call shot tolk about good thing disses people death in he/her life.

B **Check your answers with your teacher. If your score is less than 70 percent, you may need to listen to the lecture again and rewrite some of your notes.**

ORAL SUMMARY

Use your notes to create an oral summary of the lecture with your partner. As you work together, add details to your notes that your partner included but you had missed.

DISCUSSION

Discuss the following statements with a classmate or in a small group.

1. Is it surprising that people in the United States, with its great racial and ethnic diversity, celebrate birth, marriage, and death in similar ways? Why?
2. Death is a topic that is very difficult for most Americans to talk about. What reasons might there be for this?
3. It is considered bad luck for the groom to see the bride in her wedding dress before the ceremony. What might be a reason for this superstition? Does your culture have superstitions connected to weddings?

PRE-READING

The following Reading is about traditional marriage customs in parts of rural Africa. Before you read, answer the following questions. Share your answers with a classmate.

1. Which of the marriage customs described in the lecture would be most likely to exist in a variety of other countries, including traditional rural cultures in Africa?
2. What is a ritual? Describe one marriage ritual that is widely practiced in your culture.

READING

Now read the article.

African Marriage Rituals

Morocco—Berber

In Morocco's High Atlas mountains, a young woman may catch the eye of an admirer at the yearly bride's fair in the village of Imilchil. If the young woman's parents' approve, a courtship begins. This is the period of time during which the couple and their families develop a relationship, in preparation for marriage. For widows and divorced women, the Imilchil fair is an open market, with marriages performed right then and there.

Before a young bride's wedding, her mother rubs her legs with henna, a flowering plant that is used to dye the skin a reddish brown color. This is a ritual that her people believe keeps evil spirits away. On the wedding day, the mother says a bittersweet good-bye to her daughter by kissing her knee. After the wedding ceremony, the young bride travels by mule to her new husband's home. Once there, one of his female relatives will lift her off the mule so that her feet don't touch the ground and risk evil spirits entering her body.

Days of parties followed by nights of singing and dancing come next for the bride, who has captured the liver—the Berber symbol of love—of the man who has promised to protect her.

Ethiopia—Karo

The beauty of Ethiopia's Orno River Valley is matched by its people, who decorate their bodies to improve their physical appearance. The 500 or so Karo have very few possessions, so they rely on nature and trade for decoration. When a Karo girl reaches puberty, razorlike cuts are made in the skin of her stomach. Ashes are then rubbed into the cuts to make them heal in a raised pattern. This, Karo men told us, increases her beauty.

Karo women also apply face paint to attract a mate, often copying the colors and patterns that are found on local birds' feathers. In addition, they wear necklaces made of banana seeds that they have collected, or glass beads that they get from trading at small markets a three-days' walk away from their homes.

When the summer has passed and the harvest is complete, courtship season begins. Unmarried Karo youth, decorated with face paint, beaded necklaces, and many bracelets, join in joyful dances. A man signals his interest to a woman during the singing and dancing. For many the excitement will lead to engagement, marriage, and a lifetime together.

South Africa—Ndebele

Ndebele weddings are celebrated in three stages, which can take years to conclude. They begin with the negotiation of *lobola*, or bride price, which is paid over time, in the form of both money and live animals, particularly cattle.

A two-week separation of the bride from her family marks the second stage, when other women teach her how to be a good Ndebele wife. When this period of separation ends, the Ndebele bride emerges wearing colorful beaded hoops around her waist and legs. These imitate the female form that the Ndebele so greatly admire. The Ndebele bride is also given a marriage blanket, which she will wear to special events for the rest of her life.

The third stage of Ndebele marriage is completed only after the woman has given birth to her first child. Up until then, she is not considered truly married.

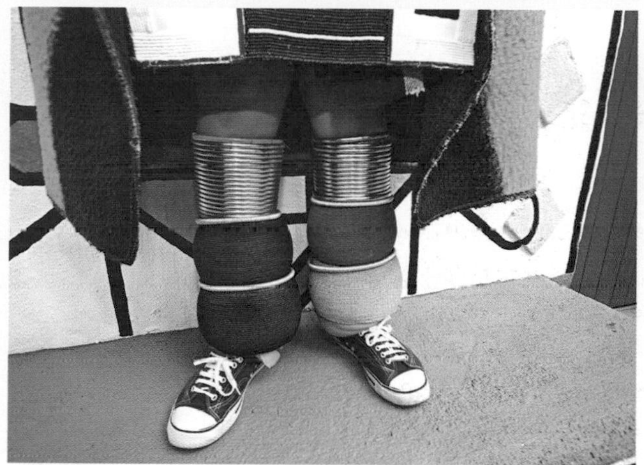

DISCUSSION

Discuss these questions with a classmate.

1. What similarities can you see between marriage customs in the United States and in parts of rural Africa—courtship and engagement, the marriage ceremony, gift giving, and so on?
2. Of the three cultures mentioned in the reading, which one has marriage customs that are most different from those in the United States? Explain.
3. Which of the marriage customs mentioned in the lecture and the reading were the most interesting or surprising to you?

PURSUING THE TOPIC

Explore the topic of this chapter further by doing the following.

Watch the movie *The Father of the Bride*, a 1991 comedy about a father whose beloved daughter is about to be married. Be prepared to discuss the movie with your classmates.

Through the Eyes of a Critic

High-fiving iguana on the Galápagos Islands, Ecuador

BEFORE VIEWING

TOPIC PREVIEW

Who is an artist's most honest critic? Rank the following people from 1 to 5 (*5* = the best or most honest critic and *1* = the worst or least honest critic). Discuss your order with a partner.

_____ a. the artist's mother or father

_____ b. the artist's husband or wife

_____ c. the artist's young son or daughter

_____ d. a stranger

_____ e. an art expert or specialist

VOCABULARY PREVIEW

A **Read the definitions of these key words and phrases that you will hear during the video.**

missing out on not able to enjoy something because of other responsibilities
hugged put one's arms around someone
never mind that don't worry about that; forget that
the surface the top or outside part of something that you can see or touch
curious wanting to learn more about someone or something
illuminating shining light on something
took me ages took me a very long time
idiot a stupid or foolish person
a high five a gesture where two people slap each other's hand above their heads in a show of greeting, pleasure, or victory

B **Work with a partner and write vocabulary from A in the blanks in the sentences.**

1. It ________________ to complete my research paper. I stayed up all night!
2. I know my son thinks I'm a(n) ________________ whenever I ask him a question about my cell phone.
3. It helps for a photojournalist to be ________________.
4. If you don't go to the club, you'll be ________________ a good time.
5. After the blackout, people started ________________ their homes with candles.
6. We won the game and everyone in the room gave each other ________________.
7. Janet cried when she broke her father's favorite sunglasses. But he just ________________ her and said, "________________."
8. Whales come to ________________ of the ocean to breathe.

VIEWING

FIRST VIEWING

Watch the video, and then compare your first impressions with a partner. Talk about what you remember, what surprised you, and what interested you.

SECOND VIEWING

Watch the video again. Listen for the missing words and write them in the blanks.

1. And then I felt a little bit ________________ for myself. It's like I'm ________________ so much.
2. So I was sitting down with a ________________ showing him this land iguana with this Galapagos mockingbird, talking about this very interesting sort of collaborative ________________.
3. It's a nice symbiotic ________________. And he was like ________________ by this.
4. And when there's a big predator, they will get very ________________. And they will hover. And the big orca will ________________ up perhaps.
5. This is a ________________ iguana. And, yeah, I was sneaking up to it.

THIRD VIEWING

Complete these notes as you watch the video. Write only important words, not full sentences, and abbreviate common words.

MK: Comes home from Galap trip
A: Dad, You're home! How was ______________________________?
MK: ______________________________
A: Any gd pics?
MK: Yeah
A: ______________________________
MK: Shows pic of mkingbd on top of liz
A: Fascinat'd
MK: Shows pic of sea lions and birds over orcas
A: ______________________________
MK: Shows last set of pics
A: Best ______________________________
MK: Why?
A: ______________________________

AFTER VIEWING

ORAL SUMMARY

Use your notes to create an oral summary of the video with your partner. As you work together, add details to your notes that your partner included but you had missed.

DISCUSSION

Discuss the following questions with a classmate or in a small group.

1. Why do you think Mattias Klum came home "feeling sorry" for himself?
2. What reaction do you think the father expected when Anskar first walked into the kitchen and saw his Dad? What was Anskar interested in instead?
3. Why did the audience find the son's questions and comments so funny?
4. What does the title of the video mean?

UNIT

3

Challenges at Home and Abroad

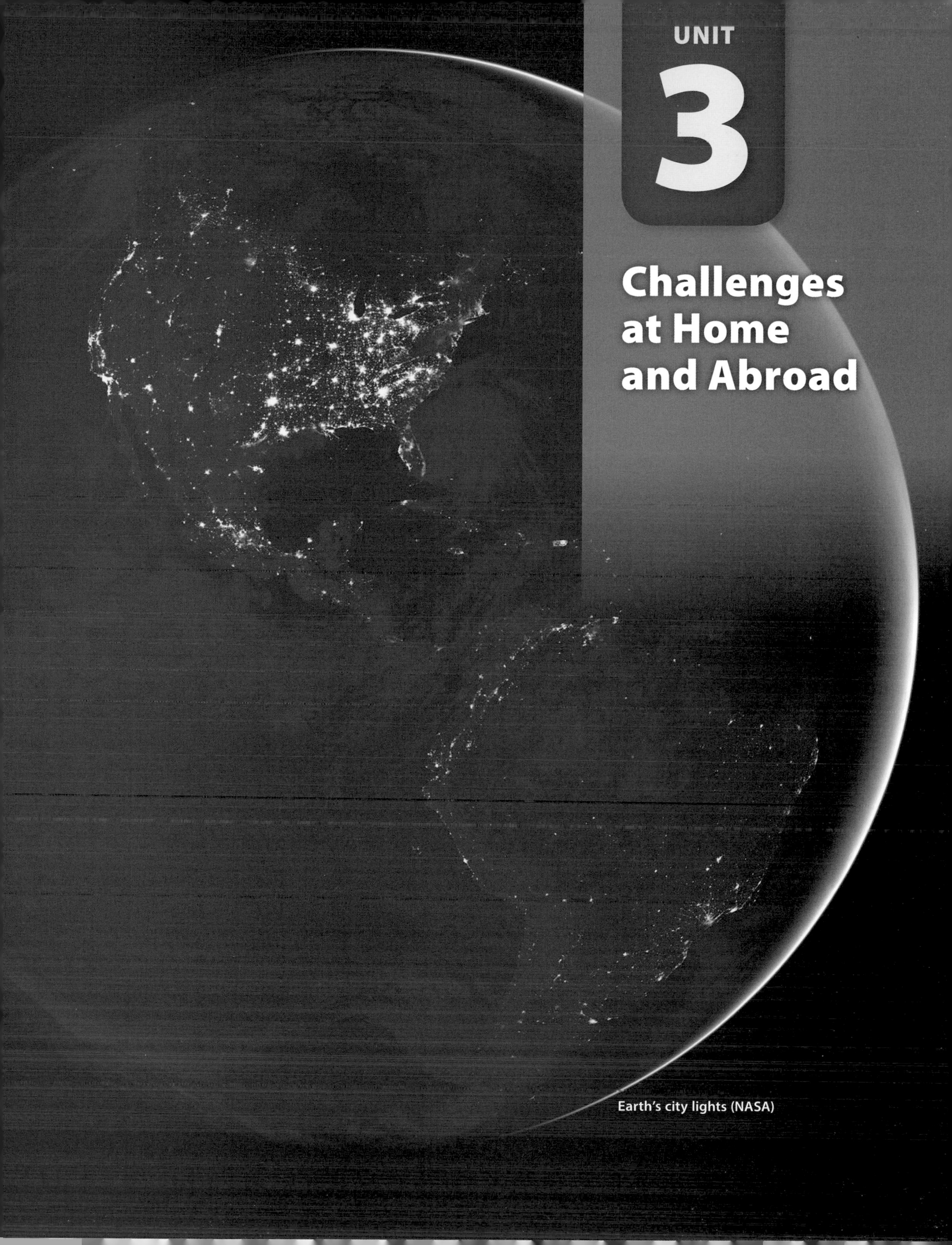

Earth's city lights (NASA)

CHAPTER

7

Multiculturalism

TOPIC PREVIEW

Answer the following questions with a partner or your classmates.

1. What happens to metals like iron and chromium put together inside a melting pot to melt?
2. Why do you think the melting pot and the patchwork quilt are often used as metaphors, or symbols, of the multicultural character of U.S. society?
3. Does cultural diversity in a society bring more benefits or more problems?

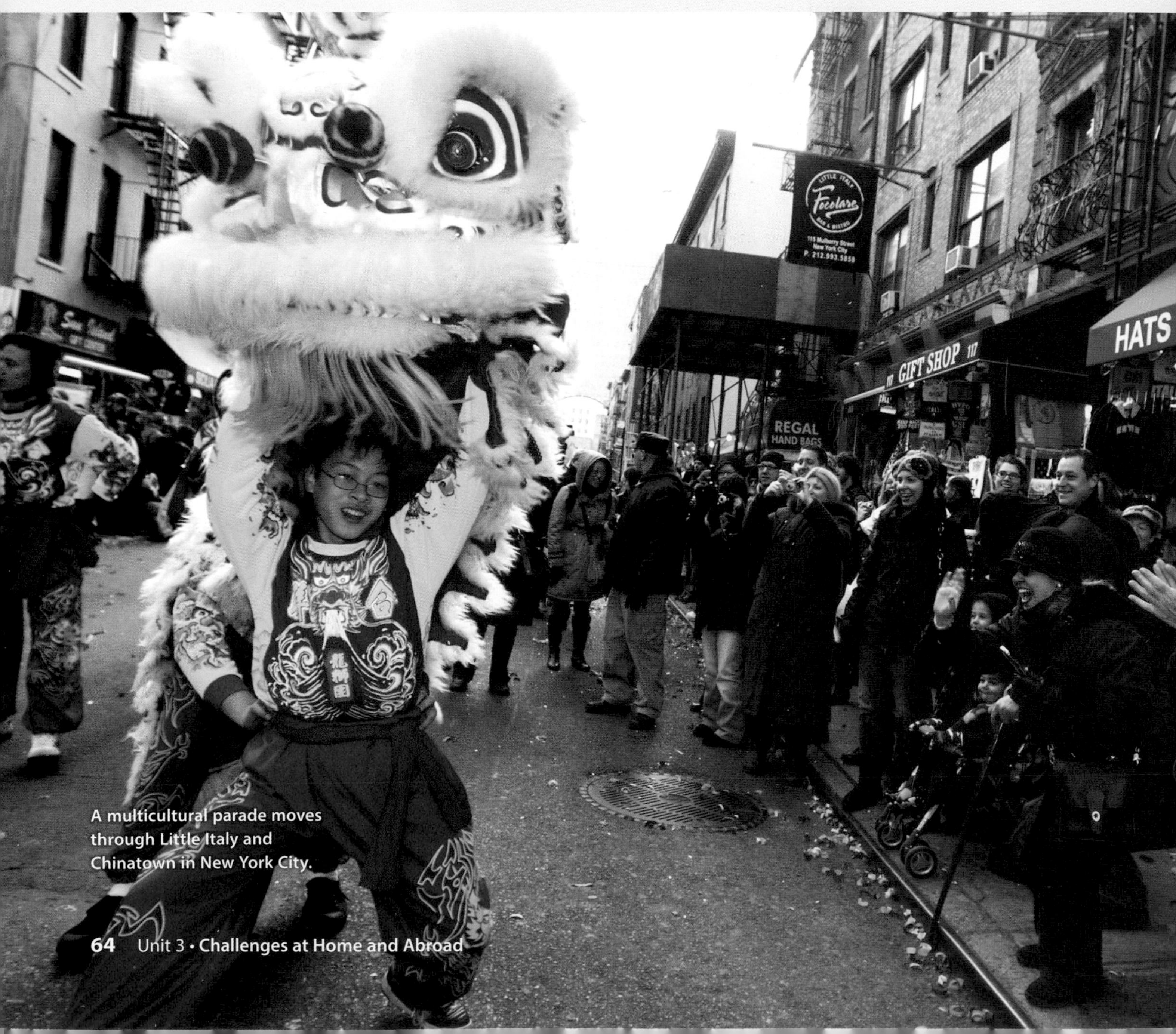

A multicultural parade moves through Little Italy and Chinatown in New York City.

VOCABULARY PREVIEW

CD 3, TR 1

A **Read through the sentences below, which are missing vocabulary from the lecture. As you read, try to imagine which words would fit in the blanks. Then listen to the sentences and write the missing words in the blanks.**

1. A melting pot is the traditional ____________ for the way different groups of immigrants came together in the United States.
2. In theory, the result of many nationalities ____________ together is one big, ____________, culture.
3. It is like an ____________, a combination of all the different parts mixed together into a single whole that is different from each of its parts.
4. Many groups, especially African, Asian, and American Indian, have at times been ____________ from participating fully in society through ____________ and discrimination.
5. U.S. society does not ____________ a new cultural group until later, after the new immigrants are viewed with less prejudice.
6. The metaphor of the patchwork quilt seems right to the multiculturalists because they see the United States as a ____________ of separate subcultures, each one distinct from the others.
7. Of the 1.6 million children in the United States who are ____________, about 18 percent are of a different race than their adopting parents, making their families ____________.
8. Cultural influences have distinct sources. We ____________ some of our culture from our families. We ____________ some of our culture subconsciously from just living in the culture—through TV and videos.
9. With ____________, individuals become part of the larger culture by accepting much, if not all, of that culture.
10. The pluralistic view differs from the single culture view in that it does not mean that immigrants must forget or ____________ their original culture.

B **Check the spelling of the vocabulary words with your teacher. Discuss the meanings of these words and any other unfamiliar words in the sentences.**

PREDICTIONS

Think about the questions in the Topic Preview on page 64 and the sentences you heard in the Vocabulary Preview. Write three questions that you think will be answered in the lecture. Share your questions with your classmates.

NOTETAKING PREPARATION

Transition Words and Phrases

Formal speech, like formal writing, is characterized by more frequent use of transition words and phrases. Transition words like such as *however, therefore,* and *in fact* help a listener understand the relationship between ideas and sentences in the lecture.

A good understanding of transition words will make a formal lecture easier to follow.

On the other hand and *however* point out contrasts between two ideas.
For instance and *for example* present examples.
In fact is used for emphasis.
Rather is used like *instead* to signal an alternative.
Furthermore is used like *also* to signal an additional point.
Therefore and *consequently* mean *for this reason* to signal a result or consequence.

A **Read through the sentences below. Choose the best transition word from the box above to complete each sentence. Write the transition word in the blank.**

1. The melting pot metaphor is a very old one. __________, it's been used since the nineteenth century.
2. Culture comes to people in different ways. __________, we inherit some, and we absorb some.
3. There are many proponents of the multiculturalist view; __________, I don't really agree with this view.
4. The multiculturalists don't use the metaphor of the melting pot. __________, they use the patchwork quilt.
5. Some existing groups were excluded from participating fully in society; __________, newly arrived groups were discriminated against.
6. We are not satisfied with the metaphors for U.S. culture in this lecture. __________, we are going to look for a new one.

B **Discourse Cues** **Number the following excerpts from the lecture from 1 to 5 in the order that you think you will probably hear them. Discuss with a partner or as a class the discourse cues that helped you figure out the order.**

_____ So, first is the single culture view of the United States as a "melting pot."
_____ This last cultural view, the pluralistic view, is a combination of the first two.
_____ To conclude, the United States has always reflected the cultures of its immigrants.
_____ Let me begin today's lecture by explaining the meaning of the word culture.
_____ Now let's move on to another view of U.S. culture.

FIRST LISTENING

CD 3, TR 2

A **Listen to the beginning of the lecture. Circle the set of notes below that best records the information you hear.**

a.

Cultr = trad + shared belfs & val
  Ex. in fam; ed; bus.; pol; ent.
US cultr ?? ppl othr countries & Am's
Contrst 3 ways US cult seen
- Sing cult (old)
- Multicult. (new)
- Pluralistic

b.

Cultr ≠ traditions; = blfs + val
  EX: fam. struc, ed. sys, etc.
Ppl fr othr cultrs, ? Am cultr
Nature US cult ? – contrast 3
  disc ↑ yrs
  decide = logical
  old (sing.), new (multi), third (pl)

CD 3, TR 3

B **Now listen to the whole lecture and take notes. Look at the lecturer's visual aids as you listen. These may help you understand parts of the lecture.**

Subtopic 1: Single Culture

Single Culture View

U.S. = Melting pot
  Homogeneous culture
Myth?
  Excluded groups

Subtopic 2: Multicultural

Multiculturalist View

U.S. = a patchwork quilt
  Many different subcultures
Opposition
  Ethnic and racial mixing

Subtopic 3: ______________________________

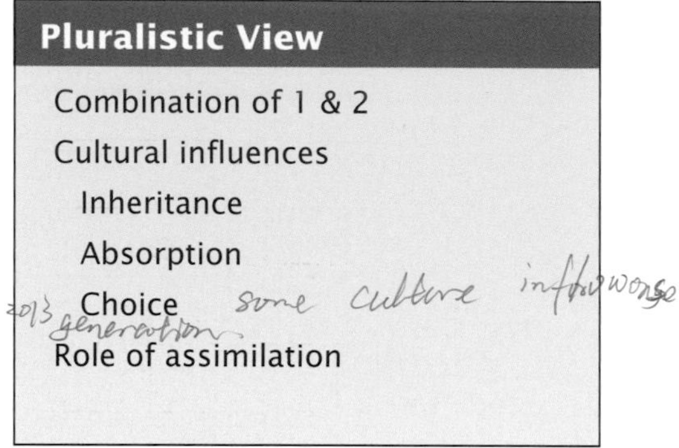

Pluralistic View

Combination of 1 & 2

Cultural influences

Inheritance

Absorption

Choice

Role of assimilation

SECOND LISTENING

CD 3, TR 4

Listen to the lecture again and make your notes as complete as possible.

THIRD LISTENING

CD 3, TR 5

A You will hear part of the lecture again. Listen and complete the notes by adding the information from the box.

i.e.	M.P.	→	cult	B.	=	diff

1. Singl. ________ view = U.S. as Melting Pot
   A. ________ = trad. metaph
      M.P. ← mix of ________ gps immigs blending
      ________ big homog. cult
   ________ comb of diff parts = new whole
   ________ Many think one cult ________ myth

B Compare your answers with a partner. Then compare the notes in A with the notes you took for this part of the lecture.

ACCURACY CHECK

CD 3, TR 6

A **Listen to the questions, and write short answers. Use your notes. You will hear each question one time only.**

1. What does coutre mean in this lecture ?
2. Which 2 groups people difficaty identy U.S coture is?
3. Which 3 views conture is old one?
4. What modifal us for single cutur view use?
5. Which 3 group people contre miss?
6. what modifal -> U.S coutur do moty coture us?
7. in 2010 what % of mary b/w people in differ or mignicyty?
8. Which part of word do U.S. children comfrom?
9. What 3 way U.S quit there coutur ploristic view?
10. Floristic view. same -> place by what generation?

B **Check your answers with your teacher. If your score is less than 70 percent, you may need to listen to the lecture again and rewrite some of your notes.**

ORAL SUMMARY

Use your notes to create an oral summary of the lecture with a partner. As you work together, add details to your notes that your partner included but you had missed.

DISCUSSION

Discuss the following questions with a classmate or in a small group.

1. Which of the three views of U.S. culture makes the most sense to you? Explain.
2. How important is it for immigrants to assimilate to the culture in a new country?
3. How open is your country of origin to influences from other cultures? Do people who spend long periods of time there assimilate to the culture, or do they maintain their own cultures?
4. Can you think of a particular metaphor that fits your culture?

PRE-READING

The following Reading is about the city of Marseille in France. Before you read, answer the following questions. Share your answers with a classmate.

1. What does the title of the article suggest to you about the population of the city of Marseille?
2. Marseille is on the sea, in the southern part of France. Where do you think immigrants to Marseille come from?

READING

Now read the article.

Marseille's Melting Pot

As more European countries become nations of immigrants, the city of Marseille in southern France may be a vision of the future, even a model of multiculturalism. In November 2005, with riots happening in just about every other French city's immigrant-filled housing projects, Marseille stayed cool.

Some local people believe that the Marseille miracle of social peace has a lot to do with its beaches, which serve as its great melting pot. Farouk Youssoufa, 25, met his 20-year-old wife, Mina, at one of Marseille's beaches. Youssoufa was born on a French island in the Comoros between Tanzania and Madagascar, and his skin is as black as anyone's in Africa. Mina is the fair-skinned French-born daughter of Algerian immigrants. "The new generation is much more of a mixture," says Youssoufa, who works with boys and girls of almost every skin tone and ethnic background at a cultural center in Marseille. On the beach, especially, "there are a lot of different communities that mix," Youssoufa says one hot afternoon in May. "Voilà: With time we've learned to live together."

Jean-Claude Gaudin, the mayor of Marseille, points out that the beach isn't the only geographic feature that has kept the city's melting pot bubbling. "Marseille's good luck is that it is surrounded by a belt of mountains." Immigrants and long-time residents have learned to live more or less on top of each other. When the country's growing economy needed foreign workers for factories, many French cities built housing projects for immigrants in distant suburbs.

"We did the opposite," says Gaudin. "We built in the city. Marseille is the oldest city in France. It's been in existence for 2,600 years. It's a port, and so we have always been used to having foreigners come here. The city itself is composed," he says, "of populations from abroad who came because of international developments." After 1915, Armenians began arriving. In the 1930s Italians who fled fascism settled in Marseille. And in 1962, after France had given up control of Algeria, Morocco, and Tunisia, tens of thousands of *pieds-noirs*, or "black feet," flooded Marseille. They were actually white French citizens fleeing newly independent Algeria, where many had lived for generations.

At the same time, Gaudin explains, Marseille gradually filled with other people—*issus de l'immigration*—produced by immigration. "That means that often the grandparents were in Algeria, the parents came here, and the grandchildren are French but have an Arab last name," says Gaudin. In other words, people who are French by birth but are still viewed as "foreigners."

Yet the mayor of Marseille can only guess how many of his city's residents are *issus de l'immigration.* He does not know how many are of Arab or African

The beach at Marseille where people of all ethnicities mix and mingle

descent. He does not know how many have Muslim roots. In France, it's against the law for any government official to record a citizen's race, religion, or ethnicity. Church and state are not only separate, but religion is officially ignored. If you are French, you are French: nothing more, nothing less, and nothing else. Yet Gaudin knows that even for the second and third generations, assimilation does not always come easily. The challenge for any city with a large immigrant population is rarely how to deal with the first wave of arrivals, but how their children and grandchildren will adapt, or not.

DISCUSSION

Discuss these questions with a classmate.

1. Based on what you learned from the lecture, which of the three ways of looking at culture—the single culture view, the multiculturalist view, or the pluralistic view—best describes the situation in Marseille?
2. In what ways do you think the French attitude toward cultural assimilation is different from the American attitude?
3. What are the differences between how the French government and the U.S. government deal with immigration?

PURSUING THE TOPIC

Explore the topic of this chapter further by doing the following.

Watch the movie *Green Card*, a 1990s romantic comedy about a French man who marries an American woman in order to be able to obtain a visa to stay in the United States. Or watch the movie *My Big Fat Greek Wedding*, a 2002 family comedy about maintaining Greek culture and tradition in modern-day America. Be prepared to discuss the movie with your classmates.

CHAPTER

8

Two Views on Crime

TOPIC PREVIEW

Answer the following questions with a partner or your classmates.

1. Do you think there has been an increase in violent crime in recent years? Why or why not?
2. What is the difference between "blue-collar" and "white-collar" crime?
3. Which of the following do you think is more responsible for whether a young person turns to crime—their family, their school, or the criminal justice system?

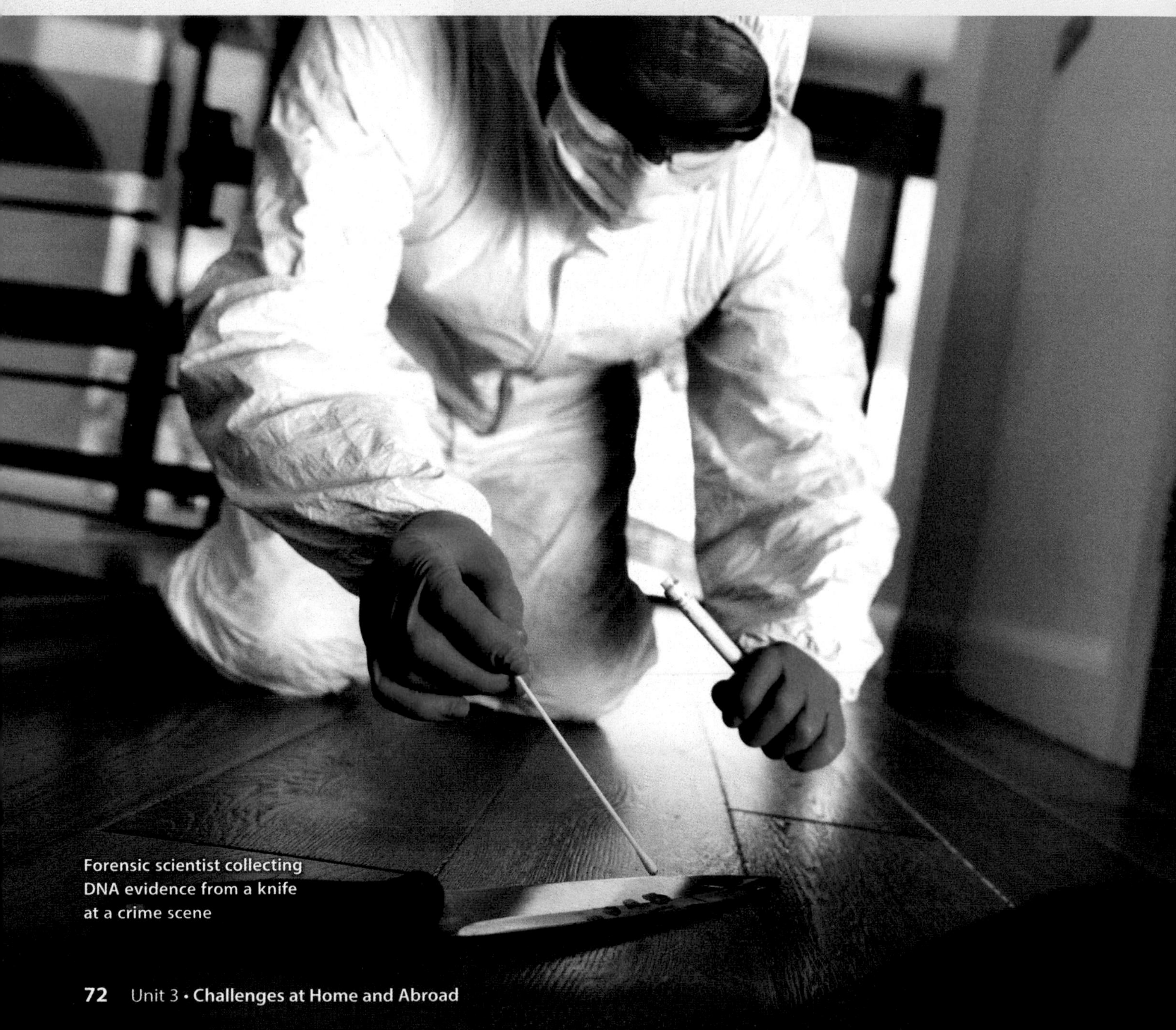

Forensic scientist collecting DNA evidence from a knife at a crime scene

VOCABULARY PREVIEW

CD 3, TR 7

A Read through the sentences below, which are missing vocabulary from the lecture. As you read, try to imagine which words would fit in the blanks. Then listen to the sentences and write the missing words in the blanks.

1. Some experts ________________ this drop in the crime rate to ________________: the U.S. population is getting older, and older people commit fewer crimes.
2. In recent years there has been stricter law ________________ in big cities, and very tough ________________ have been imposed on repeat offenders in general.
3. The encouraging statistics for violent crime may not be true for white-collar crime, crimes that include ________________, political corruption, ________________, and corporate policies that endanger workers and the public.
4. So, some people ________________ criminal behavior on society's ________________, or failures.
5. There are root causes like racism, poverty, and ________________.
6. In this theory, people become ________________ from society because they do not have many of the benefits that most Americans have.
7. The ________________ is that part of the population that typically fits the following profile: poor, unemployed, badly educated, nonwhite, and living in older city neighborhoods.
8. According to this theory, society tries to ________________ this aggressiveness and potential violence in two ways: by socializing us and, if that fails, by punishing us.
9. Society ________________ us by giving us values—values to prevent killing and stealing, for example. And society also gives us values for honesty, ________________, and kindness.
10. Our ________________ functions as a deterrent to violence and criminal behavior because we have been taught right from wrong.

B Check the spelling of the vocabulary words with your teacher. Discuss the meanings of these words and any other unfamiliar words in the sentences.

PREDICTIONS

Think about the questions in the Topic Preview on page 72 and the sentences you heard in the Vocabulary Preview. Write three questions that you think will be answered in the lecture. Share your questions with your classmates.

NOTETAKING PREPARATION

Using Indentation to Organize Notes 2

In chapter 5, you learned to organize your notes visually with indents and bullets. Ideas and information you hear can have more than two levels of importance. These less important details, examples, and ideas can be further indented to the right. A symbol, such as a hyphen (–) or a plus sign (+), can be used to indicate these other levels.

For example, information about solutions to crime in a part of this lecture could be organized like this:

Possible solutions to crime
- • the family's role
    - – socializing the children
        - + children respect themselves and others

A **Read the phrases below and decide their order of importance. Then complete the note outline by adding the phrases. Show order of importance with indenting and symbols.**

~~help them feel like part of society~~ / good education / good health care / overcome the alienation of the underclass / ~~society's role~~ / give them the same benefits that others have / ~~employment~~

society's role

        – help them feel like part of society

            + employment

B **Discourse Cues** **Number the following excerpts from the lecture from 1 to 5 in the order that you think you will probably hear them. Discuss with a partner or as a class the discourse cues that helped you figure out the order.**

_____ Well, let's go on and take a closer look at both theories.

_____ Today we're going to look at American attitudes about human nature and crime.

_____ OK, to start off with, people who believe social problems are caused by unequal opportunities prefer the first theory: that people are good by nature.

_____ Today I'd like to take a look at two different theories.

_____ Now, to go back to something I talked about earlier. This second theory helps us understand white-collar crime, I think.

FIRST LISTENING

CD 3, TR 8

A **Listen to the beginning of the lecture. Circle the set of notes below that best records the information you hear.**

a.

Am att to hum ntr & crime
CR 13.4% 2010
CR ↓ old ppl < yng ppl
Law enfrmnt & penalts ↑
Wh-collar cr ↑
• pub not afrd
• incld disc. of cr in US
Theor of cr = belief, hum ntr
• ppl good
• ppl aggress & violent
Solutns to cr in US

b.

Am attitudes abt human nature & crime
• stats
– FBI: v. cr. ↓ 13.4% 2001–10 (ex: ag, aslt, rob, murd, etc.)
+ US pop older / older= ↓ cr,
+ ↑ enfrcmnt & >penalts rep. cr
– Wht coll. C ↑ or ↓ ? (stats hard to get) (ex: brib, pol corrup, embez., dang. corp pol's)
• 2 theor C bsd on hum ntr — look at
– Theory 1: ppl good
– Theory 2 ppl aggress, so can be v.
– Pos. solutions to C in US

CD 3, TR 9

B **Now listen to the whole lecture and take notes. Look at the lecturer's visual aids as you listen. These may help you understand parts of the lecture.**

Subtopic 1: ______________________________

Environment → Criminal behavior
- Root causes in U.S. society
- Existence of an underclass

Subtopic 2: ______________________________

Aggressive nature → Violent behavior
- Socialization
- Punishment
- Connection to white-collar crime

Subtopic 3: ______________________________

Meeting the Challenge
- Role of family
- Role of government

SECOND LISTENING

CD 3, TR 10

Listen to the lecture again and make your notes as complete as possible.

THIRD LISTENING

CD 3, TR 11

A **You will hear part of the lecture again. Listen and complete the notes by adding the information from the box.**

BUT	ex	NO	polit.	SO	→	wh-coll

Theor #2 explains __________ C
- wh-collar crim. not usully under-class
  - busnssmn
  - __________
  - bankrs
- have benef's of soc., __________ good ed, good neigh.
- __________ for ? reason
  - __________ well-dev. conscience
  - __________ ntrl aggress
    - \+ __________ C

B **Compare your answers with a partner. Then compare the notes in A with the notes you took for this part of the lecture.**

AFTER LISTENING

ACCURACY CHECK

CD 3, TR 12

A **Listen to the following questions and write short answers. Use your notes. You will hear each question one time only.**

1. ______________________
2. ______________________
3. ______________________
4. ______________________
5. ______________________
6. ______________________
7. ______________________
8. ______________________
9. ______________________
10. ______________________

B **Check your answers with your teacher. If your score is less than 70 percent, you may need to listen to the lecture again and rewrite some of your notes.**

ORAL SUMMARY

Use your notes to create an oral summary of the lecture with your partner. As you work together, add details to your notes that your partner included but you had missed.

DISCUSSION

Discuss the following questions with a classmate or in a small group.

1. Which type of crime, violent crime or white-collar crime, causes the most damage to society? Explain.
2. Have you seen examples of how racism and poverty can lead people to crime?
3. Which do you think is more effective in keeping most people from committing crime: a strong conscience or a fear of punishment?
4. Should governments spend more money on keeping criminals in prison or on improving public education?

PRE-READING

The following Reading is about the nation of Singapore. Before you read, answer the following questions. Share your answers with a classmate.

1. What do you know about Singapore? For example, where is it located? Is it a rich or a poor country? What kind of government does it have? Is there any crime?
2. Look at the title of the article. The word *solution* implies that there is or was a problem. What do you think the problem could be?

READING

Now read the article.

The Singapore Solution

Singapore is often called the Switzerland of Southeast Asia. The tiny island gained independence from Britain in 1963 and, in one generation, transformed itself into a country where the income for its 3.7 million citizens is larger than in many European countries. Singapore also has excellent education and health systems and almost no government corruption; 90 percent of people own their own homes, and you never see homeless people.

Achieving all this has involved a delicate balance between what some Singaporeans refer to as "the big stick and the big carrot." First of all, the carrot: rapid financial growth. And the stick? Strict government control of citizens' lives. Racial and religious disharmony? They're simply not allowed, and no one steals anyone else's wallet.

The Singapore Flyer, the world's tallest Ferris wheel

Behind the "Singapore Model," a unique mix of economic empowerment and tightly controlled personal liberties, is Lee Kuan Yew. From a wealthy Chinese family, Cambridge University graduate Lee was Singapore's first prime minister, serving for 26 years and then as senior minister for another 15. His current title of minister mentor (MM) was established when his son, Lee Hsien Loong, became prime minister in 2004.

In creating the "Singapore Model," the MM turned a tiny country with no natural resources and a mix of ethnic groups into "Singapore, Inc." He attracted foreign investment, made English the official language, created a superefficient government, and eliminated corruption.

To lead a society, the MM says "one must understand human nature." He says, "The Confucian theory was man could be improved, but I'm not sure he can be. He can be trained, he can be disciplined." In Singapore that has meant lots of rules (no gum chewing and spitting on sidewalks) with fines and occasional notices in the newspaper about those who break the rules. Following the rules becomes automatic; you don't see very many police in Singapore. As one resident says, "The cop is inside our heads."

Singapore, maybe more than anywhere else, raises a basic question: Are financial success and personal security worth the extreme limits placed on individual freedom?

The Singapore government is aware that there are problems with its highly controlled society. One concern is the "creativity crisis." This is the fear that Singapore's schools, with their traditional educational methods, do not produce original thinkers. Another concern is a direct result of Singapore's overly successful population-control program, started in the 1970s. Today Singaporeans are simply not having enough children, so immigrants are needed to keep the population growing.

But there is a positive side. You could feel it during the "We Are the World" performance in the National Day show. On stage were representatives of Singapore's major ethnic groups: the Chinese, Malays, and Indians. After violent protests in the 1960s, the government started a strict system in public housing that required the different ethnic groups to live together. The purpose of this system may have been to control the population, but the apparently sincere expression of racial harmony at the performance was impressive.

Sculpture in Central Singapore

There is something called Singaporean, and it is real. Whatever people's complaints, Singapore is their home, and they love it despite everything. It makes you like the place, too.

DISCUSSION

Discuss these questions with a classmate.

1. Do any of the reasons mentioned in the lecture for a recent drop in crime in the United States also apply to Singapore? Which reasons? Explain your answer.
2. Which of the two theories of crime discussed in the lecture would Lee Kuan Yew of Singapore be most likely to agree with? Explain your answer using information in the reading and in the lecture.
3. Would the ways in which the Singaporean government has addressed social problems such as crime work in the United States? Why or why not? Use examples from the lecture to support your opinion.

PURSUING THE TOPIC

Explore the topic of this chapter further by doing the following.

The Web site for the Federal Bureau of Investigation (FBI) has a large amount of information about all aspects of crime in the United States. Individually or with a partner, choose a topic that interests you and read about it. Write up the details for a short presentation to the class.

www.fbi.gov

CHAPTER

9

The United States and the World

TOPIC PREVIEW

Discuss the following questions with a partner or your classmates.

1. Ten years from now, which country, or countries, do you think will be the most powerful in the world?
2. What kinds of responsibilities, if any, do powerful countries have to other countries?
3. Rank these three kinds of power in order from most to least important: (a) military, (b) economic, (c) political. Explain your reasons.

Coke bottle design contest held In Nanjing, China

BEFORE LISTENING

VOCABULARY PREVIEW

CD 3, TR 13

A **Read through the sentences below, which are missing vocabulary from the lecture. As you read, try to imagine which words would fit in the blanks. Then listen to the sentences and write the missing words in the blanks.**

1. Some experts are ________________ that China will become the new global leader because of its size as well as its economic and military strength.
2. It seems very likely that the United States will remain very important globally, at least for the ________________ future.
3. The United States can also help maintain financial ________________ in the world because of the size of its economy.
4. I'm describing hard power—that is, the ________________ or use of force.
5. This force can be economic, which would include ________________ against trading with a country.
6. For better or for worse, the United States has taken on the role of keeping a certain ________________ of power in many parts of the world.
7. The United States is also a member of NATO, an organization of mostly European nations ________________ to keeping peace in the world.
8. ASEAN countries like Indonesia and Malaysia engage in massive trade with China and may at times feel a little ________________ by China's size and power.
9. Soft power does not come from economic or military threat, but from how attractive or ________________ a country's culture, political ideals, and policies are.
10. The United States is still a ________________ to immigrants for both political and economic reasons.
11. My goal today was to give you a ________________ for understanding some of what you learn in the media about the U.S. economic, military, and political influence in the world today.

B **Check the spelling of the vocabulary words with your teacher. Discuss the meanings of these words and any other unfamiliar words in the sentences.**

PREDICTIONS

Think about the questions in the Topic Preview on page 80 and the sentences you heard in the Vocabulary Preview. Write three questions that you think will be answered in the lecture. Share your questions with your classmates.

NOTETAKING PREPARATION

Acronyms and Abbreviations 1

Acronyms are formed from the first letter of each word in a group or name. They are pronounced as words. For example, BRIC, which stands for Brazil, Russia, India, and China, is pronounced /brɪk/.

Abbreviations, like UN (United Nations), are different from acronyms and are pronounced letter by letter. Two common abbreviations usually used only in written language come from Latin: *e.g.*, used for "for example," and *i.e.*, used for "that is."

A Practice saying these acronyms and abbreviations with a partner.

1. NATO (North Atlantic Treaty Organization /ˈneɪ.t̬oʊ/)
2. ASEAN (Association of Southeast Asian Nations /əˈziː.ən/),
3. UNESCO (United Nations Educational, Social, and Cultural Organization /juːˈnes.koʊ/)
4. EU (European Union)

CD 3, TR 14

B Listen and complete the following sentences using acronyms and abbreviations.

1. Many countries have better economies, ______________, ______________.
2. ______________ is an important arm of the ______________.
3. France is a member of ______________.
4. Some ______________ countries are small, ______________, Cambodia.
5. Some people think the ______________ countries should become a federation, ______________, have a political structure that is similar to the ______________.

C Discourse Cues Number the following excerpts from the lecture from 1 to 5 in the order that you think you will probably hear them. Discuss with a partner or as a class the discourse cues that helped you figure out the order.

_____ First, let me give you some of the economic reasons Yetiv gives for why the United States will probably continue to be an important player globally.

_____ Now let's move on to the United States' use of what I'm describing today as hard power—that is, the threat or use of force.

_____ Professor Steve Yetiv of Old Dominion University in Virginia wrote three articles in which he gave a number of reasons why believes the United States will remain a global leader.

_____ Today I'd like to discuss the role of the United States in the world.

_____ Soft power does not come from economic or military threat, but from how attractive or persuasive a country's culture, political ideals, and policies are.

FIRST LISTENING

CD 3, TR 15

Listen to the lecture and take notes. Look at the lecturer's visual aids as you listen. These may help you understand parts of the lecture.

Introduction

The U.S. and the World

- Introduction
- The U.S. economy
- U.S. hard power
- U.S. soft power

Subtopic 1: ______________________________

Economic Reasons

- Ability to help others in crisis
- Ability to maintain financial stability
- U.S. dollar = global currency

Subtopic 2: ______________________________

Hard Power

- Middle East
- NATO
- ASEAN

Subtopic 3: ______________________________

Soft Power

- Democracy
- Economic competitiveness
- Education

SECOND LISTENING

CD 3, TR 16

Listen to the lecture again and make your notes as complete as possible.

THIRD LISTENING

CD 3, TR 17

A **You will hear part of the lecture again. Listen and complete the notes by adding the information from the box.**

ASEAN	econ	force	Mid	NATO	wrld	&

Hard Power = threat or use of __________

- __________
  sanctions
- mil
  US role = bal of power in __________
  - __________ East (free flow of oil)
  - Europe – __________ (organ of Eur ntns keep peace in wrld)
  - Asia – bal bet. ASEAN __________ China
    __________ incld e.g. Indonesia, Malaysia

B **Compare your answers with a partner. Then compare the notes in A with the notes you took for this part of the lecture.**

ACCURACY CHECK

CD 3, TR 18

A **Listen to the following questions, and write short answers. Use your notes. You will hear each question one time only.**

1. ______________________________
2. ______________________________
3. ______________________________
4. ______________________________
5. ______________________________
6. ______________________________
7. ______________________________
8. ______________________________
9. ______________________________
10. ______________________________

B **Check your answers with your teacher. If your score is less than 70 percent, you may need to listen to the lecture again and rewrite some of your notes.**

ORAL SUMMARY

Use your notes to create an oral summary of the lecture with your partner. As you work together, add details to your notes that your partner included but you had missed.

DISCUSSION

Discuss the following questions with a classmate or in a small group.

1. Which of the four BRIC nations, besides China, is most likely to be the next superpower?
2. Would the world be a safer place if the United States were less powerful?
3. In what ways are economic sanctions preferable to military force?
4. What are the advantages of having more than one superpower in the world? What are the disadvantages?

PRE-READING

The following Reading is about China's rapid economic growth. Before you read, answer the following questions. Share your answers with a classmate.

1. Look at the title of the article. What do you think "Go Green" means?
2. Scan the article for sentences that mention the United States. What comparisons does the writer make between the United States and China?

READING

Now read the article.

Can China Go Green?

Rizhao, in Shandong Province, is one of the hundreds of Chinese cities beginning to really grow. The road into town is eight-lanes wide, even though at the moment there's not much traffic. But the port is very busy. A big sign tells the residents to "build a civilized city and be a civilized citizen."

Rizhao is the kind of place that has scientists around the world deeply worried—China's rapid growth and new wealth are pushing carbon emissions higher and higher. It's the kind of growth that has led China to pass the United States to become the world's largest source of global warming gases.

And yet, after lunch at the Guangdian Hotel, the city's chief engineer, Yu Haibo, led me to the roof of the restaurant for another view. First we climbed over the hotel's solar-thermal system, a system that takes the sun's energy and turns it into all the hot water the kitchen and 102 rooms can possibly use. Then, from the edge of the roof, we looked at the view of the spreading skyline. On top of every single building a similar solar system could be seen. Solar is in at least 95 percent of all the buildings, Yu said proudly. "Some people say 99 percent, but I'm shy to say that."

Whatever the percentage, it's impressive—outside Honolulu, no city in the United States even comes close. China now leads the planet in energy produced by renewable solar and wind energy sources.

So, which is true? Is China the world's largest producer of global warming gases? Or is it the world's largest producer of renewable energy? The truth is, it's both.

Here's what we know: China is growing faster than any other big country has ever grown before, and that growth is opening real opportunities for environmental progress. Because it's putting up so many new buildings and power plants, the country can incorporate the latest technology more easily than countries with more mature economies. It's not just solar and wind energy. Some 25 Chinese cities are putting in subway systems or adding to existing ones. High-speed rail tracks are spreading in every direction. But all that growth takes lots of steel and cement, and as a result pours carbon into the air, which overwhelms the environmental progress. According to many energy experts, China's carbon emissions will continue to rise until at least 2030. This means that environmental progress in China will probably come too late to prevent more dramatic global warming, which could lead to environmental disasters such as the melting of the Himalayan glaciers and the rise of the seas.

It's a dark picture. Changing it in any real way will require change beyond China—most important, some kind of international agreement involving economies that use the most carbon—including of course the United States. At the moment China is taking steps that make sense for both the environment and its economy. "Why would they want to waste energy?" Deborah Seligsohn of the World Resources Institute asked, adding that "if the U.S. changed the game in a fundamental way—if it really committed to dramatic reductions—then China would look beyond its domestic interests and perhaps go much further." But for the moment, China's growth will continue, a roaring fire that throws off green sparks but burns with dangerous heat.

DISCUSSION

Discuss these questions with a classmate.

1. How is the focus of the lecture different from the focus of the article? Are there topics in the reading that are not mentioned in the lecture? Are there topics in the lecture that are not mentioned in the reading?
2. Do you think the author of the article would agree with the lecturer's view of the importance of the United States as a global power? Why or why not?
3. Do you think the lecturer would agree with the author of the article about the importance of China as a global power? Why or why not?

PURSUING THE TOPIC

Explore the topic of this chapter further by doing the following.

Watch a short YouTube video in which Professor Joseph Nye from Harvard's Kennedy School of Government speaks to Knoowii TV about the use of hard power, soft power, and smart power in international relations. Be prepared to discuss the ideas in the video with your classmates.

www.youtube.com/watch?v=cH9hn3_Q4qQ

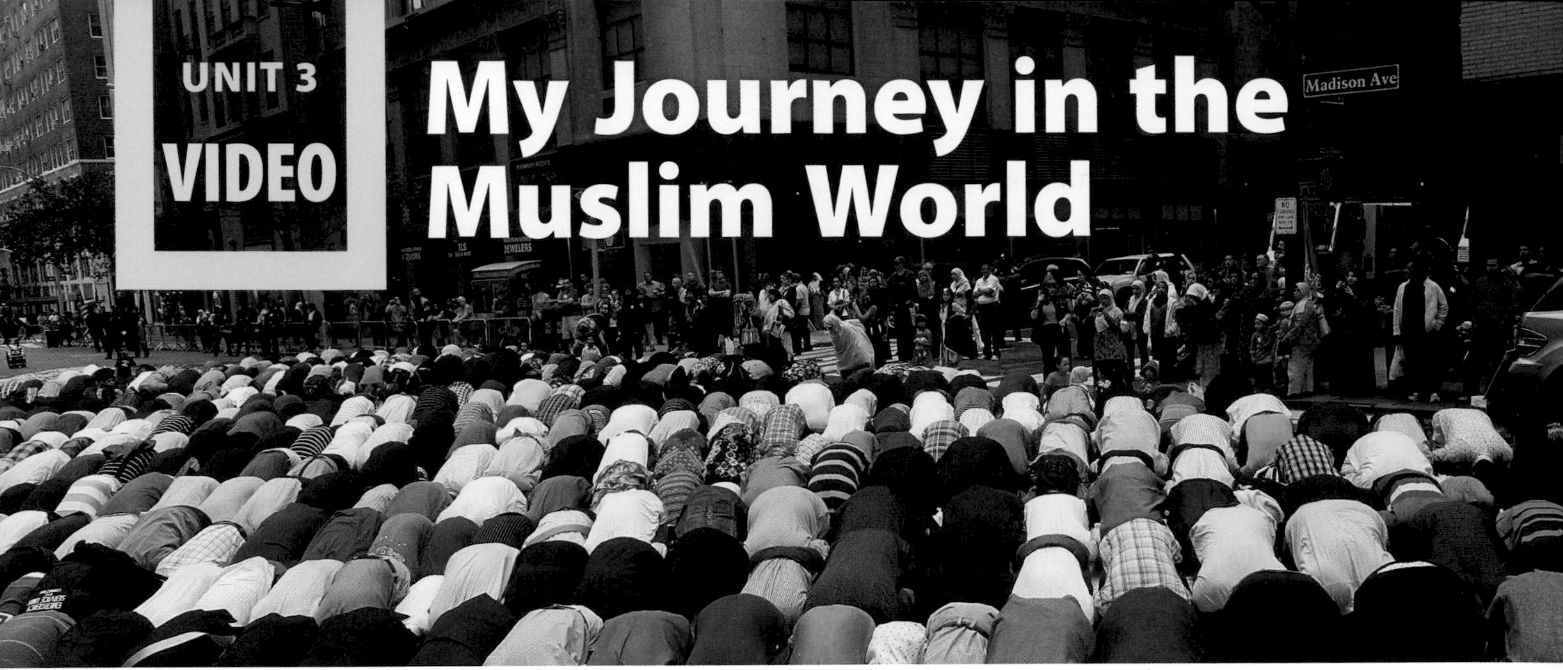

UNIT 3 VIDEO My Journey in the Muslim World

BEFORE VIEWING

TOPIC PREVIEW

Alexandra Avakian is a photojournalist. She was asked to take photographs of Muslims living in the United States. Answer the following questions with a partner.

1. What images or scenes would you expect to see in her photographs?
2. What different types of people would you expect to see in her photographs?
3. Do you think that Muslims in America have more or fewer difficulties than other immigrants living in the United States? Why or why not?

VOCABULARY PREVIEW

A **Read the definitions of these key words and phrases that you will hear during the video.**

engaged in actively involved in or part of something
an expert a person having a lot of knowledge about a particular topic
post 9/11 after the September 11, 2001, attack on the United States
fled left an area quickly in order to escape danger
reflected shown on a surface such as a mirror; seen in a person's expression
mainstream average; usual for the typical people in a group
are converting to are changing from one belief system, such as a religion, to a new one
maximum-security prison a prison where the most dangerous criminals are kept
protective keeping someone or something safe from harm

B **Work with a partner and write in the blank the word from the box that completes the sentence.**

artistic	civil war	pressure	security
Catholics	granddaughter	relatives	village

1. The ________________ she was under was **reflected** in her face.
2. The man was not an **expert** photographer, but his photos were very ________________.
3. The ________________ were very **protective** of their young ________________.
4. **Post 9/11**, there has been increased ________________ at U.S. airports.
5. There are **mainstream** ________________ who **are converting to** Islam.
6. The whole ________________ was very **engaged in** preparations for the fair.
7. Some people **fled** during the ________________; others were placed in a **maximum-security prison**.

VIEWING

FIRST VIEWING

Watch the video, and then compare your first impressions with a partner. Talk about what you remember, what surprised you, and what interested you.

SECOND VIEWING

Watch the video again. Listen for the missing words and write them in the blanks.

1. I hope to ________________ a wider view of a group of people much misunderstood, especially ________________ 9/11.
2. And these are Ryazan ________________, and they're an alternative, Islamic alternative to Barbie.
3. And you know Muslim Americans, like all Americans, have fled civil war, dictatorship, ________________ hardship.
4. These are Persian Americans, Iranian Americans, and they jump over ________________ on their New Year to cast off the bad luck of the previous year, you know, for good luck in the ________________ year.

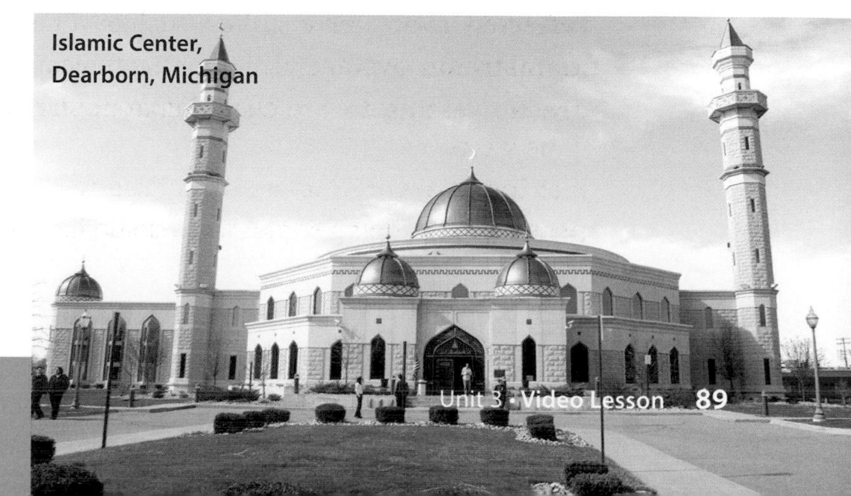
Islamic Center, Dearborn, Michigan

THIRD VIEWING

Complete these notes as you watch the video. Write only important words, not full sentences, and abbreviate common words.

Book = not all Ms
- not an expt.
- about misunderstood ppl after 9/11

Photos:
1) Dolls
2) Ldy fled CW:
3) Latif M. and Flo M.:
4) Zulia:
5) Penn.
6) Los Angeles:

AFTER VIEWING

ORAL SUMMARY

Use your notes to create an oral summary of the video with your partner. As you work together, add details to your notes that your partner included but you had missed.

DISCUSSION

Discuss the following questions with a classmate or in a small group.

1. What information about Alexandra Avakian's personal life do you learn during her lecture?
2. The speaker says that Muslims are a "group of people much misunderstood." What do you think makes her feel this way?
3. Which of the photos of Muslim Americans most interested you? Explain.

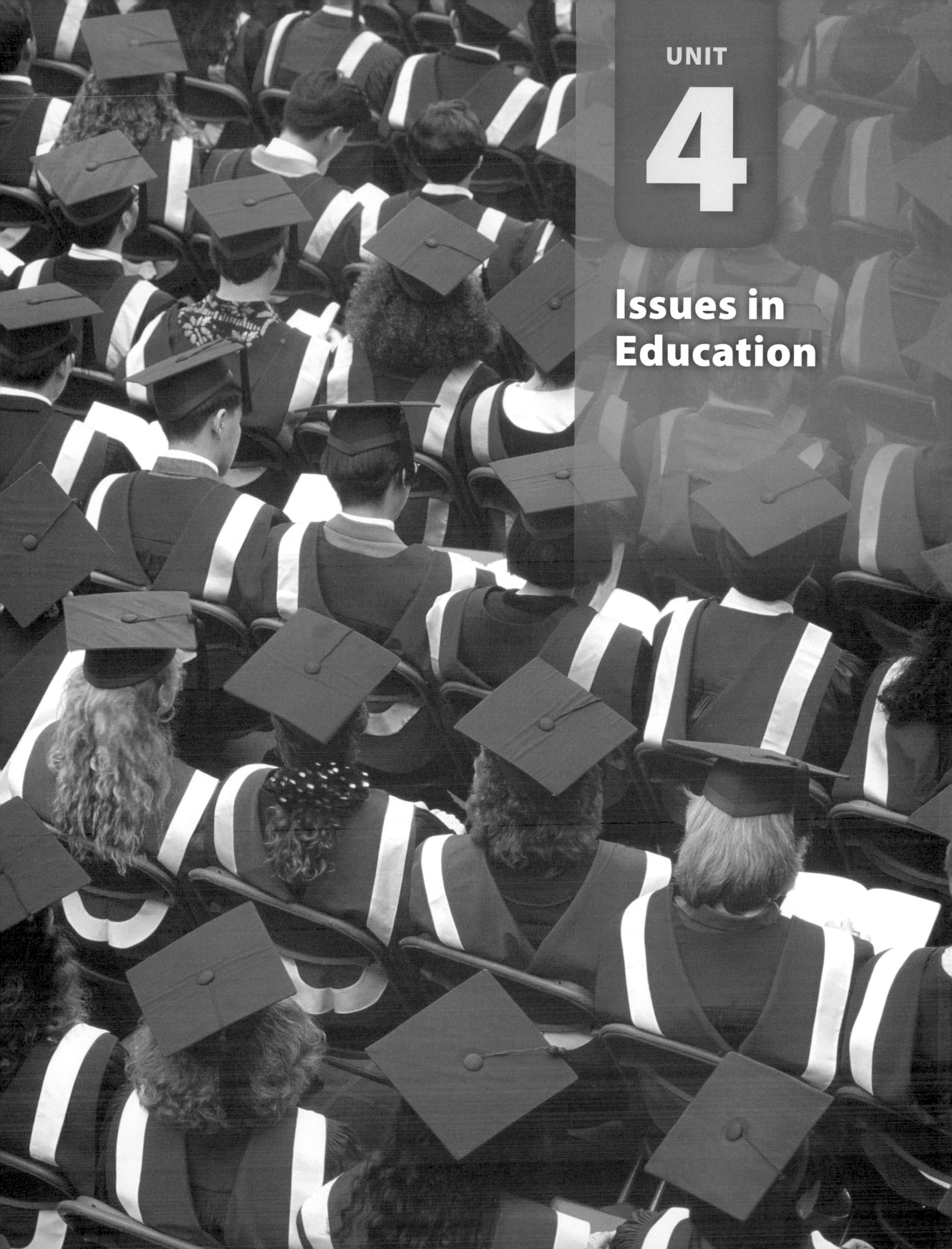

UNIT

4

Issues in Education

CHAPTER

10

Public Education in the United States

TOPIC PREVIEW

Discuss the following questions with a partner or your classmates.

1. Are children in your country of origin required to attend school? If so, until what age?
2. How are public schools in your country of origin funded, that is, where does the money come from to run the schools?
3. Where do most parents in your country of origin prefer to send their children: private schools or public schools? Why?

A student gets off the school bus in McCool Junction, Nebraska.

BEFORE LISTENING

VOCABULARY PREVIEW

CD 4, TR 1

A Read through the sentences below, which are missing vocabulary from the lecture. As you read, try to imagine which words would fit in the blanks. Then listen to the sentences and write the missing words in the blanks.

1. In the United States, attending school is ________________—children have to attend school, in most states to the age of 16.
2. A small percentage of American students attend private schools, either religious or ________________.
3. One unusual feature of U.S. public education is that there is no nationwide ________________ set by the federal government. And, there are no particular nationwide ________________ examinations.
4. Although the ________________ government provides ________________ to schools for special programs, it does *not* determine the curriculum or the examinations.
5. The state sets the number of ________________ a student must complete in order to graduate high school, and the credits include both required courses and ________________.
6. The school board is ________________ by the citizens of the district or ________________ by local officials.
7. Because private schools are not funded from taxes, parents pay ________________ to send their children to them.
8. The basic idea behind school ________________ is that parents choose the school their children will attend—public or private—and that school receives a set amount of money per student from public school funds.
9. Voucher schools are usually private schools, which are usually ________________ with religious organizations.
10. Congress passed an education bill called No Child Left Behind (NCLB), which required each state to develop and ________________ testing programs.

B Check the spelling of the vocabulary words with your teacher. Discuss the meanings of these words and any other unfamiliar words in the sentences.

PREDICTIONS

Think about the questions in the Topic Preview on page 92 and the sentences you heard in the Vocabulary Preview. Write three questions that you think will be answered in the lecture. Share your questions with your classmates.

NOTETAKING PREPARATION

Using Outline Form with Letters and Numbers

You have already practiced organizing your notes by writing the most important information to the left and less important information to the right. As you develop this skill, you can use numbers and letters to make the organization even clearer. You can use Roman numerals (I, II, etc.); capital letters; Arabic numerals (1, 2, etc.); and small letters to identify the levels of detail, from general to specific, in an outline. For example:

I. Economic reasons for U.S. remaining a global player
    A. Enough money to help others in a crisis
        1. natural disasters
            a. tsunami
            b. volcanic eruption
        2. countries in bad financial situation
        3. countries with political problems
    B. U.S. helps maintain stability as a market for the world's goods

A **Look at the lecture notes in the box above. Answer the questions about the notes by writing the letters or numerals of the correct notes.**

1. Which point in the outline is the most general, that is, the main idea?

    ____

2. Which points explain the main idea?

    ____

    ____

3. Which points give a third level of detail about the main idea?

    ____

    ____

    ____

4. Which points are specific examples?

    ____

    ____

CD 4, TR 2

B **Listen to part of the lecture. Write notes to complete the outline below. Some information is already filled in for you. Fill in the rest of the information as you listen.**

I. Three levels of control within states
   A. ______________________
      1. Responsibilities
         a. Sets curriculum requirements
         b. ______________________
   B. School district
      1. Numbers depend on ______________________
      2. School board is elected or appointed
      3. Responsibilities
         a. ______________________
            i. required courses
            ii. ______________________
         b. ______________________
   C. ______________________
      1. Teachers' responsibilities
         a. ______________________
         b. ______________________

C **Discourse Cues** **Number the following excerpts from the lecture from 1 to 5 in the order that you think you will probably hear them. Discuss with a partner or as a class the discourse cues that helped you figure out the order.**

_____ The first issue is inequality of educational opportunity.

_____ Let's talk first about charter schools.

_____ Today, I'd like to discuss two educational issues and efforts to solve them.

_____ The second issue involves private schools.

_____ Two efforts to deal with these issues are charter schools and school vouchers.

FIRST LISTENING

CD 4, TR 3

A **Listen to the beginning of the lecture. Circle the set of notes below that best records the information you hear.**

a.

I. School Compul in US
  A. 16 or 9th gr
  B. K–12
  C. Pub schl
    1. 90% sec
  D. Priv schl
    2. rel/sec
II. US pub ed
  A. No ntl curric & exams
  B. Spec prgs–hndcp, biling
  C. States contrl
    1. 3 levels
    2. Funding
    3. Issues & efforts

b.

US public schools – intro
  A. Compul. (must att) to age 16 or gr 9
  B. fr K/1st (age 5/6) to 12th gr (18) = "K through 12"
  C. 90% stud in pub. sch; sm no. priv sch.
    1. priv, relig or secu; pub, all secu
  D. No national curric or exams
    1. Fed gov. fund special prog
      a. handicap
      b. bilingual
Control of ed by indiv states (today)
I. 3 levels of contrl w/in a state
II. How ed funded
III. Issues + efforts (st & nat) to fix

CD 4, TR 4

B **Now listen to the whole lecture and take notes. Look at the lecturer's visual aids as you listen. These may help you understand parts of the lecture.**

Subtopic 1: Three Levels of Control in Each State

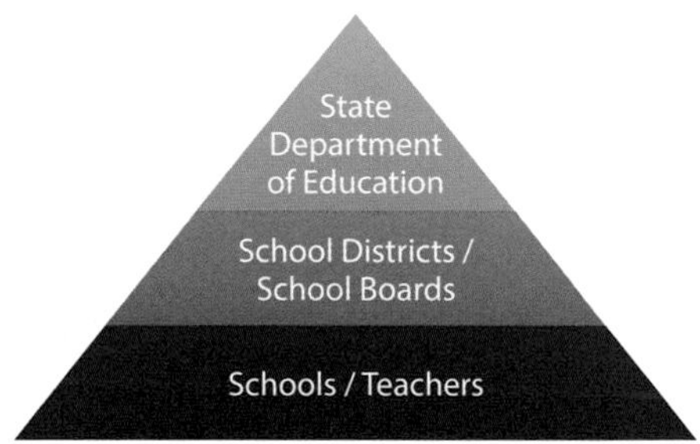

Subtopic 2: How Ed. Is Funded

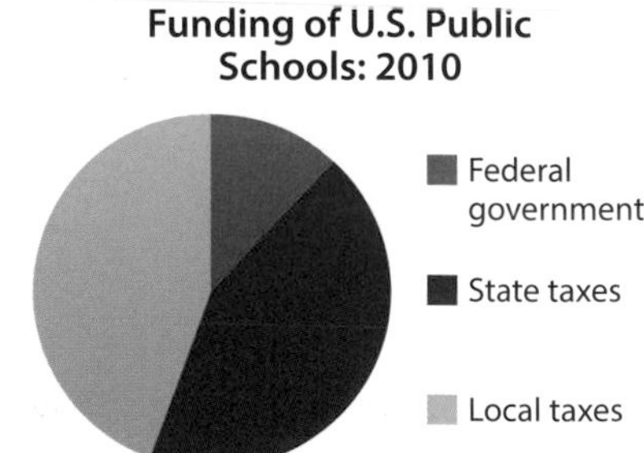

Subtopic 3: Ed. Issues & Efforts to Solve Them

Issues and Solutions

Inequality of Educational Opportunity
- Charter schools
- School vouchers

Educational Standards
- No Child Left Behind (NCLB)
- Common Core State Standards (CCSS)

SECOND LISTENING

CD 4, TR 5

Listen to the lecture again and make your notes as complete as possible.

THIRD LISTENING

CD 4, TR 6

A You will hear part of the lecture again. Listen and complete the notes by adding the information from the box.

AY	critics	pub	Ss	↑	>	??	$$

A. Chart Schs = type ________ sch
  1. funding fr taxes
  2. compt w/ reg pub schls for ________
  3. operate
    a. chrtr/contr fr St/lcl sch bd/oth pub org
    b. ________ indep
      • selectng Ts
      • curric
      • ________
  4. CSs-Stats
    a. 1st @ end 1980s
    b. AY 1999/2000 → 2009/10 # Ss ↑ fr 0.3M to 1.6M (4X ________)
    c. ________ 2009/10 CSs = ~5% of all pub sch's
  5. effective ________ – studies mixed
  6. ________ fear CSs mngd by priv comp's w/ intrst in $$ not ed

B Compare your answers with a partner. Then compare the notes in A with the notes you took for this part of the lecture.

ACCURACY CHECK

CD 4, TR 7

A **Listen to the following questions and write short answers. Use your notes. You will hear each question one time only.**

1. ______
2. ______
3. ______
4. ______
5. ______
6. ______
7. ______
8. ______
9. ______
10. ______

B **Check your answers with your teacher. If your score is less than 70 percent, you may need to listen to the lecture again and rewrite some of your notes.**

ORAL SUMMARY

Use your notes to create an oral summary of the lecture with your partner. As you work together, add details to your notes that your partner included but you did not.

DISCUSSION

Discuss the following questions with a classmate or in a small group.

1. Should people who don't have children attending public schools have to pay the same taxes as people who do? Why or why not?
2. Should all children nationwide be receiving exactly the same education? Why or why not?
3. What other reasons besides less funding for schools in poor areas might also contribute to poorer educational outcomes?
4. Would you send your children to a public school or a private school? Why?

PRE-READING

The following Reading is about pressures faced by Chinese school children. Before you read, answer the following questions. Share your answers with a classmate.

1. Look at the title of the Reading article. What is prosperity? Anxiety? What types of anxieties might sudden prosperity bring?
2. In what ways do you think the lives of school children can be affected by a country's rapid economic growth?

READING

Now read the article.

China's Sudden Prosperity Brings New Freedoms and Anxieties

The past decade has seen the rise of a Chinese middle class, now estimated to number between 100 million and 150 million people. These days, Chinese people are free to choose where to live, work, and travel, and economic opportunities grow year by year. However, if you pick up a Chinese newspaper, what comes through is a sense of discomfort at the speed of social change. Parents struggle to teach their children but feel their own knowledge is out of date. Children often guide their parents through the complications of modern life. "Society has completely turned around," says Zhou Xiaohong, a sociologist at Nanjing University. "Fathers used to give orders, but now fathers listen to their sons."

Because their parents have such high hopes for them, children are among the most pressured. They live in a world that combines old and new, with the most punishing elements of both. The traditional examination system that selects a favored few for higher education remains: The number of students

entering college in a given year is equal to 11 percent of the college-freshman-age population, compared with 64 percent in the United States. Yet the desire to develop well-rounded students has also led to an explosion of activities—music lessons, English, drawing, and martial arts classes—all of which are highly competitive.

The life of Zhou Jiaying, a Chinese girl from Shanghai, is typical. At the age of four, Zhou Jiaying was enrolled in two classes—Spoken American English and English Conversation—and given the English name Bella. Her parents hoped she might go abroad for college. When she turned eight, she started on the piano, which taught discipline and developed the brain. In the summers she went to the pool for lessons; swimming, her parents said, would make her taller. Bella wanted to be a lawyer, and to be a lawyer you had to be tall.

By the time she was 10, Bella lived a life that was rich with possibility and as strictly regulated as a soldier's. After school she did homework until her parents got home. Then came dinner, bath, piano practice. Sometimes she was permitted television, but only the news. On Saturdays she took a private essay class followed by Math Olympics, and on Sundays a piano lesson and a prep class for her entrance exam to a Shanghai middle school. The best moment of the week was Friday afternoon, when school let out early. Bella might take a deep breath and look around, like a man who discovers a glimpse of blue sky from the prison yard.

The effort to shape Bella is full of contradictions. Her parents encourage her independence but worry that school and the workplace will punish her for it. They are concerned about how much homework she has, but they then add more assignments on top of her regular schoolwork. "We don't want to be brutal to her," says Bella's father, Zhou Jiliang. "But in China, the environment doesn't let you do anything else."

DISCUSSION

Discuss these questions with a classmate.

1. Do you think Bella goes to a public school or a private school? Use specific information from the reading and the lecture as well as your own knowledge to explain your answer.
2. Compare and contrast the information in the lecture and Reading about the importance of standardized testing in schools in the United States and China.
3. In what ways are Bella's experiences similar to those of an American school child? In what ways are they different?

PURSUING THE TOPIC

Explore the topic of this chapter further by doing the following.

Watch the movie *The Joy Luck Club*, a 1993 movie about the lives of four immigrant Chinese mothers raising their daughters in San Francisco. Be prepared to discuss the movie with your classmates.

CHAPTER 11

The College Admissions Process

TOPIC PREVIEW

Discuss the following questions with a partner or your classmates.

1. In your culture, what is the most important exam that a high school student takes?
2. What happens if students do not do well on the exam?
3. How difficult is it to be admitted to a university in your culture? Why?

Students taking an exam in a college lecture hall

BEFORE LISTENING

VOCABULARY PREVIEW

CD 4, TR 8

A **Read through the sentences below, which are missing vocabulary from the lecture. As you read, try to imagine which words would fit in the blanks. Then listen to the sentences and write the missing words in the blanks.**

1. Most colleges are ________________, which means the schools meet certain standards set by outside ________________.
2. Over three-quarters of all students—76 percent—are ________________ in public colleges and universities.
3. The average cost in 2012 for tuition and room and board at a four-year college for a student living on ________________ in a ________________ varies a lot.
4. With such a wide variety of schools of different sizes, types, and locations, it probably won't surprise you to find out that admissions ________________ at these colleges and universities can vary, too.
5. Four-year colleges and universities will all require an ________________ and a high school ________________, which is a record of the applicant's grades and rank in their high school class.
6. Very often applicants for an ________________ program must also include an essay and recommendations from high school teachers
7. Some people say standardized exams don't fairly evaluate a student's ________________ for college.
8. Even the most ________________ and most highly competitive colleges and universities will consider other factors.
9. Admissions standards at community colleges are usually more ________________ than those at four-year colleges and universities.
10. Many community college programs are vocational in nature, that is, they train students to become medical technicians, office assistants, cooks, airline mechanics, or other ________________ workers needed by the community.
11. Students in the United States have many ________________ in pursuing higher education.

B **Check the spelling of the vocabulary words with your teacher. Discuss the meanings of these words and any other unfamiliar words in the sentences.**

PREDICTIONS

Think about the questions in the Topic Preview on page 101 and the sentences you heard in the Vocabulary Preview. Write three questions that you think will be answered in the lecture. Share your questions with your classmates.

NOTETAKING PREPARATION

Acronyms and Abbreviations 2

You have learned that acronyms are words formed by the first letters of the words in the name of something and are pronounced as words, not individual letters. For example, IELTS (International English Language Testing System) is an acronym and it is pronounced /ˈaɪ.ɛlts/.

Abbreviations like EFL (English as a Foreign Language) and ESL (English as a Second Language) are different because they are pronounced letter by letter (*E-F-L*; *E-S-L*). Some other short forms are a combination—part abbreviation and part acronym. For example, MCAT (Medical College Admission Test) is pronounced *M-cat*, like the letter *M* and the word *cat*.

CD 4, TR 9

A **Listen to a part of the lecture. Write the short form—abbreviation, acronym, or combination—that you hear next to what it represents.**

1. Standardized admission tests for college ____________ ____________
2. Standardized admission test for many graduate schools ____________
3. Graduate business degree program ____________
4. Standardized admission test for graduate business school ____________
5. Standardized admission test for law school ____________
6. Standardized English-language exams required of foreign students

   ____________ ____________

B **Discourse Cues** **Number the following excerpts from the lecture from 1 to 5 in the order that you think you will probably hear them. Discuss with a partner or as a class the discourse cues that helped you figure out the order.**

_____ With such a wide variety of schools of different sizes, types, and locations, it probably won't surprise you to find out that admissions requirements at these colleges and universities can vary, too.

_____ Let's begin with some facts and figures.

_____ In this lecture, I'm going to talk to you about postsecondary education in the United States, that is, education that students pursue after high school.

_____ Very often applicants for an undergraduate program must also include an essay and recommendations from high school teachers with their application.

_____ In brief, you can see that educational opportunities and admissions standards at postsecondary schools vary greatly in the United States.

FIRST LISTENING

CD 4, TR 10

A **Listen to the beginning of the lecture. Circle the set of notes below that best records the information you hear.**

a.

Postsecondary Ed in US
I. Facts and figures
II. Gen info abt admiss policies
III. Comm Coll

b.

Postsecondary Ed in US = HS Ed
Most coll accrdtd (outside eval standrds)
1. Gen info abt admiss policies
2. Community Coll

c.

I. Postsecondary Ed in US
II. Facts and Figures
III. Gen info abt admiss policies
IV. Commun Coll

CD 4, TR 11

B **Now listen to the whole lecture and take notes. Look at the lecturer's visual aids as you listen. These may help you understand parts of the lecture.**

Subtopic 1: ______________________________

Colleges & Universities
- Private vs. public
- Size
- Student body
- Programs of study
- Location
- Cost

Subtopic 2: ______________________________

Requirements
- Application
- Standardized tests
- Diversity
- High school rank

Subtopic 3: ______________________

Two-Year Colleges

- Admissions standards
- Cost
- Vocational training
- Reasons for attending

SECOND LISTENING

CD 4, TR 12

Listen to the lecture again and make your notes as complete as possible.

THIRD LISTENING

CD 4, TR 13

A **You will hear part of the lecture again. Listen and complete the notes by adding the information from the box.**

HS	req	Ss	Ts	IELTS	LSAT	SAT

II. Admissions: __________ vary dep on type—2-yr coll few req, but 4-yr req:
  A. Application
    1. __________ transcript
    2. Undergrad – essay + rec fr HS __________
  B. Standardized tests
    1. Undergrad: __________ & ACT
    2. Grad: GRE, GMAT (for MBA), __________ (for law)
    3. Foreign __________: TOEFL, __________

B **Compare your answers with a partner. Then compare the notes in A with the notes you took for this part of the lecture.**

ACCURACY CHECK

CD 4, TR 14

A **Listen to the following questions and write short answers. Use your notes. You will hear each question one time only.**

1. ______________________________
2. ______________________________
3. ______________________________
4. ______________________________
5. ______________________________
6. ______________________________
7. ______________________________
8. ______________________________
9. ______________________________
10. ______________________________

B **Check your answers with your teacher. If your score is less than 70 percent, you may need to listen to the lecture again and rewrite some of your notes.**

ORAL SUMMARY

Use your notes to create an oral summary of the lecture with your partner. As you work together, add details to your notes that your partner included but you had missed.

DISCUSSION

Discuss the following questions with a classmate or in a small group.

1. What are the advantages and disadvantages of a highly competitive examination system that limits the number of students who can enter the university?
2. What are the advantages and disadvantages of a less competitive system that allows more students to continue their education after secondary school?
3. In your opinion, which should college admissions officers look at more carefully: a student's transcript, extra-curricular activities, teacher recommendations, or standardized test scores?

PRE-READING

The following Reading is about a global ranking of higher education systems. Before you read, answer the following questions. Share your answers with a classmate.

1. Look at the table at the beginning of the article. Are you surprised by the rankings? Are there any countries missing that you expected to find? Explain.
2. What types of information do you think the authors of the report used to determine the rankings?

READING

Now read the article.

International Ranking of Systems of Higher Education

Universitas 21 (U21) is a global network of universities. Its purpose is to promote global citizenship through international research collaboration. In May 2012, U21 released a report containing the first international ranking of higher education systems, a project carried out at the Institute of Applied Economic and Social Reasearch at the University of Melbourne. Forty-eight countries were included. Four variables were considered in determining the rankings: resources, environment, connectivity, and output. The top 10 countries overall are listed in the table.

U21 Rankings 2012

RANK	COUNTRY	SCORE
1	United States	100.0
2	Sweden	83.6
3	Canada	82.8
4	Finland	82.0
5	Denmark	81.0
6	Switzerland	80.3
7	Norway	78.0
8	Australia	77.8
9	Netherlands	77.4
10	United Kingdom	76.8

Resources include the amount of money spent on higher education, per country and per student. This is money spent on educating students and conducting research. It includes money spent by the government, private citizens, businesses, and the educational institutions themselves. The country that spent the most on higher education was Canada, followed by Denmark, Sweden, and the United States. It is interesting to note that Great Britain, the country that ranked tenth overall, ranked quite low in this category, twenty-seventh.

The second category, environment, includes an evaluation of government regulations on higher education. In particular, the authors were looking at measures to ensure quality education and to what degree government regulations restricted academic freedom. Included under environment are variables such as the number of female students and academic staff as compared to male students and staff, the availability of government data on higher education, and information about governmental control over the selection of academic staff at individual institutions. The Netherlands came out on top in this category, with New Zealand and the United States coming in second and third.

The third category, connectivity, measures interaction with institutes of higher education in other countries. It takes into account the number of international students enrolled in higher education in the country and the number of articles coauthored with collaborators from other countries. Austria, Singapore, and Australia were ranked as the top three countries. Interestingly, the United States was not among the top 10 countries in this category. According to the report's authors, this is because so many top research institutions are located within the United States.

The final category, output, looks at three things. First, does the higher education system provide the country with a workforce educated to meet the country's needs? Second, does it provide opportunities to people with different interests and skills? Finally, does it contribute to national and world knowledge? Output takes into account, among other things, the number of academic researchers and the number of articles produced, per country and per student; the quality of the research produced; the percentage of the population enrolled in higher education; and unemployment rates of people with degrees from institutions of higher education. In output, the United States came out on top, followed by the United Kingdom, Canada, Finland, and Sweden.

It is interesting that some neighboring countries had similar overall rankings. For example, the Eastern European countries of Ukraine, the Czech Republic, Poland, and Slovenia ranked between 25 and 28. The Latin American countries of Chile, Argentina, Brazil, and Mexico also ranked close together. The report's authors say, "It would seem that while many countries may feel they cannot hope to match the higher education system in the United States, they do want to match that of their neighbors."

DISCUSSION

Discuss these questions with a classmate.

1. What information from the lecture would you include for each of the variables discussed in the article—resources, environment, connectivity, and output? Make a list on a separate paper.
2. Think about what you learned from the lecture and the article. Why do you think the United States has a highly regarded system of higher education?
3. How is the system of higher education in the United States different from the system of higher education in your country or in another country with which you are familiar?

PURSUING THE TOPIC

Explore the topic of this chapter further by doing the following.

Individually or with a partner, look at the most recent U21 ranking of national higher education systems at the following Web address. Choose a topic or country that interests you and read more about it. Write up the details for a short presentation to the class.

www.universitas21.com/article/projects/details/152/u21-ranking-of-national-higher-education-systems

CHAPTER

12

International Students

TOPIC PREVIEW

Discuss the following questions with a partner or your classmates.

1. Which countries do you think most postsecondary international students in the United States come from?
2. What do you suppose are the most popular fields of study for these international students?
3. What benefits do you think these international students bring to their new U.S. college or university?

VOCABULARY PREVIEW

CD 4, TR 15

A **Read through the sentences below, which are missing vocabulary from the lecture. As you read, try to imagine which words would fit in the blanks. Then listen to the sentences and write the missing words in the blanks.**

1. The number of international students studying in the United States has risen quite __________________ over the last 50 to 60 years, with an occasional small __________________ due to political or economic reasons.
2. In number of students, China only recently __________________ ahead of India, which had been number one for most of the previous decade.
3. Social sciences include such __________________ as sociology, psychology, and political science.
4. Building "bridges," or relationships, between the United States and other countries, and bringing global ways of looking at things are the types of benefits __________________ everyone mentions when talking about students going to different countries to study.
5. As one benefit, NAFSA, an association of international educators, __________________ the contribution international students make with their local spending on shopping, housing, and so forth.
6. In the academic year of 2010–2011, international students and their families made a __________________ contribution to the U.S. economy of about 20 billion dollars.
7. Some criticisms have been raised about __________________ that encourage not only the admission of so many international students, especially to graduate schools, but also ones that encourage some of these students to remain after completing their degrees.
8. According to NAFSA, international students have only increased the size of Ph.D. programs, not taken __________________ places from U.S. students.
9. Employers do not have to pay some taxes for certain foreign employees that they would have to pay for American employees, which critics believe is an unfair economic __________________ to hire foreign graduates.

B **Check the spelling of the vocabulary words with your teacher. Discuss the meanings of these words and any other unfamiliar words in the sentences.**

PREDICTIONS

Think about the questions in the Topic Preview on page 109 and the sentences you heard in the Vocabulary Preview. Write three questions that you think will be answered in the lecture. Share your questions with your classmates.

NOTETAKING PREPARATION

Reviewing Basic Notetaking Skills

No two people will take exactly the same notes on any lecture. However, most people will use at least some of the same skills, such as abbreviating words, using conventional symbols, and organizing information in a way that shows main ideas and details. This means that if you miss a class and have to review a classmate's notes, you should be able to interpret them, even if the classmate uses a slightly different system of notetaking from yours.

A **Read and interpret the notes below that a classmate took during a lecture on distance education. As you read, think about what abbreviations such as *Int'd*, *req*, *trad*, *disc*, and *ind* would mean.**

Classmate's notes

6 Things for P'ple Int'd in DE to Consid

1. many DE progs have res reqs
2. DE courses & progs have ti limits
3. DE adm's reqs = on-campus reqs
4. DE can save $ sometimes
    - Don't need to travel to class
    - But academic fees = trad ed
    - Res reqs can be costly
5. Online DE means stud needs access to comp w/ min reqs
    - e.g., latest version of Windows
        - a microph, snd card & speakers
        - adequate hard drive & RAM, modem, browser, & Internet
    - Connection speed very imp
        - cable modem
        - DSL
6. Stud need to be disc & ind
    - DE not easier than trad ed
    - dropout rate > than trad ed

B **Now complete the homework assignment. Use your classmate's notes to answer the homework questions.**

Homework assignment

1. Do all distance education programs have a residency requirement?

   ____

2. Do DE students have to follow a timetable similar to on-campus students?

   ____

3. Is it easier to be admitted to a distance program than to an on-campus programs?

   ____

4. What is the main way DS can save a student money?

   ____

5. What are three examples of computer requirements that online study might require?

   ____

6. Is distance education easier than traditional education (i.e., on campus)?

   ____

7. Are students more likely to complete distance education programs or traditional programs?

   ____

C **See how well you were able to interpret your classmate's notes by looking at the lecture transcript on page 180 in appendix A.**

D **Discourse Cues** **Number the following excerpts from the lecture from 1 to 5 in the order that you think you will probably hear them. Discuss with a partner or as a class the discourse cues that helped you figure out the order.**

_____ OK, let's begin with the number of international students studying in the United States.

_____ Well, we've covered a lot today. I hope I've at least given you some food for thought about the impact that international students have.

_____ Next I would like to discuss the benefits these students bring to the States, according to NAFSA, an association of international educators.

_____ Today I'd like to spend some time discussing international students—in this case, students from other countries studying at U.S. colleges and universities.

_____ NAFSA also addresses some of the criticisms that have been raised about policies that encourage the admission of so many international students.

CD 4, TR 16

FIRST LISTENING

Listen to the lecture and take notes. Look at the lecturer's visual aids as you listen. These may help you understand parts of the lecture.

Introduction

International Students

Introduction
Facts and figures
Benefits from foreign students
Three criticisms

Subtopic 1: ______________________________

International Students
Place of Origin, AY 2011/2012

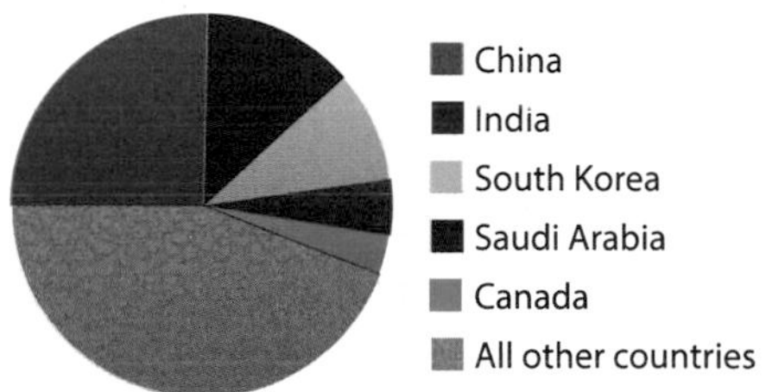

Subtopic 2: ______________________________

Five Benefits

1. Building bridges
2. Global perspective
3. Science & engineering courses
4. Tuition income
5. Local spending

Subtopic 3: ______________________________

Three Criticisms

1. Compete with U.S. students for admission
2. Compete with U.S. citizens for jobs
3. Brain drain

CD 4, TR 17

SECOND LISTENING

Listen to the lecture again and make your notes as complete as possible.

THIRD LISTENING

CD 4, TR 18

A **You will hear part of the lecture again. Listen and complete the notes by adding the information from the box.**

Areas	Comp	Eng	Manag	Phys	Soc	Sc

C. Interntl Ss—__________ of Study
   1. Bus & __________
   2. __________
   3. Math & __________ Sc
   4. __________ (phys, chem, astron) & Life __________, (biol, microbiol, biochem)
   5. __________ Sc (soc, psych, pol sc)

B **Compare your answers with a partner. Then compare the notes in A with the notes you took for this part of the lecture.**

AFTER LISTENING

ACCURACY CHECK

CD 4, TR 19

A **Listen to the following questions and write short answers. Use your notes. You will hear each question one time only.**

1. ______________________________
2. ______________________________
3. ______________________________
4. ______________________________
5. ______________________________
6. ______________________________
7. ______________________________
8. ______________________________
9. ______________________________
10. ______________________________

B **Check your answers with your teacher. If your score is less than 70 percent, you may need to listen to the lecture again and rewrite some of your notes.**

ORAL SUMMARY

Use your notes to create an oral summary of the lecture with your partner. As you work together, add details to your notes that your partner included but you had missed.

DISCUSSION

Discuss the following questions with a classmate or in a small group.

1. What are the most important benefits of having international students in a school?
2. Looking ahead 20 years, where do you think most international students in the United States will come from? Why?
3. How would you advise a young person from your culture to study: (a) at home, at a university; (b) in the United States; (c) at home through distance education? Explain.
4. If you were a university or ministry of education official in your culture, would you try to attract more international students? Why or why not?

PRE-READING

The following Reading is about American university students studying abroad. Before you read, answer the following questions. Share your answers with a classmate.

1. Look at the chart of the top five countries hosting American students. Why do you think these five countries are at the top of the list?
2. Are there any countries missing from the list that you would expect to find there? Which?

READING

Now read the article.

Rising Numbers of Americans Study Abroad

According to the 2012 Open Doors Report on International Educational Exchange, in academic year 2011–2012 the number of Americans studying for academic credit at foreign universities rose by about 1 percent to an all-time high of 273,996. This increase, although small, is a part of a two-decades-long trend in which the total number of U.S. students participating in study-abroad programs has more than tripled.

Top Five Countries Hosting U.S. Students, 2011/12

1. United Kingdom
2. Italy
3. Spain
4. France
5. China

This upward trend is welcomed by many political, business, and education leaders, who believe that in order for the United States to remain competitive in an increasingly global economy, young Americans must become more globally aware. Groups with an interest in promoting study-abroad programs speak of a "global divide" emerging between those with access to a global education and those whose education is more traditionally focused in and on the United States. They compare this to the so-called digital divide of the last decade between people who had access to personal computers and those who did not.

Commenting on the importance of a global education, U.S. Assistant Secretary of State for Educational and Cultural Affairs Ann Stock said, "Today's youth are tomorrow's leaders. International education creates strong, lasting relationships between the U.S. and emerging leaders worldwide. Students return home with new perspectives and a global skill set that will allow them to build more prosperous, stable societies."

According to the International Institute on Education (IIE), out of the 25 most popular study abroad destinations for American university students, 17 countries reported an increase in American participants in 2011–2012. The most popular region for study abroad participants remains Europe, with 54.6%, followed by Latin America with 14.6%, and Asia with 11.7%. In 2011–2012, there were increases in several less traditional destinations, including Brazil, China, Costa Rica, India, and South Korea, with particularly significant increases from the previous year in India (up 12%) and China (up 5% to 14,000 students).

In 2010, during a trip to China, President Obama set a goal of doubling the number of Americans studying in that country by 2014. While this goal was praised by organizations committed to study abroad programs, some experts criticized it as being too ambitious. One criticism is that the president has not committed any government funding to achieve this goal, which the U.S. State Department estimates

Oxford University, England

would cost at least $68 million. So far, American corporations have committed $3.25 million according to Carola McGiffert, director of the initiative. Another challenge is that very few U.S. universities have the language programs in place to prepare American students to function in classrooms where only Chinese is spoken. In addition to increasing the number of Chinese language courses, American universities will need to increase course offerings in Chinese literature, history, political science, and economics. "Otherwise, the study-abroad experience just isn't connected to a student's broader educational experience," Brian J. Whalen, president of the Forum on Education Abroad, said.

DISCUSSION

Discuss these questions with a classmate.

1. Compare the information in the Reading with what you heard in the lecture. What are the similarities and differences between Americans studying abroad at foreign universities and international students studying at American universities?
2. Why do you think President Obama was interested in increasing the number of Americans studying in China? Consider what you learned in the lecture about the benefits of international education, as well as your own ideas.
3. Based on what you learned in the lecture, what are some of the potential benefits to other countries of having Americans enrolled in their universities?

PURSUING THE TOPIC

Explore the topic of this chapter further by doing the following.

The Web site for the Institute of International Education has a lot of information on study abroad in both the United States and other countries. Individually or with a partner, choose a country or region that interests you and read about it. Write up the details for a short presentation to the class.

www.iie.org/en

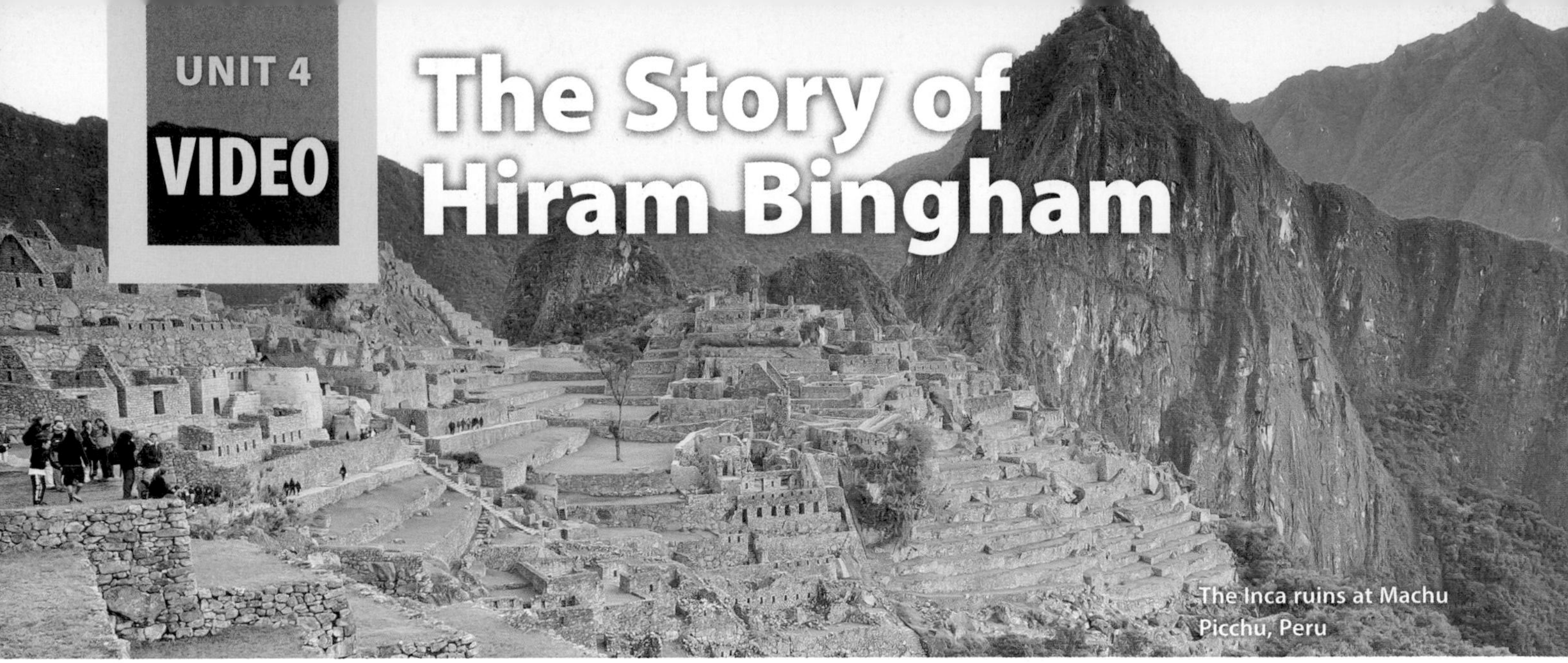

The Story of Hiram Bingham

The Inca ruins at Machu Picchu, Peru

BEFORE VIEWING

TOPIC PREVIEW

The speaker talks about the life of Hiram Bingham. Work with a partner and number the events in Bingham's life from 1 through 6 in what you think is the most likely order.

_____ had seven sons

_____ taught Latin American history at university

_____ received a doctorate degree

_____ became an explorer

_____ went to Harvard graduate school

_____ was a freshman at Yale University

VOCABULARY PREVIEW

A **Read the definitions of these key words and phrases that you will hear during the video.**

heading off to college beginning study at a college, usually away from home
got into college was accepted into a college
end up finally become something after effort, time, or academic studies
senior year the final year of high school or college
advisor a person who helps students plan their academic studies
ambitious wanting to succeed and do very well, usually professionally
fellow students classmates
barrier something in your path that makes it difficult to get where you want to go
be hired be given a job for which you are paid

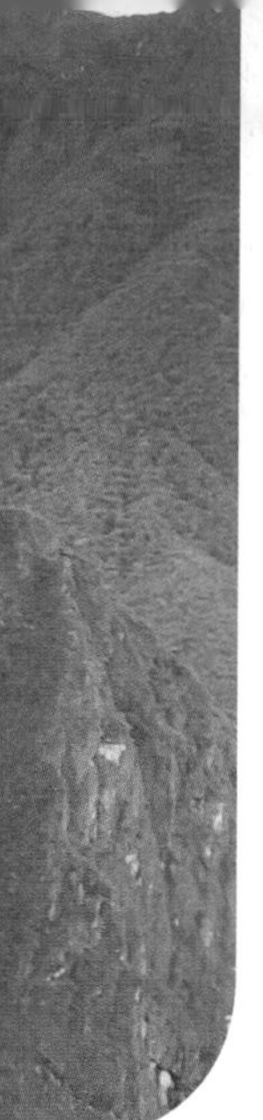

B **Work with a partner and discuss answers to the following questions.**

1. When children **head off to college**, do you think it is a difficult time for their parents?
2. Who do you know who **got into college** to study one subject but **ended up** with a degree in another subject?
3. What is a student's **senior year** of high school or college usually like? Do students usually work harder or less hard than in other years? Explain.
4. What is the role of an **advisor** at a school?
5. Do you consider yourself an **ambitious** person? What is your ambition?
6. Do you meet socially with any of your **fellow students**? If so, what do you do together?
7. What are some **barriers** for poorer people to get into a good college or to **be hired** for a well-paying job?

VIEWING

FIRST VIEWING

Watch the video, and then compare your first impressions with a partner. Talk about what you remember, what surprised you, and what interested you.

SECOND VIEWING

Watch the video again. Listen for the missing words and write them in the blanks.

1. I mean, he's very ________________; he's six feet four. He's ________________. He wears jodhpurs like the best of them.
2. Hiram Bingham, in a ________________, was a whirlwind. He was a force of ________________.
3. There still was a barrier of both wealth and prestige at Yale that he couldn't quite ________________ through.
4. Now, his decision to study ________________ at Harvard was actually a fairly radical one.
5. He wasn't doing European history. He wasn't doing ________________ history. He was doing ________________ American history.

Hiram Bingham

THIRD VIEWING

Complete these notes as you watch the video. Write only important words, not full sentences, and abbreviate common words.

Hiram Bingham
- striking and ______________________
- Yale's Ind. Jones
- whirlwind/force of nature/smart/ambitious/gd. ______________________
- gd at ______________________
- poor ______________________
- barriers at Y. ______________________
- after coll ______________________

Fell in love w/ Alfreda M.
- chngd his life
- met in ______________________
- m. soon after – 7 ______________________
- lvd in ______________________ – at Harvard

Study hist. at Harv.
- not Euro or US – ______________________
- 1st pers ______________________
- bel. ______________________

AFTER VIEWING

ORAL SUMMARY

Use your notes to create an oral summary of the video with your partner. As you work together, add details to your notes that your partner included but you had missed.

DISCUSSION

Discuss the following questions with a classmate or in a small group.

1. What do you think were the three most impressive achievements in Bingham's life?
2. Why was Hiram Bingham known as "Yale's Indiana Jones"?
3. The speaker says that many students "fear" moving back to their parents' house after college. Why do you think he says that and do you agree that it is something to fear?

UNIT

5

The Official Side

Fourth of July fireworks over Washington, DC

The Role of Government in the Economy

TOPIC PREVIEW

Discuss the following questions with a partner or your classmates.

1. Do you think the oil fields in Texas or the oil platforms in the Gulf of Mexico are owned by the U.S. government or by private companies?
2. Are energy industries (oil, gas, electricity) privately or publicly owned in your country of origin?
3. What role should the government play if certain industries pollute the environment or try to create a monopoly by driving others out of business? No role? A big one? Why?

Hibernia oil platform, Grand Banks, Atlantic Ocean

VOCABULARY PREVIEW

CD 5, TR 1

A Read through the sentences below, which are missing vocabulary from the lecture. As you read, try to imagine which words would fit in the blanks. Then listen to the sentences and write the missing words in the blanks.

1. One of the important characteristics of American-style ____________ is individual ____________ of property.
2. Another important characteristic is free ____________: This means the freedom to produce, buy, and sell goods and labor without government ____________.
3. The idea in a pure capitalist system is for the government to take a laissez-faire ____________ toward business.
4. Because the costs of ____________ the environment can affect all members of society, the government uses various legal means to try to protect the environment and make companies ____________ with certain government regulations.
5. You may remember the BP oil ____________ in the Gulf of Mexico in 2010, which resulted in the worst environmental ____________ in U.S. history.
6. The company was charged with ____________ safety and environmental regulations in building and managing the well that spilled the oil.
7. The government intervenes to see that businesses remain ____________; antitrust laws were passed to prevent companies from joining together to unfairly control prices, what we call price-____________.
8. The second method government uses to maintain ____________ in the economy is ____________, the money that the government spends.
9. The government can raise taxes to take money out of the economy and lower the ____________ rate.
10. When the president and Congress do not work together, or when the two parties do not work together, a political ____________ can occur.

B Check the spelling of the vocabulary words with your teacher. Discuss the meanings of these words and any other unfamiliar words in the sentences.

PREDICTIONS

Think about the questions in the Topic Preview on page 122 and the sentences you heard in the Vocabulary Preview. Write three questions that you think will be answered in the lecture. Share your questions with your classmates.

NOTETAKING PREPARATION

Preparing for the Lecture by Reading

Most U.S. college and university teachers plan their lectures assuming that students will have read assigned chapters before class.

A lecture will usually deal with points in the assigned text, so you will be better prepared for the lecture by doing the reading ahead of time. When you read to prepare for a lecture, you may want to take reading notes. A good reader-notetaker needs to decide which points are main ones and which are details. If you take reading notes, you should use abbreviations and key words for efficiency and use indentation for better organization and clarity.

A **Read the following text carefully.**

The Role of Government

1 Americans have been debating the role of the federal government ever since the American Revolution in the 1770s. The 13 original colonies, which banded together to declare their independence from Britain, were very suspicious of a strong central government and protective of their individual rights as states. The Confederation government they formed saw the 13 original colonies through the Revolution.

2 A few years after the end of the Revolutionary War, though, the Confederation was unable to solve many problems facing the new nation, and the need for a stronger central government led to a new Constitution, which expanded the power of the national government. Still, the debate about the role of government went on in many areas, including the economic sphere. Thomas Jefferson, the third U.S. president, was a believer in laissez-faire economics; that is, he believed the government should not interfere in the economy. His general philosophy was "Government that governs least, governs best."

3 By today's standards, the role of the national, or federal, government in the economy was very small, consisting largely of setting tariffs and excise taxes as well as issuing currency. It wasn't until the time of the Civil War in the 1860s that the first income tax was instituted. Before that time, the government did not have money for internal improvements to the country.

4 After that time, the government began to expand its role in the economy. The Industrial Revolution, which was occurring at the same time, led to demands for the government to expand its role in the regulation of railroads and other big business. During these years, the government tended to support big business rather than organized labor. During the early years of the twentieth century, the government began to debate its role in the economy more sharply. President Theodore Roosevelt and President Woodrow Wilson took steps toward controlling the excessive power of big business.

5 However, it was the Great Depression of the 1930s that led most people to give up the idea of a laissez-faire economy. President Franklin Roosevelt led the

government to take an increased role in the welfare of the people. His New Deal instituted programs by which the government provided employment for large numbers of unemployed people and provided support through welfare for others. His administration also instituted the Social Security system, by which workers pay into a fund that then provides a kind of insurance protection for older, retired workers and disabled workers. In the years following the New Deal, the role of the government in the economy continued to expand. During the 1960s there emerged a new conservative viewpoint, and efforts were made by many in politics to loosen the control of the government on the economy and to return to a more laissez-faire economy. This issue is still being debated.

B For questions 1 and 2, circle the correct answer. For questions 3, 4, and 5, write short answers.

1. In general, has the role of the federal government become

   a. stronger b. weaker c. varied in degree d. stayed the same over the years?

2. Which paragraph 2 notes seem most accurate?

   a. Cent govt = weaker – P. Jefferson agreed
   b. Cent govt = stronger – P. Jefferson opposed
   c. Cent govt = stronger b/c of laissez-faire

3. What details in paragraph 3 support the main idea of the paragraph?

   ____

4. Write a note for the main idea of paragraph 4, in your own words.

   ____

5. What details in paragraph 5 support the idea that government expanded in the 1930s?

   ____

C Discourse Cues Number the following excerpts from the lecture from 1 to 5 in the order that you think you will probably hear them. Discuss with a partner or as a class the discourse cues that helped you figure out the order.

__1__ Let me begin today by saying that the American economy is basically a capitalist economy.

__4__ So, these three methods—taxation, expenditure, and setting the interest rate—are the government's main means of maintaining the economy's stability.

__2__ An important reason that the government tries to regulate the economy is to protect the environment.

__3__ Another reason the government intervenes in the economy is to help people who for some reason beyond their control earn little or no income.

__5__ The last reason for the government's intervention in the economy is to maintain economic stability.

FIRST LISTENING

CD 5, TR 2

A **Listen to the beginning of the lecture. Circle the set of notes below that best records the information you hear.**

a.

I. Am econ = cap. econ
  A. Am cap – indiv own prop
    1. house, land, business, intel prop (song/poem/bk/inven)
  B. free ent = make/buy/sell goods & lab
  C. free, compet markets
    1. bus suc, stay market; bus fail, leave
  D. not ev/o find job; not all bus sec
  E. gov does not intf in eco
II. Pure cap syst
  A. l-f att = limtd gov role
    1. nat def
    2. laws protect own & use prv prop
    3. prov wh bus doesn't, ex. rds
  B. US not pure cap econ or comp l-f att
    1. govt role bus ↑ 20th c, esp. 1930s
    2. US expanded role compli
Discuss 4 reasons govt intervenes

b.

Cap. econ
- indiv own prop
- intell prop =song, poem, etc.
- free prod/buy/sell gds
- bus succd, sty; fail, lve

I. Pure captlst econ
- natl def
- laws protct prv prop
- bld rds, schls (bus won't provd)

II. US not cap syst
- US not LF att to bus
- gov role in bus 20th C↑
  1. start 1930s
- issues today

CD 5, TR 3

B **Now listen to the whole lecture and take notes. Look at the lecturer's visual aids as you listen. These may help you understand parts of the lecture.**

Subtopic 1: Protecting the Environment

Protecting the Environment

- Regulations
  - Pollution control equipment
  - Disposal of toxic waste
- BP oil spill

Subtopic 2: Helping People

Public Assistance Programs/ Welfare

- Children
- The elderly
- The ill/disabled
- The unemployed

Subtopic 3: Protecting Competition

Protecting Competition

- Antitrust laws
- Monopoly regulation
- Financial crisis of 2008

Subtopic 4: Maintaining Economic Stability

Maintaining Economic Stability

- Taxation
- Government expenditures
- Control of interest rates

SECOND LISTENING

CD 5, TR 4

Listen to the lecture again and make your notes as complete as possible.

THIRD LISTENING

CD 5, TR 5

A **You will hear part of the lecture again. Listen and complete the notes by adding the information from the box.**

↑	→	↓	BUT	condtns	Expend	indus	"

Stabilizing Econ

A. Taxes

1. econ grow too fast ________ inflat, so . . .
2. gov't ________ taxes – take $ out of econ & ________ inflat
3. ________ danger of unemploy, so . . .
4. gov't uses taxes to bal unemploy & inflat

B. ________

1. gov't – huge amnt of $
2. how to spend $ dep on econ ________ in
   a. diff ________
   b. ________ parts of cntry

B **Compare your answers with a partner. Then compare the notes in A with the notes you took for this part of the lecture.**

ACCURACY CHECK

CD 5, TR 6

A **Listen to the following questions and write short answers. Use your notes. You will hear each question one time only.**

1. ______________________________
2. ______________________________
3. ______________________________
4. ______________________________
5. ______________________________
6. ______________________________
7. ______________________________
8. ______________________________
9. ______________________________
10. ______________________________

B **Check your answers with your teacher. If your score is less than 70 percent, you may need to listen to the lecture again and rewrite some of your notes.**

ORAL SUMMARY

Use your notes to create an oral summary of the lecture with your partner. As you work together, add details to your notes that your partner included but you had missed.

DISCUSSION

Discuss the following questions with a classmate or in a small group.

1. Which of the four reasons for government intervention in the economy makes the most sense to you? Why?
2. What are the advantages of a laissez-faire economy? What are the disadvantages?
3. If a government has to decide between creating jobs in mining and industry and protecting the environment, which should they choose? Explain.
4. Should government provide welfare support to people who are unable to support themselves, or is this the responsibility of the family? Explain.

PRE-READING

The following Reading is about the Himalayan nation of Bhutan. Before you read, answer the following questions. Share your answers with a classmate.

1. Scan the article. What kind of government did Bhutan have in the past? What kind of government does it have now?
2. Based on what you learned in the lecture, do you expect that the government of Bhutan will play a larger or smaller role in the country's economy under the new type of government than it did under the old type of government? Why?

READING

Now read the article.

Bhutan's Enlightened Experiment

Bhutan is a country that is attempting the impossible: to jump from the Middle Ages to the twenty-first century without losing its balance.

For more than a thousand years, this tiny country has survived in magnificent isolation, a place the size of Switzerland set between two giants, India and China. Closed off from the outside world both by geography and deliberate policy, the country had no roads, no electricity, no motor vehicles, no telephones, no postal service until the 1960s. It looks like a place that time forgot: ancient temples high on cliffs; unclimbed mountain peaks rising above unpolluted rivers and forests.

But not everything was perfect in Bhutan. When King Jigme Singye Wangchuck became king in 1972, Bhutan had some of the highest poverty, illiteracy, and infant-mortality rates in the world—a result of the policy of isolation. His father, Bhutan's third king, had begun opening up the country in the 1960s, building roads, establishing schools and health clinics, pushing for United Nations membership. King Jigme Singye Wangchuck would go much further. He has tried to control Bhutan's opening to the world—and in the process redefine the very meaning of development. The phrase he invented to describe his approach: Gross National Happiness.

Guided by the "four pillars of Gross National Happiness"—sustainable development, environmental protection, cultural preservation, and good governance—Bhutan has pulled itself out of terrible poverty without harming its natural resources. Nearly three-quarters of the country is still covered by forests, with more than 25 percent protected from development—among the highest percentages in the world. Rates of illiteracy and infant mortality have fallen dramatically, and the economy is booming. Tourism is growing, too. In 1999, Bhutan granted its citizens access to television—the last country on the planet to do so.

Now comes the most important step in Bhutan's experiment: the move to

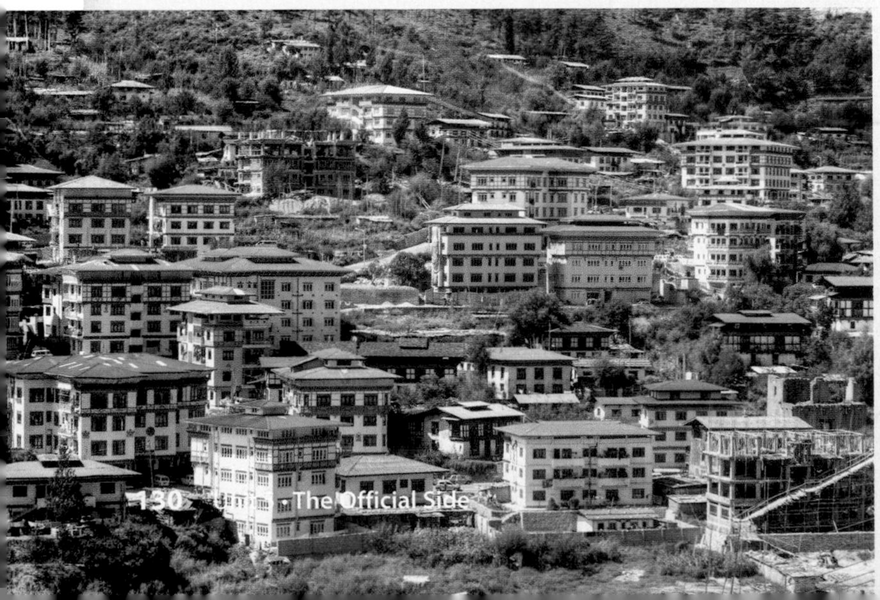

democracy. In 2006, King Jigme Singye Wangchuck decided to give up his throne to give power to the people, setting up a series of events for the year 2008 that ended in the formation of the country's first democratic government.

The real test of Gross National Happiness, then, has just begun. Bhutan's new leaders will face many challenges. One challenge is that the citizens loved their king and are suspicious of democracy. The outside world is watching closely, wondering if this tiny Himalayan nation might help answer some of humankind's most difficult questions: How can a society maintain its identity in the face of globalization? How can it take advantage of the good of the modern world without being overwhelmed by the bad? And can there ever be a happy balance between tradition and development?

To survive in democratic politics, Bhutan's new government will have to make the people happy. As the country modernizes, that may depend on relations with the outside world. As of 2008, Bhutan had established connections with only 21 countries; the most important is India, which provides military security and buys 80 percent of Bhutan's exports. Most big powers, including the United States, aren't on the list, because Bhutan worries about being controlled by others. However, Bhutan is moving toward membership in the World Trade Organization (WTO). In a globalized economy, no country can fully protect itself from trade—and, therefore, the WTO. "Our greatest fear," government minister Jigme Y. Thinley said, "comes from the unknown."

DISCUSSION

Discuss these questions with a classmate.

1. Does the economy of Bhutan fit the definition of a capitalist economy given in the lecture? Explain your answer.
2. Which of the reasons for regulating the economy mentioned in the lecture were also mentioned in the Reading? Compare examples about the United States to examples about Bhutan.
3. What are some of the advantages that a monarchy has over a democracy when it comes to making widespread, rapid changes to a country's economy?

PURSUING THE TOPIC

Explore the topic of this chapter further by doing the following.

Individually or with a partner, choose one of the issues mentioned in the lecture and research the positions of the two major political parties in the United States, the Democrats or the Republicans. Take notes and prepare a short presentation comparing and contrasting their views on the issue.

www.ontheissues.org/democratic_party.htm
www.ontheissues.org/republican_party.htm

CHAPTER

14

Government by Constitution

TOPIC PREVIEW

Discuss the following questions with a partner or your classmates.

1. What are the benefits of a written constitution, a document that the government must follow? What disadvantages might there be?
2. In your culture, where do the laws come from? Can a law change over time, that is, can it ever be seen as illegal?
3. Should branches of government—for example, the executive, legislative, and judicial branches—have equal power? Explain.

Tourists view historical U.S. documents at the National Archives, Washington, DC.

VOCABULARY PREVIEW

CD 5, TR 7

A Read through the sentences below, which are missing vocabulary from the lecture. As you read, try to imagine which words would fit in the blanks. Then listen to the sentences and write the missing words in the blanks.

1. Before we begin our discussion of the two important ________________ of the U.S. government, let's take a look at the three ________________ that make up the U.S. government.
2. The Congress is primarily responsible for ________________, or making, new laws that are to be followed by the 50 states of the country.
3. The executive branch ________________ the laws that ________________ in the legislature.
4. After the president has signed a new law, the executive branch of the government is responsible for seeing that the new law is ________________, or carried out.
5. The judicial branch decides any kind of legal issue that falls under federal ________________.
6. A president who feels very strongly that a new law is wrong may refuse to sign it. Congress can ________________ a presidential ________________, but it is a very difficult thing to do.
7. If an investigation shows that illegal activities probably did take place, Congress has the power to ________________, or charge, the person. This did not happen to President Nixon, who ________________ before Congress could act.
8. The U.S. Supreme Court, the highest court in the judicial branch, hears cases involving the ________________ of federal laws enacted by Congress.
9. In 2012, the Court heard arguments that challenged parts of a controversial health-care bill that was ________________ passed by the legislature.
10. The president can check the power of the judicial branch because he is the person who ________________ candidates to be federal judges, including those on the Supreme Court.

B Check the spelling of the vocabulary words with your teacher. Discuss the meanings of these words and any other unfamiliar words in the sentences.

PREDICTIONS

Think about the questions in the Topic Preview on page 132 and the sentences you heard in the Vocabulary Preview. Write three questions that you think will be answered in the lecture. Share your questions with your classmates.

NOTETAKING PREPARATION

Pre-Lecture Reading and Key Words

As mentioned in the previous chapter, U.S. university students most often prepare for each class with an assigned reading—a text chapter, an article, or even a case study. This preparation makes the instructor's lecture, which is usually on a topic related to the reading, easier to follow and to take notes on. You will notice how this pre-lecture reading will aid your comprehension of the lecture.

Using key words in your lecture notes allows you to take down important information quickly. You can also use key words to take notes on a reading. Think of the key words as notes on the reading that you can use to study in the future.

A Read the following passage carefully.

Judicial Review

Judicial review is the power of a court to invalidate, or overturn, any law passed by the legislature that the court believes to be unconstitutional. The concept of judicial review as exercised by the Supreme Court of the United States is almost unique in the world. It can be called an American invention. Nowhere else does the judiciary of a country exercise final say over laws passed by the legislature. This enormous power of judicial review by the Supreme Court was established in a famous case several years after the Constitution was written, *Marbury v. Madison* (1803). The Court stated that the Constitution was superior to any acts by the legislature and that it was the Court's duty to void any laws that went against the Constitution. This power was not explicitly expressed in the Constitution, and even today, almost 200 years later, the Supreme Court's power to void laws passed by the legislature is still controversial.

If we compare judicial review in the United States with that in a few other countries, we will see just how unusual it is. In Great Britain, the right of Parliament (the legislature) to make any law it wants to make cannot be challenged by the courts. The courts can interpret a law but not decide if a law is valid. In Germany, the judiciary has had the power of judicial review since shortly after World War II, but it has been slow to exercise judicial review for cultural and historical reasons. The judiciary in Canada has had this judicial review power since 1982.

B Write answers to the following comprehension questions using key words.

1. What is judicial review?

____

2. Is judicial review guaranteed by the U.S. Constitution? Explain.

____

3. Which of the following countries has no provisions for judicial review—Britain, Canada, or Germany?

____

4. Do Germany and Canada exercise judicial review more or less frequently than the United States does? Explain.

____

C **Study the chart below and answer the two questions that follow. The chart shows some of the powers of each branch of the U.S. government and how some of these powers may be limited by the other two branches.**

The U.S. Government		
Executive Branch	**Legislative Branch**	**Judicial Branch**
• Proposes new legislation to Congress • May veto bills passed by Congress • Nominates judges • Makes treaties with other countries • Prepares federal budget	• Approves federal budget • Approves treaties • Sends bills it has passed to president for signature • May override a president's veto by a two-thirds majority • Must approve appointment of judges • May impeach the president	• Interprets laws • May declare a law unconstitutional • Interprets treaties

1. Which powers in each branch are checked by another branch?

____

2. Which powers seem to have no checks against them?

____

D **Discourse Cues** **Number the following excerpts from the lecture from 1 to 5 in the order that you think you will probably hear them. Discuss with a partner or as a class the discourse cues that helped you figure out the order.**

_____ In addition to separation of powers, a system of checks and balances was written into the Constitution.

_____ You might wonder what check the executive or the legislative branch has on the judicial branch.

_____ To start, the Constitution provides for three branches of government: one, the legislative; two, the executive; and three, the judicial.

_____ First, let's consider how the executive branch can check the power of the legislative branch.

_____ Knowing the three branches, you'll already have an idea of what is meant by *separation of powers*.

FIRST LISTENING

CD 5, TR 8

A **Listen to the beginning of the lecture. Circle the set of notes below that best records the information you hear.**

a.

US Constitution
- >225 yrs basis for stable govt
- basically unchanged
- oldest written const

Look @ 2 imp principals
- (1) Sep of powers
- (2) Sys of cks and bal
- 1st—3 branches of gov't

b.

US Constitution
- >225 yrs basis for stable govt
- basically unchanged
- US young cntry, but oldest written const

I. 2 imp princpls in Const
   A. 1 Sep of powers and 2 sys cks and bal

II. 3 branches of gov't

c.

US Constitution
1987=200th anniv
basically unchanged
US oldest const in wrld
A. 2 imp prncpls in Const
B. 3 branches of gov'

CD 5, TR 9

B **Now listen to the whole lecture and take notes. Look at the lecturer's visual aids as you listen. These may help you understand parts of the lecture.**

Subtopic 1: ____________________________

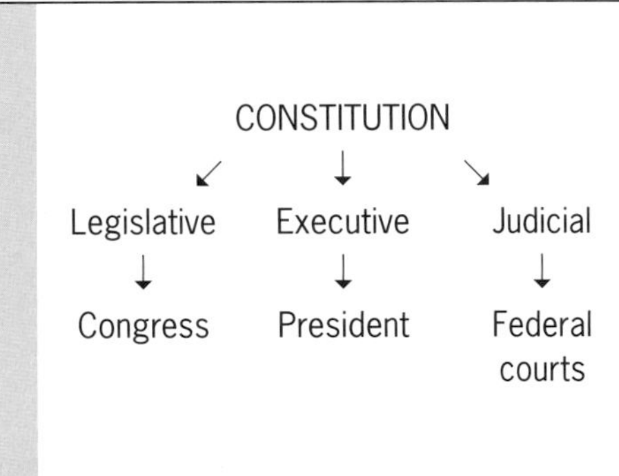

Subtopic 2: ____________________________

Constitution
- Each branch has its own power
- No single branch can have all the power
- Checks and balances prevent abuse of power

Subtopic 3: ______________________________

Executive → Legislature
Legislature → Executive
Judiciary → Legislature
Executive and Legislature → Judiciary

SECOND LISTENING

CD 5, TR 10

Listen to the lecture again and make your notes as complete as possible.

THIRD LISTENING

CD 5, TR 11

A You will hear part of the lecture again. Listen and complete the notes by adding the information from the box.

apprvd	oppty	Jud	SC	?ed	abt	sep	√

Exec & Leg Ck on __________
- Pres nom fed judgs, inc __________ (9 judgs)
  - __________ to chng bal of SC
- Senate apprvs Pres's nom = __________ on both Exec & Jud
  - Nom for SC __________ by Senate
    - e.g. ? __________ record & opinions: abortin, gun contrl, __________ of church & state, etc.
  - Most nom __________, but not all

B Compare your answers with a partner. Then compare the notes in **A** with the notes you took for this part of the lecture.

AFTER LISTENING

ACCURACY CHECK

CD 5, TR 12

A **Listen to the following questions and write short answers. Use your notes. You will hear each question one time only.**

1. ______________________________
2. ______________________________
3. ______________________________
4. ______________________________
5. ______________________________
6. ______________________________
7. ______________________________
8. ______________________________
9. ______________________________
10. ______________________________

B **Check your answers with your teacher. If your score is less than 70 percent, you may need to listen to the lecture again and rewrite some of your notes.**

ORAL SUMMARY

Use your notes to create an oral summary of the lecture with your partner. As you work together, add details to your notes that your partner included but you had missed.

DISCUSSION

Discuss the following questions with a classmate or in a small group.

1. Do the two principles of (1) separation of powers and (2) checks and balances make the United States easier or more difficult to govern? Why?
2. How is the power to make and enforce laws in your culture divided? Explain.
3. Can a law be overturned by the courts or another branch of government in your culture?
4. Do you think a branch of government should have the power to remove a president from office? Explain.

PRE-READING

The following Reading is about the government of ancient Rome. Before you read, answer the following questions. Share your answers with a classmate.

1. Why do people continue to study ancient Roman civilization? What contributions did the ancient Romans make to the world?
2. What type of government did the ancient Romans have? Discuss what you know about the executive, legislative, and judicial functions of ancient Roman government.

READING

Now read the article.

The World According to Rome

Fifteen centuries after the fall of Rome, the influence of the Roman Empire—in language, literature, legal codes, government, architecture, medicine, sports, arts, engineering, etc.—can still be felt in the daily lives of people all over the world. One Roman ideal in particular has had a large impact on American government: that of the written law used to protect individuals against one another and against the power of the state. In fact, the Romans took this practice from the Greeks, but it was Rome that put this abstract idea into daily practice. A Latin inscription at Harvard Law School expresses the idea very clearly: *Non sub homine sed sub deo et lege*—It is not by men but by God and the law we are governed.

In the ongoing struggle between the ordinary people of Rome and those in power, the ordinary people, called the *plebeians*, or *plebs*, decided they would much rather rely on laws than their all-too-human rulers. Under pressure from the plebs, the governing class was repeatedly forced to issue written codes. In 450 BC, the first of these documents, the Twelve Tables, came out, and the Romans continued to publish legal codes for the next thousand years. A collection of these codes, completed by the emperor Justinian in AD 534, has served as the foundation of Western law ever since.

The ancient Roman process of making laws also had a deep influence on the American system. During the era of the Roman Republic (509 to 49 BC), lawmaking involved two houses of government, just as it does in the United States today. Legislation was first passed by the *comitia*, the assembly of citizens, then approved by the members of the upper class, the senate, and finally issued in the name of the senate and the people of Rome.

Centuries later, when the American Founding Fathers began their bold experiment in democratic government, they took republican Rome as their model. American laws must also be approved by two legislative bodies. The House of Representatives is similar to the Roman assembly of citizens. The U.S. Senate, like the Roman senate, was originally established as a body of members of the social and political elite. (It was not until the Seventeenth Amendment to the Constitution was passed that ordinary American citizens were allowed to vote for their senators.) Impressed by the checks and balances of the Roman system, the authors of the American Constitution made sure that an official could be "impeached," or removed from office. The word *impeached* is a word that is taken from the Latin *in pedica*.

This genuine respect for the power of law was reflected in the behavior of the otherwise all-powerful Roman emperors, who for the most part felt obligated to obey these written codes. And if the emperor himself had to honor the law, the obligation fell even more heavily on lower-ranking officials and colonial governors. Any official who violated the law could be called back to Rome, where he would be put *in pedica*, into chains. In fact, the establishment in the United States Constitution of an independent judicial branch with judges and juries has its roots in these ancient Roman legal practices.

DISCUSSION

Discuss these questions with a classmate.

1. What similarities and differences are there between the executive power of the emperor in ancient Rome, and the executive branch of the U.S. government?
2. What similarities and differences are there between the legislature in ancient Rome, and the legislative branch of the U.S. government?
3. How did ancient Roman ideals affect the development of the judicial system of the United States?

PURSUING THE TOPIC

Explore the topic of this chapter further by doing the following.

Watch the movie *All the President's Men*, a movie about President Richard Nixon, who resigned before being impeached for an abuse of presidential power. Be prepared to discuss the movie with your classmates.

CHAPTER

15

Common Law and the Jury System

TOPIC PREVIEW

Discuss the following questions with a partner or your classmates.

1. If you were accused of a crime and went to court, who would you prefer to decide if you were innocent or guilty, a judge or a group of your peers on a jury?
2. Do you think of laws as something written and unchangeable? Or can laws change over time according to changes in a culture?
3. Should criminals receive lighter sentences for their crimes for cooperating with the police, for example, by telling them about another person who did something illegal?

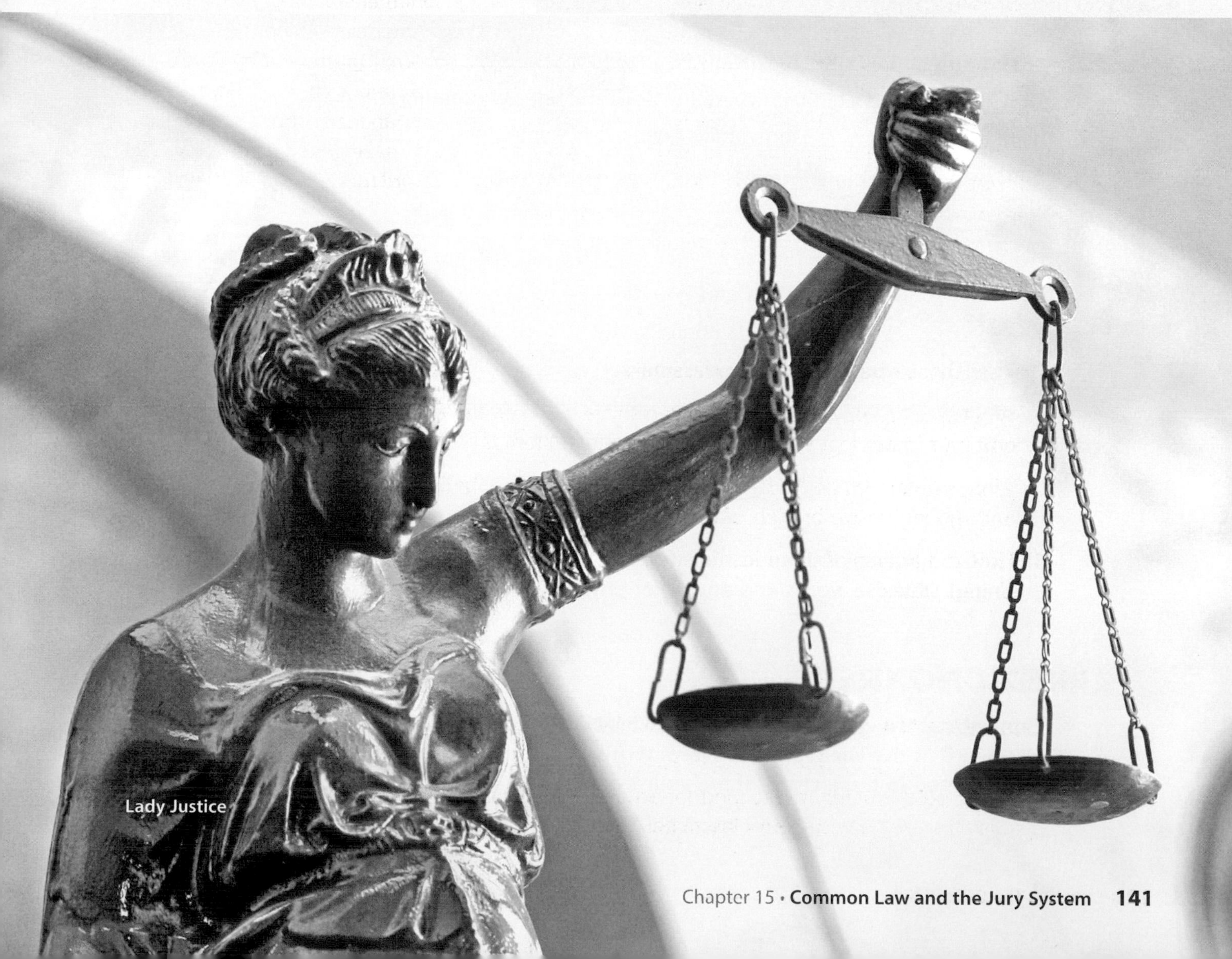

Lady Justice

VOCABULARY PREVIEW

CD 5, TR 13

A **Read through the sentences below, which are missing vocabulary from the lecture. As you read, try to imagine which words would fit in the blanks. Then listen to the sentences and write the missing words in the blanks.**

1. The basic principle of the U.S. legal system is that an accused person is ________________ until proven ________________.
2. In deciding a case, under ________________ law, the judge consults a ________________, a complex set of written laws.
3. The judge also decides what ________________ the defendant, that is, the person accused of wrongdoing, will be given if guilty.
4. To determine the defendant's guilt under common law, the judge also considers the ________________ set by other court decisions.
5. Very often, it is not the judge who gives a ________________, but the jury, a group of six or twelve ordinary citizens, who decide the defendant's guilt or innocence and, in civil cases, how much money should be paid in ________________.
6. In either civil or criminal trials, the jury hears ________________ from people with information about the case; these people are called ________________.
7. Criminal trials are ones where the government, representing the public, ________________ individuals accused of committing a crime.
8. The defendant in a criminal case does not have to ________________; it is the government's job to ________________ the person is guilty.
9. The reason that the degree of ________________ is much higher in a criminal trial is that a person's freedom and even life can be taken away if he or she is ________________, that is, found guilty, of a crime.
10. Michael Jackson's doctor was convicted of ________________ manslaughter, meaning he caused his patient's death without intending to.
11. Often the defendant is allowed to ________________ bargain only if he or she also cooperates with the ________________ in bringing other criminals to justice.

B **Check the spelling of the vocabulary words with your teacher. Discuss the meanings of these words and any other unfamiliar words in the sentences.**

PREDICTIONS

Think about the questions in the Topic Preview on page 141 and the sentences you heard in the Vocabulary Preview. Write three questions that you think will be answered in the lecture. Share your questions with your classmates.

NOTETAKING PREPARATION

Pre-Lecture Reading and Abbreviations and Symbols

As mentioned in previous chapters, U.S. university students are expected to arrive in class with some background on the topic that the professor will lecture on or that students will be asked to apply to questions or problems posed by the professor in class. Doing the reading will help you put the parts of the lecture together in your mind.

Besides preparing you for class, the notes you take on the reading will give you an efficient record of what you've read. Using abbreviations and symbols and organizing the information on the page will make it easier to review the notes before class or before a quiz.

A **Read the following passage carefully.**

Jury Selection

Serving on a jury in the United States to determine the guilt or innocence of an accused person is one of the most important civic duties a citizen can perform. Jurors are randomly selected from voter registration—and sometimes drivers' license—lists. To serve on a jury, a person must be a U.S. citizen, be at least 18 years old, live in the judicial district for a year, and know English well enough to follow the court proceedings. People with a serious mental or physical condition or with a felony record are disqualified from serving on a jury. Members of the military on active duty, police and firefighters, as well as public officials may not serve on federal juries. Also, people for whom jury duty would cause a severe hardship or inconvenience are often excused. Employers by law cannot penalize an employee for missing work to serve on a jury, but someone who lost wages to serve on a jury would be under a hardship to serve. Potential jurors fill out questionnaires to see if they are qualified to serve. These methods help to ensure that jurors represent a cross section of the community without consideration of race, gender, national origin, age, or political affiliation.

Being called for jury duty does not mean a person will actually serve. The judge and lawyers involved in an actual case have the opportunity to question potential jurors in order to exclude those who may not be able to decide the case fairly. Potential jurors who know someone in the case, who have information about the case, or who may have strong prejudices about the case will typically be excused by the judge. The lawyers for the defense and the prosecution may also exclude a certain number of jurors without giving a reason. A person who is against the death sentence would probably be excluded by the judge in a capital case, in other words, a case that could call for the death penalty if the defendant were found guilty. This is a clear-cut example. Lawyers defending or prosecuting a defendant will often have far less obvious reasons for excluding a potential jury member.

B **Write answers to the following comprehension questions using abbreviations and symbols. Write headings to the left and details under the heading to the right, as shown under question 1.**

1. What four criteria must a person in the U.S. meet to serve on a jury?

   1. 4 criteria to be a U.S. juror

      a. ______________________________

      b. ______________________________

      c. ______________________________

      d. ______________________________

2. Who is disqualified from serving on a jury?

3. Which potential jurors are excluded as being unable to decide a case fairly?

C **Discourse Cues** **Number the following excerpts from the lecture from 1 to 5 in the order that you think you will probably hear them. Discuss with a partner or as a class the discourse cues that helped you figure out the order.**

_____ Although different from many legal systems, the U.S. system of justice is not unique.

_____ To start out today, let me say that the legal system of a country—that is, its system of justice—reflects the history and culture of the country just as much as the other topics we have discussed so far.

_____ I don't want to leave you with the impression that every legal case is tried in court with a jury in the United States.

_____ Now that you've had a chance to think about these philosophical questions, let's begin by looking at the U.S. legal system in terms of what makes it different from legal systems in many other countries.

_____ Now I'd like to discuss two other big differences, namely between criminal and civil trials.

CD 5, TR 14

FIRST LISTENING

Listen to the lecture and take notes. Look at the lecturer's visual aids as you listen. These may help you understand parts of the lecture.

Introduction

Common Law and the Jury System

Introduction
1. Common law vs civil law
2. Jury system
3. Plea bargaining

Subtopic 1: ______________________________

Civil Law
- Code of laws
- Judge

Common Law
- Case by case
- Judge
- Jury

Subtopic 2: ______________________________

The Jury System
- Civil trials
- Criminal trials
- Judge vs. jury
- Criticisms

Subtopic 3: ______________________________

Plea Bargaining/Settlements
- Criminal cases
- Civil cases

SECOND LISTENING

CD 5, TR 15

Listen to the lecture again and make your notes as complete as possible.

THIRD LISTENING

CD 5, TR 16

A You will hear part of the lecture again. Listen and complete the notes by adding the information from the box.

bet	citz	def	not	Rt	vs.	$	++

__________ to trial by jury guarntd by US Const
Jury = 6 or 12 ordin __________; hear testmny in civil or crim trials & reach verdct
I. Civil trial: disp __________ prvt ind re: contrcts, prop. rts
 A. jury decd who wins—which side > evidnce?
 B. __________ must testify
 C. jury decd __________ to winner
II. Crim trial: gov't __________ accusd of crim
 A. jury decd guilt or innoc—"beyond a reason. doubt"
 B. gov't must prv guilt—__________ def prv innoc
 C. def doesn't have to testify
 D. deg of proof __________ bec if convctd, crim's free or life taken away

B Compare your answers with a partner. Then compare the notes in A with the notes you took for this part of the lecture.

ACCURACY CHECK

CD 5, TR 17

A **Listen to the following questions and write short answers. Use your notes. You will hear each question one time only.**

1. ______
2. ______
3. ______
4. ______
5. ______
6. ______
7. ______
8. ______
9. ______
10. ______

B **Check your answers with your teacher. If your score is less than 70 percent, you may need to listen to the lecture again and rewrite some of your notes.**

ORAL SUMMARY

Use your notes to create an oral summary of the lecture with your partner. As you work together, add details to your notes that your partner included but you had missed.

DISCUSSION

Discuss the following questions with a classmate or in a small group.

1. Which principle of law do you think is fairer, "innocent until proven guilty" or "guilty until proven innocent"? Why?
2. Compare the advantages of having a judge decide a case without a jury to the advantages of having a jury decide a case.
3. In plea bargaining, is it fair to the victim of a crime if the guilty person receives a less severe punishment for cooperating with the state? Explain.

PRE-READING

The following Reading is about the countries that are beginning to use juries in their legal system. Before you read, answer the following questions. Share your answers with a classmate.

1. Are juries used in your country of origin? If so, how are they used? Are you aware of any countries other than the United States that use a jury system?
2. Look at the title. Why do you think a country would want to try using juries as a part of its legal system?

READING

Now read the article.

Experimenting with the Jury System

When you hear the word *jury*, what image comes to mind? Most likely, you will picture an American courtroom drama as seen in countless movies and television programs. It is indeed true that the jury system is an essential part of the U.S. legal system; a majority of both civil and criminal cases in the United States every year are heard by a jury. It is perhaps less well-known that a number of other countries in the world also use juries in their legal systems. In fact, despite criticisms of the U.S. jury system, more and more countries around the world are beginning to experiment with the use of juries.

In 2009, Japan reinstated the jury system, after having abandoned it in 1943. The jury system in

Japan is far more limited than in the United States, however. Juries are used only in criminal cases involving serious crimes such as murder and rape. In such cases, six citizen jurors randomly chosen from among those registered to vote serve alongside three professional judges. The jurors must be at least 20 years old and have at least a junior high school education. In order to find a defendant guilty, at least one of the professional judges must agree with all six of the citizen jurors. On the other hand, a not-guilty verdict by at least five of the jurors will stand, even if all three of the professional judges vote for a guilty verdict.

South Korea has also recently begun to use juries. Starting in 2008, the country began a five-year experiment using American-style jury trials. South Korean juries have five to nine members. During this experimental period, the decision of the jury is considered advisory; that is, the judge does not have to follow the jury's decision. At the end of the experimental period, the South Korean Supreme Court will decide which, if any, aspects of the new system will be permanently adopted.

In Hunan Province in China, home to some 100 million citizens, the use of a "people's jury" has been in place since 2007. Jurors are randomly chosen from a large pool of people who are selected by local officials. Usually, but not always, the pool consists of people who live in the town or city where the crime was committed. Typically seven to nine (but sometimes as many as thirteen) people are randomly chosen from the pool to sit on the jury. These jurors attend the court proceedings. At the end, they give their opinions on both the facts and an appropriate sentence. They are not required to reach a unanimous decision, and as in South Korea, their decisions are merely advisory. The people's jury is typically used in criminal cases involving what are considered to be sensitive or difficult matters that have the potential to affect group harmony or stability. They often involve cases that could result in the death penalty.

As you can see, there are many differences in the ways juries function in the U.S., Japan, South Korea, and China. However, one common theme seems to be a belief that at least in theory, ordinary citizens have an important role to play in the judicial process.

DISCUSSION

Discuss these questions with a classmate.

1. What are the differences between the jury system in the United States and the new jury system in Japan?
2. What are the differences between the way juries are used in South Korea and China and the jury system in the United States?
3. Considering the criticisms that are made of the jury system in the U.S., why do you think some countries are starting to use juries in a limited way?

PURSUING THE TOPIC

Explore the topic of this chapter further by doing the following.

Watch the movie *12 Angry Men*, either the original 1957 version or the 1997 HBO remake. This drama is about a jury deciding a murder case. Be prepared to discuss the movie with your classmates.

Demon Fish

BEFORE VIEWING

TOPIC PREVIEW

Read the situation below. Then discuss with a partner what *a representative of the hotel industry, a local politician,* and *a tourist* in the town would want to see happen.

A small beach town on the U.S. Atlantic coast depends on tourism as its main industry. It is tourist season and a shark has been seen swimming near the beach for two days.

VOCABULARY PREVIEW

A **Read the definitions of these key words and phrases that you will hear during the video.**

a natural transition a reasonable or normal change from one thing to another
time and time again over and over again; repeatedly
abstract threat a danger that exists in one's mind rather than based on a real event
familiar with knowing someone or something fairly well
within a span of during the period of time of
stamp out remove; put an end to something
halt stop something or someone
hold politicians accountable for force politicians to take responsibility for something
political penalty the consequence for a politician of an unpopular decision or bad behavior

B **Work with a partner and write vocabulary from A in the blanks in the sentences.**

1. The ________________ for voting against the president was losing reelection.
2. There were four shark attacks ________________ twelve days, but the local politicians did nothing to try to ________________ them.
3. Are you ________________ the movie *Jaws*, which is about a shark attack?
4. This is not a(n) ________________. People are dying and something must be done.
5. The police are trying hard to ________________ drug dealing in the area.
6. ________________ voters want to ________________ events that they really cannot control.
7. When the senator lost the election, she made ________________ from politics to business.

VIEWING

FIRST VIEWING

Watch the video, and then compare your first impressions with a partner. Talk about what you remember, what surprised you, and what interested you.

SECOND VIEWING

Watch the video again. Listen for the missing words and write them in the blanks.

1. I've spent the vast majority of my reporting career here in ________________ covering politicians.
2. The first recorded shark ________________ in history in the late 1500s comes from a Portuguese sailor who had the misfortune to ________________ overboard.
3. This in some ways was the inspiration for the ________________ *Jaws*.
4. In fact, Woodrow Wilson, who was ________________ at the time and started his political career in New Jersey, actually came under attack for the fact that he did ________________ to halt these shark strikes.
5. And so it was just interesting to see how voters really did ________________ Woodrow Wilson and thought that, you know, there was something he could do to ensure that they could be ________________ at sea.

President Woodrow Wilson

THIRD VIEWING

Complete these notes as you watch the video. Write only important words, not full sentences, and abbreviate common words.

1) Early sh. attks
    - late 1500s ______________________
    - many tales ______________________
    - capts ______________________
2) Abst. threat — but changed
    - beachgoers ______________________
    - front pg Phil. Inq. ______________________
    - ppl more aware, but ______________________
3) Then 4 ppl ______________________ in 12 ______________________
    - Woodrow Wilson, pres: ______________________
    - voters ______________________ WW

AFTER VIEWING

ORAL SUMMARY

Use your notes to create an oral summary of the video with your partner. As you work together, add details to your notes that your partner included but you had missed.

DISCUSSION

Discuss the following questions with a classmate or in a small group.

1. The speaker says jokingly, "Many people said it was obviously a natural transition from politicians to sharks." Why is this funny?
2. Why did Woodrow Wilson lose some votes during his election?
3. What can the government do to make beaches safe places in many different ways, not just from the threat of sharks?

Audioscripts

UNIT 1

The Face of the People

CHAPTER 1

The Population

VOCABULARY PREVIEW Page 3

1. Most countries take a census every 10 years or so in order to count the people and to know where they are living.
2. A country with a growing population is a country that is becoming more populous.
3. A person's race is partly determined by skin color and type of hair as well as other physical characteristics.
4. The majority of the U.S. population is of European origin.
5. The geographical distribution of a country's population gives information about where the people are living.
6. Many different kinds of people comprise the total U.S. population. In other words, people of different races and ages make up the population.
7. The median age of the U.S. population, which is a relatively large one, has been getting progressively higher recently.
8. Metropolitan areas are more densely populated than rural areas. That is, they have more people per square mile.
9. I want to discuss the distribution of the U.S. population in terms of age and gender.
10. In fact, statistically, women generally live longer than men worldwide.
11. A country whose birth rate is higher than its death rate will have an increasing population.
12. On the average, women have a higher life expectancy than men do.

NOTETAKING PREPARATION Page 4

1. 27 million
2. three and a half
3. 2 out of 10
4. 0.2 percent
5. 80.8 percent
6. 75.7 percent
7. one-half
8. 145 thousand
9. 0.9 percent
10. 9 out of 10

FIRST LISTENING Page 5

Today we're going to talk about population in the United States. According to the most recent government census, in 2010, the population is almost 309 million people, an increase of about 27 million people since the 2000 census. A population of close to 309 million makes the United States the third most populous country in the whole world. Now, as you probably know, the People's Republic of China is the most populous country in the world. Do you know which is the second most populous? If you thought India, you were right. The fourth, fifth, and sixth most populous countries are Indonesia, Brazil, and Pakistan. Now let's get back to the United States and look at the U.S. population in three different ways. The first way is by race and origin. Here we're talking about the percentages of whites, blacks, and so on—and from the parts of the world that they or their ancestors came from. Second, we'll look at the population by geographical distribution. In other words, where people live. And the third way is by the age and gender of the population. Let me make sure you got all of those down in your notes. First, we'll look at the population by race and origin. Second, by geographical distribution. And last, by age and gender.

Today we're going to talk about population in the United States. According to the most recent government census, in 2010, the population is almost 309 million people, an increase of about 27 million people since the 2000 census. A population of close to 309 million makes the

United States the third most populous country in the whole world. Now, as you probably know, the People's Republic of China is the most populous country in the world. Do you know which is the second most populous? If you thought India, you were right. The fourth, fifth, and sixth most populous countries are Indonesia, Brazil, and Pakistan. Now let's get back to the United States and look at the U.S. population in three different ways. The first way is by race and origin. Here we're talking about the percentages of whites, blacks, and so on—and from the parts of the world that they or their ancestors came from. Second, we'll look at the population by geographical distribution. In other words, where people live. And the third way is by the age and gender of the population. Let me make sure you got all of those down in your notes. OK. First, we'll look at the population by race and origin. Second, by geographical distribution. And last, by age and gender.

First of all, let's take a look at the population by race and origin. The 2010 U.S. census reports that 72.4 percent of the population is white, whereas 12.6 percent is black. About 4.8 percent are of Asian origin, Native Hawaiians and other Pacific Islanders comprise 0.2 percent, and Native Americans are 0.9 percent. Two point nine percent of the population is a mixture of two or more races, and 6.2 percent report themselves as "of some other race." Let's make sure your figures are right: white, 72.4 percent; black, 12.6 percent; Asian, 4.8 percent; Native Hawaiian and other Pacific Islanders, 0.2 percent, Native American, 0.9 percent; a mixture of two or more races, 2.9 percent; and people who say they're of some other race, 6.2 percent. Interestingly, Hispanics, whose origins lie in Spanish-speaking countries, comprise whites, blacks, and Native Americans, so they are already included in the above figures. However, it is important to note that Hispanics make up 16.3 percent of the present U.S. population.

Another way of looking at the population is by geographical distribution. Do you have any idea which states are the five most populous in the United States? Well, I'll help you out there. The five most populous states are California, with more than 37 million people; Texas, with more than 25 million; New York, with a little more than 19 million; Florida, with a little less than 19 million; and finally, Illinois with almost 13 million people. These figures are surprising to many people because, although over half of the total U.S. population lives in the South and West, the East is more densely populated. Nevertheless, there are more people all together in the South and West. To understand this seeming contradiction, one need only consider the relatively larger size of many southern and western states, so although there are more people, they are distributed over a larger area. By the way, the South and the West are growing much faster than any other area of the country. Now to finish up this section on geographical distribution, consider that about 83 percent of the people live in metropolitan areas like Los Angeles, New York, Chicago, and Houston. That means that fewer than two out of ten people live in rural areas.

Before we finish today, I want to discuss the distribution of the U.S. population in terms of age and gender. Just for interest, would you say there are more men or more women in the United States? Well, according to the 2010 census, there are more women. In fact, there are more than 5 million more women than men in the United States. If we consider that more males than females are born each year, how can this difference be explained? Well, one important reason is that there is a progressively higher death rate for males as they get older. As of 2010 the life expectancy for women was 80.8 years, whereas for men it was only 75.7 years. In fact, statistically, women generally live longer than men worldwide. A 2011 estimate of the average life expectancy worldwide for the total population is about 69 for females and 65 for males.

You don't need to take notes on this, but I thought you might be interested in the life expectancy for the total population in the other five most populous countries I mentioned earlier: China: about 75 years of age, India: about 67, Indonesia: about 71, Brazil, about 72 and a half, and Pakistan, about 70.

Now, to finish up, let's look at the median age of the whole population. The median age is the age that half of the population is older than and half is younger than. Overall, the median age of the U.S. population is increasing: from 35.3 years in 2000 to 37.2 years in 2010. The median age has been slowly, but steadily, increasing over the past several decades. This trend toward a higher median age can be explained by a decreasing birth rate and an increasing life expectancy for the population as a whole. I'd like to investigate these two subjects further, but I see our time is up, so we'll have to stop now.

SECOND LISTENING Page 6

See First Listening B, above.

THIRD LISTENING Page 6

Another way of looking at the population is by geographical distribution. Do you have any idea which states are the five most populous in the United States? Well, I'll help you out there. The five most populous states are California, with more than 37 million people; Texas, with more than 25 million; New York, with a little more than 19 million; Florida, with a little less than 19 million; and finally, Illinois with almost 13 million people. These figures are surprising to many people because, although over half of the total U.S. population lives in the South and West, the East is more densely populated. Nevertheless, there are more people all together in the South and West. To understand this seeming contradiction, one need only consider the relatively larger size of many southern and western states, so although there are more people, they are distributed over a larger area. By the way, the South and the West are growing much faster than any other area of the country. Now to finish up this section on geographical distribution, consider that about 83 percent of the people live in metropolitan areas like Los Angeles, New York, Chicago, and Houston. That means that fewer than two out of ten people live in rural areas.

ACCURACY CHECK Page 7

A

1. Which two countries have a larger population than the United States?
2. What was the population of the United States in the 2010 census?
3. Which group is bigger, blacks or Hispanics?
4. Which state is more populous, Florida or Texas?
5. In what two regions of the country do most Americans live?
6. What ratio of the population lives in rural areas?
7. How many more women than men are there in the U.S. population?
8. About how many years longer do women live than men in the United States?
9. What was the increase in the median age from 2000 to 2010?
10. What two factors account for the increase in the median age?

CHAPTER 2

Immigration

VOCABULARY PREVIEW Page 11

1. Sometimes people immigrate to a new country to escape political or religious persecution.
2. Rather than immigrants, the early settlers from Great Britain considered themselves colonists; they had left home to settle new land for the mother country.
3. The so-called Great Immigration, which can be divided into three stages, or time periods, began about 1830 and lasted till about 1930.
4. The Industrial Revolution, which began in the nineteenth century, caused widespread unemployment as machines replaced workers.
5. The scarcity of farmland in Europe caused many people to immigrate to the United States, where there was an abundance of available land.
6. Land in the United States was plentiful and available when the country was expanding westward. In fact, the U.S. government offered free public land to citizens in 1862.
7. The failure of the Irish potato crop in the middle of the nineteenth century caused widespread starvation.
8. The first law that limited the number of immigrants coming from a certain part of the world was the Chinese Exclusion Act of 1882, but in 1965 strict quotas based on nationality were eliminated.
9. This is the largest number of immigrants in history, although the share of the total population today, 12.8 percent, has been larger in the past.
10. Strict anti-immigration laws at the state or federal level and sanctions against employers who hire illegal immigrants could lead to a decline in immigration to the United States.

NOTETAKING PREPARATION Page 12

1. 1850
2. 1915
3. the 1840s
4. from 1890 to 1930
5. between 1750 and 1850
6. 1776
7. 1882
8. 1929
9. 1860
10. from approximately 1830 to 1930

B

1. France	the French
2. Germany	Germans
3. Scotland	Scots or the Scottish
4. Ireland	the Irish
5. Great Britain	the British or Britons
6. Denmark	Danes
7. Norway	Norwegians
8. Sweden	Swedes
9. the Netherlands or Holland	the Dutch
10. Greece	Greeks
11. Italy	Italians
12. Spain	the Spanish or Spaniards
13. Portugal	the Portuguese
14. China	the Chinese

15. the Philippines	Filipinos
16. Mexico	Mexicans
17. India	Indians
18. Russia	Russians
19. Poland	Poles
20. Vietnam	the Vietnamese

FIRST LISTENING Page 14

The subject of immigration is quite fascinating to most Americans because they view themselves as a nation of immigrants. However, the early Britons who came to what is today the United States considered themselves "settlers" or "colonists," rather than immigrants. These people did not think they were moving to a new country; instead, they thought they were settling new land for the "mother country." There were also large numbers of Dutch, French, German, and Scotch-Irish settlers, as well as large numbers of blacks brought from Africa as slaves. At the time of independence from Britain in 1776, about 40 percent of people living in what is now the United States were not British. The majority of people, however, spoke English, and the traditions that formed the basis of life were mainly British traditions. This period we have just been discussing is usually referred to as "the Colonial period." Today, we're a little more interested in actual immigration after this period. Let's first take a look at what is often called the Great Immigration, which began about 1830 and ended in 1930. Then let's consider the reasons for this so-called Great Immigration. Third, I'll make a few brief remarks about a decrease in immigration between 1940 and 1970. Finally, we'll talk about the immigration situation in the United States today.

The subject of immigration is quite fascinating to most Americans because they view themselves as a nation of immigrants. However, the early Britons who came to what is today the United States considered themselves "settlers" or "colonists," rather than immigrants. These people did not think they were moving to a new country; instead, they thought they were settling new land for the "mother country." There were also large numbers of Dutch, French, German, and Scotch-Irish settlers, as well as large numbers of blacks brought from Africa as slaves. At the time of independence from Britain in 1776, about 40 percent of people living in what is now the United States were not British. The majority of people, however, spoke English, and the traditions that formed the basis of life were mainly British traditions. This period we have just been discussing is usually referred to as "the Colonial period." Today, we're a little more interested in actual immigration after this period. Let's first take a look at what is often called the Great Immigration, which began about 1830 and ended in 1930. Then let's consider the reasons for this so-called Great Immigration. Third, I'll make a few brief remarks about a decrease in immigration between 1940 and 1970. Finally, we'll talk about the immigration situation in the United States today.

As I said, we'll begin our discussion today with the period of history called the Great Immigration, which lasted from approximately 1830 to 1930. It will be easier if we look at the Great Immigration in terms of three major stages, or time periods. The first stage was from approximately 1830 to 1860. Before this time, the number of immigrants coming to the United States was comparatively small, only about 10,000 a year. However, the rate began to climb in the 1830s when about 600,000 immigrants arrived. The rate continued to climb during the 1840s with a total of 1,700,000 people arriving in that decade. The rate went on climbing during the 1850s, when 2,600,000 immigrants arrived. During this first stage of the Great Immigration, that is, between the years 1830 and 1860, the majority of immigrants came from Germany, Great Britain, and Ireland. Now let's consider the second stage of the Great Immigration. The second stage was from 1860 to 1890, during which time another 10 million people arrived. Between 1860 and 1890 the majority of immigrants continued to be from Germany, Ireland, and Great Britain. However, during the second stage, a smaller, but significant, number of immigrants came from the Scandinavian nations of Denmark, Norway, and Sweden. The third stage of the Great Immigration, which lasted from 1890 to 1930, was the era of heaviest immigration. Between the years 1890 and 1930, almost 22 million immigrants arrived in the United States. Most of these new arrivals came from the Southern European countries of Greece, Italy, Portugal, and Spain and the Eastern European countries of Poland and Russia.

Now that we know something about the immigrants who came to the States during the Great Immigration, let's consider the reasons why most of these people immigrated. Why did such large numbers of Europeans leave their homes for life in an unknown country? It would be impossible to discuss all the complex political and economic reasons in any depth today, but we can touch on a few interesting facts that might help to clarify the situation for you. First of all, one of the most important reasons was that the population of Europe doubled between the years 1750 and 1850. At the same time that the population was growing so rapidly, the Industrial Revolution in Europe was causing widespread unemployment. The combination of increased population and the demand for land by industry also meant that farmland was becoming increasingly scarce in Europe. The scarcity of farmland in Europe meant that the abundance of available land in the growing country of the United States was a great attraction. During these years, the United States was an expanding country, and it seemed that there was no end to land. In fact, in 1862 the government offered public land free to citizens and to immigrants who were planning to become citizens. In addition to available farmland, there were also plentiful jobs during these years of great economic growth. Other attractions were freedom from religious or political persecution. Some other groups also came to the United States as the direct results of natural disasters that left them in desperate situations. For example, the frequent failure of the potato crop in Ireland between the years 1845 and 1849 led to widespread starvation in that country, and people were driven to emigrate. Another factor that affected the number of immigrants coming to the United States was improved ocean transport beginning in the 1840s. At that time, ships big enough to carry large numbers of people began to make regular trips across the ocean. Now let's summarize the reasons for the high rate of immigration to the United States during the years we discussed: first, the doubling of the population in Europe between 1750 and 1850; second, the unemployment caused by the Industrial Revolution; and third, the land scarcity in Europe, followed by religious and political persecution and natural disaster. These reasons combined with improved transportation probably accounted for the largest number of immigrants.

Immigration declined somewhat after the Great Immigration. During the decades between 1940 and 1970, the total immigrant population varied from 9 to 11 million people. There are several reasons for this decline. This decline was in part due to various laws whose aim was to limit the number of immigrants coming from different parts of the world to the United States. The first law that limited the number of immigrants coming from a certain part of the world was the Chinese Exclusion Act of 1882. This law was followed by many other laws that also tried to limit the numbers of people immigrating from various countries or parts of the world. In addition to such laws, certainly economic and geopolitical events as important as the Great Depression which began in 1929, and World War II, which lasted from about 1937 to 1945, also contributed to the decline in immigration.

Now that we've talked about the historical situation, let's discuss the current situation with respect to immigration, which is quite different from that in the past. To understand some of the changes, it's important to note that in 1965 strict quotas based on nationality were eliminated, and immigration has increased in every decade since. Let's see how different things are today from the past. In 2010, the number of immigrants living in the United States was 40 million, or 12.8 percent of the total population. This is the largest number of immigrants in history although the share of the total population, 12.8 percent, has been larger in the past. The 40 million figure includes both legal and illegal immigrants, and the census reports that three-quarters of these immigrants came to the United States legally. These recent immigrants are seldom Europeans as they were in the Great Immigration. Rather, immigration from Latin America was responsible for 58 percent of immigrants from 2000 to 2010. Mexico, the origin of close to 12 million, was the top country to send immigrants in that decade. The second largest group came from China. Third was India, and the fourth and fifth largest groups of immigrants were from the Philippines and Vietnam.

Do immigrants today migrate for the same reasons as in the past? Not exactly, according to information immigrants reported to the Census Bureau. There were three main reasons for immigrating to the United States in the decade 2000 to 2010: (1) access to public services; (2) political problems in their home countries; and (3) the desire to join relatives living in the States. Interestingly, none of these reasons is directly related to the U.S. economy, which actually lost jobs during the decade. We'll talk more about that in the next lecture.

Last, it might be interesting to speculate on immigration in the future. Complicated issues worldwide may cause an increase in immigration—or they may cause a decrease. Global warming and social unrest in other countries could lead to an increase in immigration to the United States. On the other hand, strict U.S. anti-immigration laws at the state or federal level, sanctions against employers who hire illegal immigrants, and improved economic conditions in home countries could lead to a decline in immigration to the United States. We can't know for sure which way the numbers will go. We've covered a lot, so let's end here for today.

SECOND LISTENING Page 16

See First Listening B, above.

THIRD LISTENING Page 16

Now that we've talked about the historical situation, let's discuss the current situation with respect to immigration, which is quite different from that in the past. To understand some of the changes, it's important to note that in 1965 strict quotas based on nationality were eliminated, and immigration has increased in every decade since. Let's see how different things are today from the past. In 2010, the number of immigrants living in the United States was 40 million, or 12.8 percent of the total population. This is the largest number of immigrants in history although the share of the total population, 12.8 percent, has been larger in the past.

The 40 million figure includes both legal and illegal immigrants, and the census reports that three-quarters of these immigrants came to the United States legally. These recent immigrants are seldom Europeans as they were in the Great Immigration. Rather, immigration from Latin America was responsible for 58 percent of immigrants from 2000 to 2010. Mexico, the origin of close to 12 million, was the top country to send immigrants in that decade. The second largest group came from China. Third was India, and the fourth and fifth largest groups of immigrants were from the Philippines and Vietnam.

ACCURACY CHECK Page 17

A

1. What did the earliest Britons who came to what is now the United States consider themselves to be?
2. Which five non-English groups came to the United States during the Colonial period?
3. Of the three stages of the Great Immigration, which had the heaviest immigration?
4. Between the years 1890 and 1930, which two areas of the world did most immigrants come from?
5. What three conditions in Europe caused a lot of immigration to the United States during the Great Immigration?
6. What conditions in the United States attracted the earliest immigrants?
7. Give an example of a natural disaster that caused immigration to the United States.
8. What three reasons are given for a decline in immigration after the period of the Great Immigration?
9. How is the origin of people who immigrate to the United States today different from those who immigrated during the Great Immigration?
10. What two factors could lead to an increase in immigration to the United States in the future?

CHAPTER 3

Work in America

VOCABULARY PREVIEW Page 21

A

1. There was also a large decrease in the number of people working in industry, that is, in making, or manufacturing, things in factories.
2. While the number of people in agriculture and manufacturing industries went down, the number of people in the services went up dramatically.
3. Over the years, child labor laws became much stricter and by 1999, it was illegal for anyone under 16 to work full-time in any of the 50 states.
4. In 1900, only 19 percent of women were employed; in 2010, almost 73 percent of women were holding down jobs.
5. For much of the twentieth century, U.S. workers saw rising wages, increased benefits like Social Security and health insurance, and better working conditions.
6. While the productivity of the U.S. workforce has continued to increase since the 1970s, wages for the working class have not increased.
7. Let me give you some statistics that may help you understand the impact of stagnant wages and high unemployment.
8. Labor unions, which protect workers' rights, have become weaker in the past decades.
9. Lack of regulation of financial institutions has led to very risky investments, which have led to loss of jobs, lost pensions, and loss of homes.
10. "Cautious optimism" about the U.S. economy seems to be the watchword of the day in newspapers and magazine articles about the economy at this time.

NOTETAKING PREPARATION Page 22

1. There was also a large decrease in the number of people working in industry.
2. It was illegal for anyone under 16 to work full-time in any of the 50 states.
3. By the end of the century, only 3 percent still worked on farms.

FIRST LISTENING Page 24

Whether you love it or hate it, work is a major part of most people's lives everywhere in the world. Americans are no exception. Americans might complain about "blue Monday," when they have to go back to work after the weekend, but most of them put a lot of importance on their job, not only in terms of money but also in terms of identity. In fact, when Americans are introduced to a new person, they almost always ask each other, "What do you do?" They are really asking, "What is your job or profession?" Today, however, we won't look at work in terms of what work means socially or psychologically. Rather, um, we're going to take a look at work in the United States today in three different ways. First, we'll take a historical look at work in America. Uh, we'll do that by looking at how things changed for the American worker from the year 1900 to the year of the latest statistics, 2010. That is, from the beginning of the twentieth century to recent times. Then we'll look at how

U.S. workers are doing today. And after that, we'll take a look at some possible reasons for the current economic situation. And finally, we'll look at what people are saying about what the government should and should not do in order to improve the country's economy.

As we look at the changes over the last century or so, we're going to use a lot of statistics to describe these changes. First, let's consider how the type of work people were involved in changed. At the beginning of the twentieth century, in 1900, about 38 percent of the workforce was involved in agriculture; that is, they worked on a farm. By the end of the century, only 3 percent still worked on farms, and by 2010, only about 1 percent worked in agriculture. There was also a large decrease in the number of people working in industry, that is, in making, or manufacturing, things in factories. The number of workers in industry is down from over 30 percent in 1900 to just over 22 percent in 2010.

While the number of people in agriculture and manufacturing industries went down, the number of people in the services went up. As you may know, services, rather than goods or products, provide other less concrete things that people need. A few examples include education, health care, transportation, tourism, banking, advertising, and legal services. Cafés, restaurants, and fast-food outlets like McDonald's are part of the service sector, as are retail sales jobs, driving taxis, and pumping gas. The services workforce jumped from 31 percent of the workforce in 1900 to 77 percent in 2010.

Let's recap the numbers: in 1900, 38 percent in agriculture; 31 percent in industry; and 31 percent in services. In 2010, about 1 percent in agriculture; 22 percent in industry; and 77 percent in services.

To put things into perspective, let's compare the United States today to China, where the picture is very different. From your experience, would you expect China to have more workers in agriculture or in industry? Well, it may or may not surprise you, but in China, agriculture takes up only 10 percent of the workforce, industry a huge 47 percent, and services 43 percent. Figures for the entire world are somewhere between China's and the United States' figures: 6 percent, 31 percent, and 63 percent for agriculture, industry, and services, respectively. Let's get back to the changes in the U.S. workforce in the last century or so.

There are just two more points I wanted to bring up. First, child labor was not unusual at the beginning of the twentieth century. In 1900, there were 1,750,000 children aged 10 to 15 working full-time in the labor force. This was 6 percent of the labor force. Over the years, child labor laws became much stricter and by 1999, it was illegal for anyone under 16 to work full-time in any of the 50 states. Second, while the number of children in the workforce went down, the number of women went up dramatically. In 1900, only 19 percent of women were employed; in 2010, almost 73 percent of women were holding down jobs.

OK, now let's take a look at how the U.S. workforce is doing today. First, let me say that for much of the twentieth century, U.S. workers saw rising wages, increased benefits like social security and health insurance, and better working conditions. However, things are not so rosy for today's workers. First, let's look at wages. The U.S. workforce is still considered extremely productive among the industrialized nations of the world, but while its productivity has continued to increase since the 1970s, wages for the working class have not increased. Also the number of unemployed has been high for some of the past few years.

Let me give you some statistics that may help you understand the impact of stagnant wages and high unemployment. Shortly after World War II, a child born in poverty, that is, to a poor family, had a 50 percent chance of being in the middle class as an adult. But by 1980, a person born in poverty had a 40 percent chance. In 2012, economists told us that his or her chance of entering the middle class was only 33 percent.

Finally, let's take a look at some of the possible reasons for the current situation. First of all, agriculture in the United States has become much more mechanized and more efficient, so fewer people are needed to grow crops and raise animals. Most people agree that outsourcing, that is, sending some U.S. manufacturing and service work overseas to countries like China and India that have lower wages, is one reason. At the same time, these countries manufacture products that they can export to the United States and other countries more cheaply than U.S. companies can manufacture them. Also we should keep in mind that some advances in technology have eliminated a lot of the jobs that required workers in the past. I'm thinking of robots in the auto industry and bank ATM machines, for example. In addition to outsourcing and advances in technology, unions, which protect workers' rights, have become weaker in the past decades. The result is lower wages and even loss of jobs for people from factory workers to teachers. Some economists point out that the American consumer has benefited from outsourcing and technology in that many products are much cheaper. That is cold comfort to millions of workers who have lost their jobs, of course. Let's look at some more reasons.

Other possible causes for the economic problems may be government policies and legislation, among them tax cuts and lack of regulation of businesses, especially large corporations and financial institutions such as banks, mortgage companies, and investment firms. Tax cuts mean the government has less money to provide programs to help people in difficulty or to invest in education and research. Lack of regulation of financial institutions has led to their making very risky investments, risky investments that have led to loss of jobs, lost pensions, and loss of homes. It's important to note, however, that many people believe that high taxes and too much regulation pulls down the economy.

These issues are very difficult ones, and discussions about how to fix the economy can get very heated. Liberals and conservatives blame each other, and the political process seems more polarized than ever before. However, let's not forget that the United States has survived many economic downturns in the past and "cautious optimism" about the U.S. economy seems to be the watchword of the day in newspapers and magazine articles about the economy at this time. Even the prestigious World Economic Forum, which met in Davos, Switzerland, in late January of 2012, expressed optimism and caution, in other words, "cautious optimism."

SECOND LISTENING Page 26

See First Listening, above.

THIRD LISTENING Page 26

OK, now let's take a look at how the U.S. workforce is doing today. First, let me say that for much of the twentieth century, U.S. workers saw rising wages, increased benefits like social security and health insurance, and better working conditions. However, things are not so rosy for today's workers. First, let's look at wages. The U.S. workforce is still considered extremely productive among the industrialized nations of the world, but while its productivity has continued to increase since the 1970s, wages for the working class have not increased. Also the number of unemployed has been high for some of the past few years.

Let me give you some statistics that may help you understand the impact of stagnant wages and high unemployment. Shortly after World War II, a child born in poverty, that is, to a poor family, had a 50 percent chance of being in the middle class as an adult. But by 1980, a person born in poverty had a 40 percent chance. In 2012, economists told us that his or her chance of entering the middle class was only 33 percent.

ACCURACY CHECK Page 27

1. What percentage of the workforce was engaged in agriculture in 1900?
2. What percentage of the workforce was still engaged in agriculture at the end of 1999?
3. Education and transportation are examples of which kind of work?
4. By 2010, what percentage of workers were in the service sector?
5. What percentage of women were in the workforce in 1900? What percentage in 2010?
6. What is one benefit that most U.S. workers received by the end of the twentieth century?
7. What were the chances of entering the middle class in 1980 for a person born in poverty?
8. What are two large countries that the United States is outsourcing a lot of work to?
9. According to the lecturer, what is the reason financial institutions in the United States have been able to make risky investments?
10. Which two words were often used to describe the economy in newspaper and magazine articles at the beginning of 2012?

UNIT 2

The American Character

CHAPTER 4

Family in the United States

VOCABULARY PREVIEW Page 35

1. Although many social scientists are concerned about the decrease in marriage and its possible negative effects on the family, others say it is wrong to assume that marriage in the United States is "on the rocks."
2. In any society, economic and cultural elements interact with each other and bring about change.
3. This was the period after World War II, a period characterized by a very strong economy, a rising standard of living, and a growing middle class.
4. The typical configuration of the family in these years was the traditional one: a married couple with children.
5. Culturally, three characteristics stand out in this period: conformity to social norms, greater male domination of the family than in the later periods, and very clear gender roles.
6. The women's liberation movement was an outgrowth of the struggle for civil rights.
7. Women's liberation challenged discrimination against women in the home, in the work place, and in society in general.

8. Three movements—the sexual revolution, women's liberation, and the antiwar movement—were typical of the nonconforming nature of these decades.
9. With more women having careers and making money, there was less economic pressure for them to stay in an unsuitable marriage.
10. Many experts claim that children have paid a high price for the social changes that took place in the second period.

NOTETAKING PREPARATION Page 36

A

1. With more women having careers and making money, there was less economic pressure for them to stay in an unsuitable marriage.
2. Young children often spend long hours away from their parents and homes in day care, and school-aged children often pass after-school hours home alone while their parents work.
3. A look at the new family shows that young people are more cautious about marriage than their parents were.

FIRST LISTENING Page 37

Let me begin today's lecture by saying that many people today are concerned about the decline in the number of people who are married in the United States. Here are some interesting statistics that explain why they are concerned: In 1960, 74 percent of whites were married, 72 percent of Hispanics were married, and 61 percent of blacks. Today, the figures are dramatically lower: only 55 percent of whites are married, only 48 percent of Hispanics, and only 31 percent of blacks. When we look at the young, that is people between 18 and 24, the figures are even more surprising. Forty-five percent of young people were married in 1960. Today by comparison only 9 percent of young people are married.

OK, what does this mean for the family? Although many social scientists are concerned about the decrease in marriage and its possible negative effects on the family, others say it is wrong to assume that marriage in the United States is "on the rocks." Rather, they argue there are changes in the culture which are contributing to different ideas about marriage and family. In any society, economic and cultural elements interact with each other and bring about change. That is what has been happening in the United States. I'll try to explain the way Americans look at family today by taking a look at how their views have changed over time. I'll depend on the writings of sociologist Barbara Dafoe Whitehead in looking at three different time periods: the mid-1940s to the mid-1960s; the mid-60s to the mid-80s; and finally the present. We'll refer to the first period as the era of the traditional family. The second period we'll call the period of individualism, and the third period we'll call the period of the new family.

Let me begin today's lecture by saying that many people today are concerned about the decline in the number of people who are married in the United States. Here are some interesting statistics that explain why they are concerned: In 1960, 74 percent of whites were married, 72 percent of Hispanics were married, and 61 percent of blacks. Today, the figures are dramatically lower: only 55 percent of whites are married, only 48 percent of Hispanics, and only 31 percent of blacks. When we look at the young, that is people between 18 and 24, the figures are even more surprising. Forty-five percent of young people were married in 1960. Today by comparison only 9 percent of young people are married.

OK, what does all this mean for the family? Although many social scientists are concerned about the decrease in marriage and its possible negative effects on the family, others say it is wrong to assume that marriage in the United States is "on the rocks." Rather, they argue there are changes in the culture which are contributing to different ideas about marriage and family. In any society, economic and cultural elements interact with each other and bring about change. That is what has been happening in the United States. I'll try to explain the way Americans look at family today by taking a look at how their views have changed over time. I'll depend on the writings of sociologist Barbara Dafoe Whitehead in looking at three different time periods: the mid-1940s to the mid-1960s; the mid-60s to the mid-80s; and finally the present. We'll refer to the first period as the era of the traditional family. The second period we'll call the period of individualism, and the third period we'll call the period of the new family.

So, let's start with the first period, the mid-1940s to the mid-1960s, the era of the traditional family. This was the period after World War II, a period characterized by a very strong economy, a rising standard of living, and a growing middle class. The typical configuration of the family in these years was the traditional one: a married couple with children where the husband worked and the wife stayed home. Of course, some women worked, but divorce rates were low, and birth rates were high. TV programs of the era depicted the family in this traditional configuration: as working father, happy housewife and mother, and children. Culturally, three characteristics stand out in this period: conformity to social norms, greater male domination of the family than in later periods, and very clear gender roles, that is, clear and separate roles for men and women at home and at work. Well, things changed quite a bit after this period.

The second period that I want to talk about today, the period of individualism, lasted from the mid-1960s to the mid-1980s. During this period of individualism, there were three important social and political movements. The first of these movements was the sexual revolution, in which sex was no longer always reserved for marriage. The second was the women's liberation movement. The women's liberation movement was an outgrowth of the struggle for civil rights. Women's liberation challenged discrimination against women at home, at work, and in society in general. The third movement, against the war in Vietnam, was more political than social. All three movements—the sexual revolution, women's liberation, and the antiwar movement—were typical of the nonconforming nature of these decades. Culturally, it is in this period where we see two important social developments. One development was a stronger focus on one's career and work. The second development was a drive for self-expression and self-fulfillment. These developments suggested that women could and should do more than raise children and take care of the family. In this period, the feminist movement challenged traditional gender roles and male domination of society. Women began to enter professions that had been generally closed to them, professions such as medicine, law, and management. Men began at least to consider a more active role in raising their children.

In addition to the cultural changes during this period of individualism, there were also economic changes that affected families. The cost of living rose rapidly, and families saw the need for women to work outside the home to help support the family. Together, these cultural and economic forces changed the picture of the family. These new configurations included families in which the husband and wife both worked, families of single parents with children, and families of unmarried couples with or without children. With more women having careers and making money, there was less economic pressure for them to stay in an unsuitable marriage. Therefore, divorce rates doubled within a decade. Rising divorce rates and more financial independence for women made marriage less attractive for many women. Consequently, the number of single-parent households tripled. Less conformity to social norms led to an increase in the number of unmarried couples living together in this period. Can you see how economic and cultural elements interact with each other to change the family? Well, let's go on to the third period.

The third period from the mid-1980s until now, what we'll call the "new family," is harder to see because we are living in this period now. However, I think that today most people are happy about the social changes that occurred in the second period of individualism. Women are not willing to give up gender equality, the freedom to leave an unsuitable marriage, or the fulfillment of an interesting job. At the same time, many experts claim that children have paid a high price for the social changes that took place in the second period. Young children often spend long hours away from their parents and homes in day care, and school-aged children often pass after-school hours home alone while their parents work. Many children grow up with only one parent or with stepparents.

A look at the new family shows that young people are more cautious about marriage than their parents were. They still very much want to get married and have children. But they are willing to wait for the right person. And they want to get educated and have good jobs before marrying. The statistics support these findings. The median age for a first marriage for men in the United States today is 28.7 and 26.5 for women, while it was 22.8 for men and 20.3 for women in 1960. Women may make more money than their husbands and share in the decision making much more than women in the traditional family. And today, the ideal family has just two children. Parents, especially fathers, spend much more time with their children than in the past. And many upper- and middle-class children have more structured activities like music lessons and sports than children used to.

The changes in the family over the last 50 years or so have caused some politicians, religious leaders, social scientists, and everyday people a lot of concern. Should we be worried about the decline in the number of people who get married today, the number of women who work outside the home, etcetera? All that statistics can show us is that our attitudes toward marriage and the family are different now than they were in 1960. I don't think there is strong evidence that marriage and family in the United States are "on the rocks." Instead, our new attitudes toward marriage and family are one example of how American society has been changing.

SECOND LISTENING Page 38

See First Listening B, above.

THIRD LISTENING Page 38

So, let's start with the first period, the mid-1940s to the mid-1960s, the era of the traditional family. This was the period after World War II, a period characterized by a very strong economy, a rising standard of living, and a growing middle class. The typical configuration of the family in these years was the traditional one: a married couple with children where the husband worked and the wife stayed home. Of course, some women worked, but divorce rates were low, and birth rates were high. TV programs of the era depicted the family in this traditional configuration: working father, happy housewife and mother, and children. Culturally, three characteristics stand out in this period: conformity to social norms, greater male domination of the family than in later periods, and very clear gender roles, that is, clear and separate roles for men and women at home and at work. Well, things changed quite a bit after this period.

ACCURACY CHECK Page 39

1. Today, in what group is the percentage of people who are married the lowest?
2. What was the typical configuration of the family during the first period of the traditional family?
3. Was it common or uncommon for women to work during the era of the traditional family?
4. What economic changes occurred during the second period?
5. What three social and political movements occurred during the second period?
6. What two cultural changes occurred during this second period?
7. In which of the three periods that the lecturer discussed did divorce rates double and the number of single-parent families increase?
8. Did people get married at a younger age in the first period or during the third period?
9. What cultural elements from the first two periods do people want to keep today?
10. Does the lecturer feel that the American family is "on the rocks" or simply changing?

CHAPTER 5

Religion

VOCABULARY PREVIEW Page 43

1. These churches generally represent the two major Christian traditions, Catholic and Protestant, but often include several different Protestant denominations.
2. Larger towns and big cities will also have other places of worship including synagogues, mosques, and temples representing other religious traditions.
3. The U.S. government cannot ask for information on religious affiliation in any official capacity, for example, on the census.
4. Statistical information must be gathered from surveys of the population done by nongovernmental agencies or from organizational reports from religious groups themselves.
5. A 2009 Gallup poll asked, "Is religion an important part of your life?"
6. Most writers and scholars agree that Europeans are generally more secular than Americans.
7. They may believe in God, but they tend to stay away from religious institutions except for certain formal occasions like weddings, baptisms, and funerals and a few very important religious days.
8. It's important to remember that freedom of worship is guaranteed by the First Amendment to the Constitution, which also establishes the separation of church and state.
9. Recently, however, there has been a trend toward an increase in the influence of religion on American political life.
10. Although religion in America seemed to be in decline during most of the last century, in the 1970s, there was a religious revival that surprised many people.

FIRST LISTENING Page 46

The subject of today's lecture is religion, and religion in the United States is a complicated topic that is often misunderstood by people from other parts of the world. One reason for this may be that people in other countries are often only exposed to American culture through television, films, and videos on the Internet. These are media that, in general, ignore the role and importance of religion in the United States.

If international visitors took a drive through small towns in the United States, they might be surprised by the number of different churches in even a small town of two or three thousand people. These churches generally represent the two major Christian traditions, Catholic and Protestant, but often include several different Protestant denominations. Larger towns and big cities will also have other places of worship including synagogues, mosques, and temples representing other religious traditions.

When you consider that people from many different countries and religious backgrounds immigrated to the United States, it probably shouldn't be surprising to find a great number of different religions in the States. That brings me to what I want to talk about today. First, I'd like to give you some facts and figures about various religious groups in the United States. Second, I'll compare the United States to other modernized Western nations. Third, I'll discuss the importance of religion, particularly about the increasing role of religion in U.S. political life in recent years. And finally, I'll talk about the increasing diversity of religion in the United States.

B

The subject of today's lecture is religion, and religion in the United States is a complicated topic that is often misunderstood by people from other parts of the world. One reason for this may be that people in other countries are often only exposed to American culture through television, films, and videos on the Internet. These are media that, in general, ignore the role and importance of religion in the United States.

If international visitors took a drive through small towns in the United States, they might be surprised by the number of different churches in even a small town of two or three thousand people. These churches generally represent the two major Christian traditions, Catholic and Protestant, but often include several different Protestant denominations. Larger towns and big cities will also have other places of worship including synagogues, mosques, and temples representing other religious traditions.

When you consider that people from many different countries and religious backgrounds immigrated to the United States, it probably shouldn't be surprising to find a great number of different religions in the States. That brings me to what I want to talk about today. First, I'd like to give you some facts and figures about various religious groups in the United States. Second, I'll compare the United States to other modernized Western nations. Third, I'll discuss the importance of religion, particularly about the increasing role of religion in U.S. political life in recent years. And finally, I'll talk about the increasing diversity of religion in the United States.

Let's start today with facts and figures. Estimating the number of people belonging to various religious groups in the States can be difficult. First of all, the U.S. government cannot ask for information on religious affiliation in any official capacity, for example, on the census. Statistical information must be gathered from surveys of the population done by nongovernmental agencies or from organizational reports from religious groups themselves on how many members they have. One major survey conducted in 2007 reported that about 78 percent of Americans identified themselves as Christian, with about 51 percent of these identifying themselves as Protestant and about 24 percent as Catholic. The same survey reported that 1.7 percent identified themselves as Jewish, 0.7 percent as Buddhist, 0.6 percent as Muslim, and 0.4 percent as Hindu.

Another major survey done in 2008 found fairly similar results. However, they also reported results that indicated that the U.S. population had been continuing to become less religious over the last few decades. Let me just say that not everyone agrees with this conclusion. Some people believe that many Americans, especially young people, are turning away from religious institutions, not from religion itself.

Now let's look at the two major ways that religion in the United States differs from religion in other modernized Western nations. The first way involves the importance of religion in people's lives and their attendance at their places of worship. A 2009 Gallup poll asked, "Is religion an important part of your life?" While 65 percent of Americans said, "yes," only 27 percent of Britons, 30 percent of the French, and 40 percent of Germans said, "yes." And, in terms of church attendance, Gallup reported that 41 percent of Americans, 15 percent of the French, and 10 percent of Britons reported that they regularly attended church (or another place of worship).

Most writers and scholars agree that Europeans are generally more secular than Americans. They may believe in God, but they tend to stay away from religious institutions except for certain formal occasions like weddings, baptisms, and funerals and a few very important religious days.

The second difference is that in many modernized, European nations, there is no clear separation of religion and government. When discussing religion in America, it's important to remember that freedom of worship is guaranteed by the First Amendment to the Constitution, which also establishes the separation of church and state. So, this amendment guarantees everyone the right to practice his or her religion, but it also says that religion should not have a place in the public sphere. For example, it should not be part of anything concerning the government or public schools. Of course, religious beliefs and values have always influenced politics and education in the United States, but generally they influence these areas in an indirect way. To sum up, then, the importance of religion and belonging to a church or religious organization seem greater to Americans than to Europeans. At the same time, however, religion has no official role in the U.S. government, and it has largely been confined to people's private lives. Recently, however, there has been a trend toward an increase in the influence of religion in politics. Let's take a closer look at this rather sudden rise in the influence of religion on American political life.

Although religion in America seemed to be in decline during most of the last century, in the 1970s, there was a religious revival that surprised many people. This religious revival became known as the "rise of the religious right." In other words, the people involved in this religious revival were politically conservative. For a while it seemed that this conservative trend would not influence politics or the legal system. Although the religious right was generally opposed to abortion, abortion was made legal by the Supreme Court. And although the religious right generally favored prayer in schools, the Supreme Court found that prayer in public schools was unconstitutional. The issues of abortion and prayer were felt by many to be matters of private concern, not serious political issues. However, these issues have become increasingly politicized recently, and because they are highly controversial issues, they have tended to divide people very sharply.

Finally, I'd like to briefly focus on religious diversity in the States. There have always been religious minorities in the States, but since immigration quotas by national origins were eliminated in 1965, more immigrants have been coming from parts of the world with many religious traditions rarely seen in the States previously.

Diana Eck, a professor at Harvard, runs a project which studies pluralism. Her research looks at the issues of a population that has become diverse because of historical events such as immigration. Her interest in pluralism began when she was doing research in the multireligious nation of India, where she met Hindus, Muslims, Sikhs, Christians, Jews, Jains, Zoroastrians, and Buddhists. Later she became aware of how her Harvard classes over the years had increasing numbers of American-born students of Indian origin. This started her thinking about and researching how the religious traditions of Indian-Americans influence American society, and how these traditions may have changed because of America's influence on them. As part of her research, she found an amazing diversity of small religious communities, first in Boston and then nationwide. I don't have time today to go more deeply into her research and findings, but the title of her book, published in 2002, says a lot. The title is *A New Religious America: How a Christian Country Has Become the World's Most Religiously Diverse Nation.*

Because religious values have always been important in the United States in one way or another, it seems likely that religion will continue to play an important role in the country well into the future. I've already mentioned the role of the religious right. However, we cannot know how much this group will be able to influence political life in the future. And of course we can't know how significant religious diversity will be in the future of American society.

SECOND LISTENING Page 48

See First Listening B, above.

THIRD LISTENING Page 48

The second difference is that in many modernized, European nations, there is no clear separation of religion and government. When discussing religion in America, it's important to remember that freedom of worship is guaranteed by the First Amendment to the Constitution, which also establishes the separation of church and state. So, this amendment guarantees everyone the right to practice his or her religion, but it also says that religion should not have a place in the public sphere. For example, it should not be part of anything concerning the government or public schools. Of course, religious beliefs and values have always influenced politics and education in the United States, but generally they influence these areas in an indirect way.

ACCURACY CHECK Page 49

1. Why do many people from other countries often have difficulty understanding the role of religion in America?
2. What are the two largest religious groups in America, and what are the percentages of people who identify themselves as belonging to these groups?
3. According to the lecturer, why are there so many different religious groups in the United States?
4. About what percentage of people are members of a church or other religious organization in the following three countries:
   a. the United States?
   b. France?
   c. Britain?
5. What right does the First Amendment to the Constitution guarantee?
6. What does "separation of church and state" mean?
7. Was the religious revival of the 1970s conservative or liberal?
8. What was the religious revival called?
9. What issues have become very important politically because of this religious revival?
10. Which country does Diana Eck say is the most religiously diverse in the world?

CHAPTER 6

Birth, Marriage, and Death

VOCABULARY PREVIEW Page 53

1. Customs vary so much from culture to culture that it's often bewildering for someone trying to understand the traditions and customs of a new place.
2. The birth of a baby is a momentous occasion in most families and is celebrated in some way or another.

3. Traditionally, Christian babies are baptized in a ceremony involving washing the baby's head with water.
4. The traditional reception that follows the ceremony can be as simple as cookies and punch in the house of worship where the ceremony took place or as elaborate as a large sit-down dinner at a local hotel.
5. Traditionally, most wedding ceremonies have been conducted in houses of worship.
6. All traditions and religions have to cope with one basic issue: how to deal with the body of the deceased person.
7. Some religions such as Judaism and Islam require that the body be very quickly buried, or put into the ground.
8. This event, sometimes called a *wake*, usually takes place at a funeral home for a day or two before the funeral ceremony.
9. At the funeral, it is customary for a religious leader to speak some words of comfort to the friends and family of the deceased. In addition, a eulogy is usually given by someone close to the deceased person.
10. If the body is cremated, the ashes are placed in a special jar, called an urn.

NOTETAKING PREPARATION Page 54

1. It's often bewildering for someone trying to understand the traditions and customs of a new place.
2. The bride should be wearing something old, something new, something borrowed, something blue.
3. The wedding ceremony can be a very simple one, with only a few family members and close friends present, or it can be very elaborate.
4. As for the actual wedding ceremony and related celebrations, traditionally it is the bride's family who pays for these expenses.

FIRST LISTENING Page 55

Today I want to talk about customs in the United States—not all customs of course, but customs surrounding certain important events in almost everyone's life. As I'm sure you know, customs vary so much from culture to culture that it's often bewildering for someone trying to understand the traditions and customs of a new place. If you ask people to explain a custom, they may be quite surprised: "Doesn't everyone do it this way?" they may ask. In a country as large as the United States, with people from so many different parts of the world and different cultures, it can be even more bewildering. But if we look at the country and its people as a whole, we can find a kind of "general" culture with traditions that are often accepted. If they're not accepted completely, they may at least be adapted to fit in with the customs and traditions of each immigrant group. So, today, let's look at some widely accepted customs and traditions of most Americans concerning three of life's most important events, or passages: birth, marriage, and death.

The birth of a baby is a momentous occasion in most families and is celebrated in some way or another. One of the most common ways in the United States is the baby shower. A shower is given by a close friend or relative of the expectant mother shortly before the baby is due. At the shower party, the mother-to-be is "showered" with gifts for the new baby. The gifts may be small ones or very expensive ones, but there is always a very emotional expression of good wishes for the expected baby and its parents. The gifts are opened, and everyone admires them. There's always a lot of advice from experienced mothers. A few years ago, it was almost unheard of for men to participate in baby showers, but men's participation at baby showers is becoming more common.

After the baby is born, most families participate in some kind of spiritual ceremony according to their religious faith. Traditionally, Christian babies are baptized in a ceremony involving washing the baby's head with water. The specific significance of baptism and other ceremonies varies from religion to religion, but they all involve celebration of the birth of a baby.

Now, marriage is another passage that has many customs and traditions surrounding it, particularly activities having to do with the wedding. Once again, it is very hard to generalize about these customs, because they vary so much among different people, but there are some customs that are often observed. It is no longer necessary for a young man to ask permission of a young woman's father for her "hand," but most young people still very much want their parents' approval of the person they hope to marry. It is also still traditional for a young man to give his fiancée a diamond ring at the beginning of their engagement period. As for the actual wedding ceremony and related celebrations, traditionally it is the bride's family who pays these expenses. The wedding ceremony can be a very simple one, with only a few family members and close friends present, or it can be very elaborate, with hundreds of people in attendance. The traditional reception that follows the ceremony can be as simple as cookies and punch in the house of worship where the ceremony took place or as elaborate as a large, sit-down dinner held at a local hotel with music and dancing following the dinner.

One very popular tradition associated with weddings is, once again, a shower. At a wedding shower, the bride-to-be receives gifts to help her set up her new household. These gifts might be electrical appliances, sheets, towels, pots and pans, and so forth. In addition to shower gifts, wedding gifts are also expected from people who receive wedding invitations and attend the wedding. Those who receive invitations but don't attend the wedding may or may not send gifts.

An interesting tradition associated with weddings probably dates back to nineteenth-century England, and possibly much earlier. It is said that a bride should be wearing or carrying "something old, something new, something borrowed, something blue." Also, on the day of the wedding, it is considered bad luck for the groom to see the bride in her wedding dress until the ceremony. Another popular tradition is the bouquet toss, when the bride turns her back to all the single women who gather behind her and tosses her bouquet over her shoulder. Tradition says that the woman who catches the bouquet will be the next one to get married.

Traditionally, most wedding ceremonies have been conducted in houses of worship. However, people occasionally choose to get married in a nonreligious ceremony conducted by a licensed public official like a judge or justice of the peace. In these cases, they may have the ceremony at home, in the official's office, or even in a public space such as a park.

The last passage I'm going to talk about today is the passage from life to death. The customs people in the United States follow in dealing with death again depend on their traditions and religious beliefs, but all traditions and religions have to cope with one basic issue: how to deal with the body of the deceased person. Some religions such as Judaism and Islam require that the body be very quickly buried, or put into the ground. Christian and various secular traditions provide an opportunity for people close to the deceased to "visit" and say good-bye to their friend or loved one. This event, sometimes called a *wake*, usually takes place at a funeral home for a day or two before the funeral ceremony.

At the funeral service, which usually takes place in the funeral home or a house of worship, it is customary for a religious leader to speak some words of comfort to the friends and family of the deceased. In addition, a eulogy is usually given by someone close to the deceased person. A eulogy is a speech in which the good things about the deceased are spoken of. Sometimes many people take turns giving short eulogies. After the religious ceremony, the body is usually taken to a cemetery, where it will be buried after another brief religious service. If the body is cremated, the ashes are placed in a special jar, called an urn, and either buried in a cemetery or kept in another special place of the family's choosing.

In recent decades, a different tradition has been developing. In this tradition, the funeral and or cremation are attended by only a few close family members, but a memorial service for the deceased is held later. Food and drink are served and the life of the deceased is celebrated with informal speeches in which people share their memories of the deceased.

As I said before, in a society so large and diverse as the United States, customs can vary greatly, but I have tried to give you some idea of customs and traditions that are generally accepted. It's always a good idea to ask someone who has had some experience with the culture for advice if you find yourself participating in any of these major life events.

SECOND LISTENING Page 56

See First Listening, above.

THIRD LISTENING Page 56

Now, marriage is another passage that has many customs and traditions surrounding it, particularly activities having to do with the wedding. Once again, it is very hard to generalize about these customs, because they vary so much among different people, but there are some customs that are often observed. It is no longer necessary for a young man to ask permission of a young woman's father for her "hand," but most young people still very much want their parents' approval of the person they hope to marry. It is also still traditional for a young man to give his fiancée a diamond ring at the beginning of their engagement period. As for the actual wedding ceremony and related celebrations, traditionally it is the bride's family who pays these expenses. The wedding ceremony can be a very simple one, with only a few family members and close friends present, or it can be very elaborate, with hundreds of people in attendance. The traditional reception that follows the ceremony can be as simple as cookies and punch in the house of worship where the ceremony took place or as elaborate as a large sit-down dinner held at a local hotel with music and dancing following the dinner.

ACCURACY CHECK Page 57

1. When are baby showers usually given?
2. What is a recent change concerning the custom of baby showers?
3. What do we call the Christian religious service held after a baby is born?
4. Who traditionally pays for an American wedding?
5. Do most American couples have a civil ceremony or a religious ceremony when they get married?
6. What four things does tradition say a bride should have at her wedding?
7. By custom, who should not see the bride in her wedding dress before the wedding ceremony?

8. Under what circumstances is a memorial service held instead of a funeral?
9. What two gestures do people outside the family often make to the family of the deceased?
10. What do we call the short talk about all the good things a deceased person did in his or her life?

UNIT 3

Challenges at Home and Abroad

CHAPTER 7

Multiculturalism

VOCABULARY PREVIEW Page 65

1. A melting pot is the traditional metaphor for the way different groups of immigrants came together in the United States.
2. In theory, the result of many nationalities blending together is one big, homogeneous, culture.
3. It is like an alloy, a combination of all the different parts mixed together into a single whole that is different from each of its parts.
4. Many groups, especially African, Asian, and American Indian, have at times been excluded from participating fully in society through segregation and discrimination.
5. U.S. society does not assimilate a new cultural group until later, after the new immigrants are viewed with less prejudice.
6. The metaphor of the patchwork quilt seems right to the multiculturalists because they see the United States as a mosaic of separate subcultures, each one distinct from the others.
7. Of the 1.6 million children in the United States who are adopted, about 18 percent are of a different race than their adopting parents, making their families multiracial.
8. Cultural influences have distinct sources. We inherit some of our culture from our families. We absorb some of our culture subconsciously from just living in the culture—through TV and videos.
9. With assimilation, individuals become part of the larger culture by accepting much, if not all, of that culture.
10. The pluralistic view differs from the single culture view in that it does not mean that immigrants must forget or deny their original culture.

FIRST LISTENING Page 67

Let me begin today's lecture by explaining the meaning of the word *culture* as I'm using it today. For this lecture, I'm using the word *culture* to mean not only traditions, but more importantly, the basic beliefs and values that people in a society share. These beliefs and values can be seen in family structure, in the educational system, in business practices, in political institutions, in entertainment—in all parts of the society. A person who focuses on "traditions" alone probably won't see the whole picture when it comes to the United States.

People from other countries have trouble identifying an American culture. To be fair, I have to say that is understandable. Not even the best minds in the country agree on the basic nature of U.S. culture. So, today I want to talk about ways of looking at U.S. culture.

I'm going to contrast three ways that U.S. culture has been seen and discussed over the years. Then you can decide which point of view seems the most logical to you. We'll take a look at the older, single culture view; a newer, multiculturalist view; and finally, a third view, which I'll call the pluralistic view.

Let me begin today's lecture by explaining the meaning of the word *culture* as I'm using it today. For this lecture, I'm using the word *culture* to mean not only traditions, but more importantly, the basic beliefs and values that people in a society share. These beliefs and values can be seen in family structure, in the educational system, in business practices, in political institutions, in entertainment—in all parts of the society. A person who focuses on "traditions" alone probably won't see the whole picture when it comes to the United States.

People from other countries have trouble identifying an American culture. To be fair, I have to say that is understandable. Not even the best minds in the country agree on the basic nature of U.S. culture. So, today I want to talk about ways of looking at U.S. culture.

I'm going to contrast three ways that U.S. culture has been seen and discussed over the years. Then you can decide which point of view seems the most logical to you. We'll take a look at the older, single culture view; a newer, multiculturalist view; and finally, a third view, which I'll call the pluralistic view.

So, first is the single culture view of the United States as a "melting pot." A melting pot—literally, a pot in which metals like iron and chromium are melted in order to blend them—is the traditional metaphor for the way different groups of immigrants came together in the United States. In theory, the result of many nationalities blending together is one big, homogeneous culture. It is like an alloy, comprised of all the parts that went into it. In other words, the culture is a combination of all the different parts mixed together into a single whole that is different from each of its parts. However, many people today believe the idea of one common U.S. culture is a myth and has always been a myth. These people point out that many groups, especially African, Asian, and American Indian, have at times been excluded from participating fully in society through segregation and discrimination. In fact, a characteristic of U.S. immigration has been that the most recently arrived group, whether Irish or Italian or Chinese, typically faced strong discrimination from those already in the United States.

We know that every group has made important contributions to the culture, but that's not the point. The point is, U.S. society does not assimilate a new cultural group until later, after the new immigrants are viewed with less prejudice. Often that happens only after the second or third generation.

Now let's move on to another view of U.S. culture. OK, the second view of U.S. culture is the multiculturalist view. The multiculturalist view focuses on the many subcultures—all the different ethnic and racial groups—that make up the population. Each group brought its own distinct culture when it immigrated to the United States. In the multiculturalist view, the United States is *not* a melting pot. Rather, the metaphor multiculturalists use is the patchwork quilt, a bedcover made of many small pieces of material of different colors and patterns. The metaphor of the patchwork seems right to the multiculturalists because they see the United States as a mosaic of separate subcultures, each one distinct from the others. U.S. culture, in this view, is a sum of the distinct parts, with little or no mixing of the different subcultures.

Opponents of this view (and there are many) say that the multiculturalist view ignores the characteristic mixing of groups, both ethnic and racial, that has been common in the United States. For instance, Americans of different European backgrounds have long intermarried. Many Americans today are a combination of four or more ethnic and racial backgrounds—and often more than they can keep track of. Now, I don't want to imply that the United States has overcome its race problems—far from it. But recent census statistics do indicate more mixing than previously.

- First, in 2010, 15 percent of new marriages in the United States were between people of different races or ethnicity. These marriages include combinations of whites, blacks, Latinos, Asians, and American Indians.
- Second, of the 1.6 million children in the United States who are adopted, about 18 percent are of a different race than their adopting parents, making their families multiracial. These children were either American children of another race or children from abroad, especially from Asia or Latin America.

Intermarriage and adoption of children of another race make a difference in how people in a family look at themselves.

So, the point here is that few individuals belong to a single ethnicity or a single race. The lack of mixing implied by this multiculturalist view is more the exception than the rule. Therefore, many people prefer another, more satisfactory, view of U.S. culture.

This last cultural view, the pluralistic view, is a combination of the first two. The pluralistic view says that individuals have a number of cultural influences. Some of these they share with others and some are different from one person to the next. These cultural influences have three distinct sources. One, we inherit some of our culture from our families. Two, we absorb some of our culture subconsciously from just living in the culture—through TV and videos, for example. And three, we choose some cultural influences that we find attractive from the many subcultures in the United States. In this way, the population shares a large portion of common culture, but people also have individual cultural characteristics that make them different from others. Furthermore, the pluralistic view recognizes the strong role of assimilation, of becoming part of the larger group. With assimilation, individuals become part of the larger culture by accepting much, if not all, of that culture. The pluralistic view differs from the single culture view in that pluralism does not mean that immigrants must forget or deny their original culture. But those immigrants do become a little less what they were—Mexican, Chinese, Russian—as they assimilate into the new culture. If assimilation doesn't take place in the first generation, it will by the second or third generation, as I mentioned earlier.

To conclude, the United States has always reflected the cultures of its immigrants and will likely continue to do so. If we accept this idea, continued immigration will always change the character of the U.S. culture somewhat. Not as much as some people fear, I think. I suspect U.S. culture, to use another metaphor, will continue to seem like the same dish—but it will be a dish with a somewhat different flavor in the future. In the future, the real challenge of the United States as a culture may well be whether its ideal of tolerance is a reality.

SECOND LISTENING Page 68

See First Listening B, above.

THIRD LISTENING Page 68

So, first is the single culture view of the United States as a "melting pot." A melting pot—literally, a pot in which metals like iron and chromium are melted in order to blend them—is the traditional metaphor for the way different groups of immigrants came together in the United States. In theory, the result of many nationalities blending together is one big, homogeneous culture. It is like an alloy, comprised of all the parts that went into it. In other words, the culture is a combination of all the different parts mixed together into a single whole that is different from each of its parts. However, many people today believe the idea of one, common U.S. culture is a myth and has always been a myth.

ACCURACY CHECK Page 69

1. What does the word *culture* mean in this lecture?
2. Which two groups of people often have difficulty identifying what the American culture is?
3. Which of the three views of culture is the oldest one?
4. What metaphor is used for the single culture view?
5. Those who claim a single culture is a myth point to which three groups of people as examples?
6. What metaphor for U.S. culture do the multiculturalists use?
7. In 2010, what percentage of marriages were between people of different races or ethnicity?
8. From which parts of the world do many adopted children in the United States come from?
9. In what three ways do Americans acquire their culture, according to the pluralistic view?
10. According to the pluralistic view, assimilation will take place by what generation?

CHAPTER 8

Two Views on Crime

VOCABULARY PREVIEW Page 73

1. Some experts attribute this drop in the crime rate to demographics: the U.S. population is getting older, and older people commit fewer crimes.
2. In recent years there has been stricter law enforcement in big cities, and very tough penalties have been imposed on repeat offenders in general.
3. The encouraging statistics for violent crime may not be true for white-collar crime, crimes that include bribery, political corruption, embezzlement, and corporate policies that endanger workers and the public.
4. So, some people blame criminal behavior on society's shortcomings, or failures.
5. There are root causes like racism, poverty, and injustice.
6. In this theory, people become alienated from society because they do not have many of the benefits that most Americans have.
7. The underclass is that part of the population that typically fits the following profile: poor, unemployed, badly educated, nonwhite, and living in older city neighborhoods.
8. According to this theory, society tries to deter this aggressiveness and potential violence in two ways: by socializing us and, if that fails, by punishing us.
9. Society socializes us by giving us values—values to prevent killing and stealing, for example. And society also gives us values for honesty, compassion, and kindness.
10. Our conscience functions as a deterrent to violence and criminal behavior because we have been taught right from wrong.

FIRST LISTENING Page 75

Today we're going to look at American attitudes about human nature and crime. But let's begin by looking at some statistics that will help you understand points I'll discuss later on.

According to FBI statistics the violent crime rate had dropped 13.4 percent between 2001 and 2010. What this means is that violent crime—aggravated assault, robbery, rape, and murder—has continued to decrease in the United States. Some experts attribute this drop in the crime rate to demographics: the U.S. population is getting older, and older people commit fewer crimes than younger people. At the same time, in recent years there has been stricter law enforcement in big cities, and very tough penalties have been imposed on repeat offenders in general. The encouraging statistics for violent crime may not be true for white-collar crime, crimes that include bribery, political corruption, embezzlement, and corporate policies that endanger workers and the public. Statistics on white-collar crime are hard to get, and the public is not as afraid of white-collar crime as they are of violent crime. But it certainly needs to be included in a discussion of crime in the United States.

Crime is a challenging issue to examine because it can be looked at in so many different ways. Today I'd like to take a look at two different theories. These two theories of crime are based on a person's beliefs about the nature of human beings. The first theory says that people are good by nature. The second theory says that people are basically aggressive by nature, and therefore, more likely to turn to violence. This second theory doesn't say that we *are* violent; rather, it says that we are naturally aggressive and *can be* violent.

Um. Before we go on, I want you to decide in your own minds which of these two theories you agree with more. One, are people basically good by nature? Or, two, are people aggressive and sometimes violent by nature?

Well, let's go on and take a closer look at both theories. Then we'll finish the day with a brief discussion of possible solutions to crime in the United States.

Today we're going to look at American attitudes about human nature and crime. But let's begin by looking at some statistics that will help you understand points I'll discuss later on.

According to FBI statistics, the violent crime rate had dropped 13.4 percent between 2001 and 2010. What this means is that violent crime—aggravated assault, robbery, rape, and murder—has continued to decrease in the United States. Some experts attribute this drop in the crime rate to demographics: the U.S. population is getting older, and older people commit fewer crimes than younger people. At the same time, in recent years there has been stricter law enforcement in big cities, and very tough penalties have been imposed on repeat offenders in general. The encouraging statistics for violent crime may not be true for white-collar crime, crimes that include bribery, political corruption, embezzlement, and corporate policies that endanger workers and the public. Statistics on white-collar crime are hard to get, and the public is not as afraid of white-collar crime as they are of violent crime. But it certainly needs to be included in a discussion of crime in the United States.

Crime is a challenging issue to examine because it can be looked at in so many different ways. Today I'd like to take a look at two different theories. These two theories of crime are based on a person's beliefs about the nature of human beings. The first theory says that people are good by nature. The second theory says that people are basically aggressive by nature, and therefore, more likely to turn to violence. This second theory doesn't say that we *are* violent; rather, it says that we are naturally aggressive and *can be* violent.

Um. Before we go on, I want you to decide in your own minds which of these two theories you agree with more. One, are people basically good by nature? Or, two, are people aggressive and sometimes violent by nature?

Well, let's go on and take a closer look at both theories. Then we'll finish the day with a brief discussion of possible solutions to crime in the United States.

OK, to start off with, people who believe social problems are caused by unequal opportunities prefer the first theory: that people are good by nature. If someone commits a crime or behaves violently, it is because that person's environment has put violence or evil into their heart. So, these people blame criminal behavior on society's shortcomings, or failures. In the United States, we don't have to look very far to find shortcomings that are likely causes of crime. There are root causes like, oh, racism, poverty, and injustice. And there are more obvious causes like unemployment, drug use, and violence on TV. Can you think of some other causes? Many people would add the breakdown of the family and poor education for some children. In this theory, people become alienated from society because they do not have many of the benefits that most Americans have. Their alienation leads them to react in violence against the society that has, in many ways, forgotten them.

Uh, well, the existence of an underclass in U.S. society lends support to this theory of crime. The underclass is that part of the population that typically fits the following profile: poor, unemployed, badly educated, nonwhite, and living in older city neighborhoods. Both gangs and drugs are common among the underclass. The shortcomings of life in the underclass help explain some research findings that link a higher crime rate to unemployment.

Like any theory, this one has critics who disagree with it. The critics point out that most people who grow up as part of the underclass do not become criminals. Also, there are people from rich families, with all the benefits of society, who do sometimes become violent criminals. So we need to look a little further into the causes of crime. So, let's look at the second theory.

The second theory sees people as basically aggressive and sometimes violent. According to this theory, society tries to deter this aggressiveness and potential violence in two ways: by socializing us and, if that fails, by punishing us. Society socializes us by giving us values—values to prevent killing and stealing, for example. And society also gives us values for honesty, compassion, and kindness. Now, this is important: It is largely the family, acting for society, that socializes us. And the result of socialization is a conscience, a sense of right and wrong. Our conscience functions as a deterrent to violence and criminal behavior because we have been taught right from wrong. If socialization fails, the fear of punishment should keep us from committing a crime, according to the theory. In this view, a criminal is someone who is not adequately socialized or one who isn't afraid of the punishment they might receive for a crime. Because of the family's role in socializing, the amount of crime and violence depends greatly on how we bring up our children—that is, how well we pass on important values. It also depends on how punishment is used as a deterrent to crime—that is, how effectively the criminal justice system works.

Now, to go back to something I talked about earlier. This second theory helps us understand white-collar crime, I think, because those who commit white-collar crime are usually not part of the underclass. Typically, white-collar criminals are businessmen, politicians, and bankers. Unlike the underclass, white-collar criminals have usually enjoyed many of the material benefits of society such as a good education and living in a peaceful neighborhood. But for whatever reason, perhaps the failure of their family to properly socialize them, they seem not to have a well-developed conscience. Without a strong conscience, a person's aggressiveness takes over and leads to crime. They might then become criminals because they feel they won't get caught, so obviously they do not fear punishment.

I think you can see that a topic like crime is far too complex to explain completely with a simple theory or two. The theories give us a way to look at possible solutions to crime. My feeling is that both the family and society have a role to play in meeting the challenge of reducing crime. I think most of us would agree that the family can play a role through socialization, which leads children to respect themselves, others, and the values of their society. Moreover, I think society, in the form of government, has a role to play in reducing crime: by overcoming the alienation of the underclass, by helping these people to feel that they are part of the society. Um. Many experts feel that ending the alienation of the underclass can come about only if the underclass has the same benefits that the majority of the population already have: good education, health care, and employment. The government, in the form of the justice system, can also contribute to curbing crime by making sure that those who might become criminals know they will be punished. In another lecture, we will look at the justice system, but we don't have any more time today.

SECOND LISTENING Page 76

See First Listening B, above.

THIRD LISTENING Page 76

Now, to go back to something I talked about earlier. This second theory helps us understand white-collar crime, I think, because those who commit white-collar crime are usually not part of the underclass. Typically, white-collar criminals are businessmen, politicians, and bankers. Unlike the underclass, white-collar criminals have usually enjoyed many of the material benefits of society such as a good education and living in a peaceful neighborhood. But for whatever reason, perhaps the failure of their family to properly socialize them, they seem not to have a well-developed conscience. Without a strong conscience, a person's aggressiveness takes over and leads to crime. They might then become criminals because they feel they won't get caught, so obviously they do not fear punishment.

ACCURACY CHECK Page 77

1. By what percentage did violent crime decrease between 2001 and 2010?
2. Give three examples of white-collar crime.
3. What three shortcomings of society are seen by some as root causes of crime?
4. Why do some criminals become alienated from society?
5. Do most people who grow up poor, unemployed, and badly educated become criminals?
6. How does the second theory of crime see people?
7. In the second theory of crime, what two ways does society attempt to deter crime?
8. How are white-collar criminals different from criminals of the underclass?
9. What three things do some experts think society should provide for the underclass?
10. Is deterring crime through punishment a feature of the first or the second theory of crime?

CHAPTER 9

The United States and the World

VOCABULARY PREVIEW Page 81

1. Some experts are predicting that China will become the new global leader because of its size as well as its economic and military strength.
2. It seems very likely that the United States will remain very important globally, at least for the foreseeable future.
3. The United States can also help maintain financial stability in the world because of the size of its economy.
4. I'm describing hard power—that is, the threat or use of force.
5. This force can be economic, which would include sanctions against trading with a country.
6. For better or for worse, the United States has taken on the role of keeping a certain balance of power in many parts of the world.
7. The United States is also a member of NATO, an organization of mostly European nations devoted to keeping peace in the world.
8. ASEAN countries like Indonesia and Malaysia engage in massive trade with China and may at times feel a little intimidated by China's size and power.

9. Soft power does not come from economic or military threat, but from how attractive or persuasive a country's culture, political ideals, and policies are.
10. The United States is still a magnet to immigrants for both political and economic reasons.
11. My goal today was to give you a framework for understanding some of what you learn in the media about the U.S. economic, military, and political influence in the world today.

NOTETAKING PREPARATION Page 82

B

1. Many countries have better economies, for example, BRIC.
2. UNESCO is an important arm of the UN.
3. France is a member of NATO.
4. Some ASEAN countries are small, for example, Cambodia.
5. Some people think the EU countries should become a federation, that is, have a political structure similar to the United States of America.

FIRST LISTENING Page 83

Today I'd like to discuss the role of the United States in the world. Let me begin by saying that in the past few decades, there has been amazing growth in the economies of many countries around the world, including some African countries and the BRIC nations—Brazil, Russia, India and, most notably, China.

In recent years, there has been a lot of attention focused on the world's two biggest economic powers, which as you probably know are China and the United States. Some experts are predicting that China will become the new global leader because of its size as well as its economic and military strength. Most experts, however, also agree that both countries have serious, but very different, economic and political challenges. Of course, no one can predict how China or the United States will respond to their respective challenges over time, or which of these two world powers, if either one, will end up the more powerful nation in the long run. However, in the shorter term, it seems very likely that the United States will remain very important globally, at least for the foreseeable future.

Let's take a look at what one professor of political science had to say on this topic. Professor Steve Yetiv of Old Dominion University in Virginia wrote three articles in which he gave a number of reasons why he believes the United States will remain a global leader. Today I'll discuss some of these reasons. In this lecture, I will take the liberty of organizing the reasons he gives into three categories. First I'll talk about economic reasons. Then I'll use the categories of hard power and soft power to discuss more of his ideas.

First, let me give you some of the economic reasons Yetiv gives for why the United States will probably continue to be an important player globally. First, it has enough money to help out other countries in a crisis. The crisis could be caused by a natural disaster, like a tsunami or volcanic eruption, or by the financial or political situation of a country. Second, the United States can also help maintain financial stability in the world because of the size of its economy. The United States is a huge market for other countries' goods. A third economic reason concerns the U.S. dollar. To date, the dollar remains the closest thing to a global currency. That is, it continues to be the currency that the world trusts the most. The world still feels that the United States will repay money that it borrows. China's currency, the yuan, may not be allowed by the Chinese government to become seriously stronger. A stronger yuan would make Chinese goods more expensive and less attractive to the world market.

Now let's move on to the United States' use of what I'm describing today as hard power—that is, the threat or use of force. This force can be economic—which would include sanctions against trading with a country—*or* military. For better or for worse, the United States has taken on the role of keeping a certain balance of power in many parts of the world. We have seen this very obviously in the Middle East, where the United States will probably continue to protect the free flow of oil in the Persian Gulf as it has done for decades. The world is very dependent on oil, and keeping it flowing is vital to many economies. The United States is also a member of NATO, an organization of mostly European nations devoted to keeping peace in the world. And in another part of the world the United States has been involved in keeping the Asian balance of power—between the ASEAN countries and China, for example. ASEAN countries like Indonesia and Malaysia engage in massive trade with China and may at times feel a little intimidated by China's size and power as is often the case with the United States' much smaller neighbors. So, having a "friend" like the United States can be a kind of comfort to the smaller countries in Asia. This friendship, while bringing comfort to some, can of course create tensions between China and the United States.

Let's move on to the United States' soft power in the world. By soft power, we mean the ability to attract or persuade a partner to do what we want through dialog or because of shared values. Soft power does not come from an economic or military threat, but from how attractive or persuasive a country's culture, political ideals, and policies are. Britain and France, for example, are leaders in a global move toward democracy because of their soft power—the fact that many admire their cultures and policies. The United States comes third in this ranking.

If one values competitive economies—economies in which it is relatively easy for an individual to start and run a business—there are other places that have more competitive economies than the United States: Singapore, for example. But the United States has the most competitive *major* economy in the world and has maintained its competitiveness at the same time that some European countries have lost it. And as we already know from a previous lecture, the United States is still a magnet to immigrants for both political and economic reasons. And although its primary and secondary education systems have problems, the United States still gets top global ratings for its colleges and universities. A lot of top scientific research is done in American universities, which lead much of the world in developing technologies like nanotechnology and biotechnology. This not only gives the United States an economic advantage, but attracts top graduate students from other countries, many of whom remain in the United States.

OK, before I finish up for today, I realize that I have presented a somewhat simplistic picture of the American role in the world. I don't have the time today to discuss the role of other major players such as the European Union, the United Nations, international business and finance, the World Trade Organization, and so many others. And you may or may not agree with Professor Yetiv's analysis of why he expects the United States to remain a global power at least for the near future, but my goal today was to give you a framework for understanding some of what you learn in the media about U.S. economic, military, and political influence in the world today.

SECOND LISTENING Page 84

See First Listening, above.

THIRD LISTENING Page 84

Now let's move on to the United States' use of what I'm describing today as hard power—that is, the threat or use of force. This force can be economic, which would include sanctions against trading with a country, *or* military. For better or for worse, the United States has taken on the role of keeping a certain balance of power in many parts of the world. We have seen this very obviously in the Middle East, where the United States will probably continue to protect the free flow of oil in the Persian Gulf as it has done for decades. The world is very dependent on oil, and keeping it flowing is vital to many economies. The United States is also a member of NATO, an organization of mostly European nations devoted to keeping peace in the world. And in another part of the world the United States has been involved in keeping the Asian balance of power—between the ASEAN countries and China, for example. ASEAN countries like Indonesia, and Malaysia engage in massive trade with China and may at times feel a little intimidated by China's size and power as is often the case with the United States' much smaller neighbors. So, having a "friend" like the United States can be a kind of comfort to the smaller countries in Asia. This friendship, while bringing comfort to some, can of course create tensions between China and the United States.

ACCURACY CHECK Page 85

1. Which four countries are represented by the acronym BRIC?
2. What two kinds of strength does China have in addition to its size?
3. Name two economic reasons the lecturer gives for U.S. power in the world?
4. What effect might a stronger yuan have on China's economy?
5. What is "hard power" according to the lecturer?
6. What organization does the United States belong to that is largely made up of European countries?
7. Which international trade organization do Indonesia and Malaysia belong to?
8. According to the lecturer, which two countries rank number 1 and number 2 in the world's admiration for cultural and political values?
9. In what two kinds of technology does the lecturer claim the United States is a leader?
10. Name three organizations in addition to NATO that the lecturer mentions as being major players in the world?

UNIT 4

Issues in Education

CHAPTER 10

Public Education in the United States

VOCABULARY PREVIEW Page 93

1. In the United States, attending school is compulsory—children have to attend school, in most states to the age of 16.
2. A small percentage of American students attend private schools, either religious or secular.

3. One unusual feature of U.S. public education is that there is no nationwide curriculum set by the federal government. And, there are no particular nationwide standardized examinations.
4. Although the federal government provides funds to schools for special programs, it does *not* determine the curriculum or the examinations.
5. The state sets the number of credits a student must complete in order to graduate high school, and the credits include both required courses and electives.
6. The school board is elected by the citizens of the district or appointed by local officials.
7. Because private schools are not funded from taxes, parents pay tuition to send their children to them.
8. The basic idea behind school vouchers is that parents choose the school their children will attend—public or private—and that school receives a set amount of money per student from public school funds.
9. Voucher schools are usually private schools, which are usually affiliated with religious organizations.
10. Congress passed an education bill called No Child Left Behind (NCLB), which required each state to develop and implement testing programs

NOTETAKING PREPARATION Page 94

Let's begin by looking at the three levels of control within each state. Notice how as we go down the levels, control becomes increasingly local.

So, starting at the top, a state department of education has two basic functions. First, it sets the state's minimum curriculum requirements for K through 12—elementary through high school. Second, it sets the number of credits a student must complete in order to graduate high school. This total number of credits includes both required courses and electives.

The second level of control is the school district. The number of school districts in a state depends on the size of the state and the size of its population. A large metropolitan area might have several school districts. A smaller community might have only one district. Each school district is run by a school board. This board is elected by the citizens of the district or appointed by local officials. Now, the school district is responsible for the specific content of courses taught in its schools. In other words, the district determines what the students will study, for example, in each year of high school English. The district also decides what electives are available to students. In addition to the content of required courses and the choice of electives, the school district is responsible for hiring teachers and administrators.

The third level of control is the school, where teachers have primary responsibility for deciding how to teach each course and for preparing and giving classroom examinations to the students.

FIRST LISTENING Page 96

Today our topic is U.S. public schools. Now, most young people in the United States today, like most young people around the world, attend school. In fact, in the United States attending school is compulsory—children have to attend school, in most states to the age of 16 or until a student reaches ninth grade. Students begin school in kindergarten or first grade, at age five or six, and continue through twelfth grade, when they are about 18 years old. These years of education are often referred to as "K through 12."

The great majority of young Americans, about 90 percent, attend public school. A small percentage attend private schools, either religious or secular. All public schools, however, are secular.

One unusual feature of U.S. public education—one that surprises many foreigners—is that there is no nationwide curriculum set by the federal government. And, there are no particular nationwide standardized examinations. Although the federal government provides funds to schools for special programs such as education for the handicapped and bilingual education, it does *not* determine the curriculum or the examinations. Control of education is largely in the hands of the individual states.

Today then I will discuss first, the three levels of control *within* each state; second, how education is funded, and finally, some issues and the efforts at both the state and national levels to solve them. Let's begin by looking at the three levels of control within each state.

Today our topic is U.S. public schools. Now, most young people in the United States today, like most young people around the world, attend school. In fact, in the United States attending school is compulsory—children have to attend school, in most states to the age of 16 or until reaching ninth grade. Students begin school in kindergarten or first grade, at age five or six, and continue through twelfth grade, when they are about 18 years old. These years of education are often referred to as "K through 12."

The great majority of young Americans, about 90 percent, attend public school. A small percentage attend private schools, either religious or secular. All public schools, however, are secular.

One unusual feature of U.S. public education—one that surprises many foreigners—is that there is no nationwide curriculum set by the federal government. And, there are no particular nationwide standardized examinations. Although the federal government provides funds to schools for special programs such as education for the handicapped and bilingual education, it does *not* determine the curriculum or the examinations. Control of education is largely in the hands of the individual states.

Today then I will discuss first, the three levels of control *within* each state; second, how education is funded, and finally, some issues and the efforts at both the state and national levels to solve them. Let's begin by looking at the three levels of control within each state. Notice how as we go down the levels, control becomes increasingly local.

So, starting at the top, a state department of education has two basic functions. First, it sets the state's minimum curriculum requirements for K through 12—elementary through high school. Second, it sets the number of credits a student must complete in order to graduate high school. This total number of credits includes both required courses and electives.

The second level of control is the school district. The number of school districts in a state depends on the size of the state and the size of its population. A large metropolitan area might have several school districts. A smaller community might have only one district. Each school district is run by a school board. This board is elected by the citizens of the district or appointed by local officials. Now, the school district is responsible for the specific content of courses taught in its schools. In other words, the district determines what the students will study, for example, in each year of high school English. The district also decides what electives are available to students. In addition to the content of required courses and the choice of electives, the school district is responsible for hiring teachers and administrators.

The third level of control is the school, where teachers have primary responsibility for deciding how to teach each course and for preparing and giving classroom examinations to the students.

Now let's move on to our second topic. Local control of schools may seem very strange to some of you, but consider how public schools in the United States are funded. As an example, in 2010 only about 12 percent of the money came from the federal government. The rest came from state and local taxes: approximately 43 percent from the states and about 44 percent from local communities—the school districts—mostly from property taxes on houses and businesses.

Finally today, I'd like to discuss educational issues and efforts to solve them, first at a state level and then at a national level.

The first issue is inequality of educational opportunity. Because public schools are funded mainly by local taxes, schools in poorer communities do not have the same amount of money as schools in wealthier communities. Therefore, children from poorer areas are less likely than children from wealthier areas to receive a good education.

The second issue involves private schools. Because private schools are not funded from taxes, parents pay tuition to send their children to them. Parents with children in private schools sometimes wonder why they have to pay taxes for public schools when their children don't use them.

The inequalities of public school education and the funding of private school education—that is, tuition costs—have led to two efforts to deal with these issues: charter schools and school vouchers. Let's talk first about charter schools.

Charter schools are a type of public school. So funding for charter schools comes from taxes. They compete with regular public schools for students. These schools operate under a charter, or contract, from a state, a local school board, or another public organization. Charter schools generally have greater autonomy—more independence in selecting teachers, curriculum, resources, and so on—than regular public schools.

The first charter schools opened toward the end of the 1980s. From the academic year 1999–2000 to academic year 2009–2010, the number of students enrolled in charter schools grew from 0.3 million to 1.6 million, over a fourfold increase. In 2009–2010, about 5 percent of all public schools were charter schools.

Studies of the effectiveness of charter schools are mixed. Also, some critics fear that these schools will be managed by private companies more interested in profit than education.

The school voucher concept is much more controversial. The basic idea behind school vouchers is that parents choose the school their children will attend—public or private—and that school receives a set amount of money per student from public school funds. Voucher schools are usually private schools, which are usually affiliated with religious organizations. Supporters of vouchers feel strongly that private schools offer a better education than public schools. Those who oppose vouchers claim it robs public schools of needed funds. They also say voucher schools do not really provide school choice because of admissions standards that exclude students based on, for example, academic performance, religion, or gender. Opponents of vouchers also strongly believe that using public money for private, religious-affiliated schools violates the constitutional separation of church and state.

I should mention here that charter schools and school vouchers are efforts to solve educational problems at the state level. The federal government is concerned about the same issues I already mentioned, but also about standards and about the accountability of states receiving federal money.

In 2002, Congress passed an education bill called No Child Left Behind (NCLB), which required each state to develop and implement testing programs and other systems to ensure adequate, yearly student progress. NCLB has been widely criticized for many reasons, mainly because people feel that standardized testing leads teachers to "teach to the test" rather than what they feel students need. Also, it didn't address the problem of differences in standards among the states.

A more recent national effort, Common Core State Standards (CCSS), is an attempt by state governors and senior state school officials to establish clear goals to ensure students are prepared for success after high school. These standards for English and math can make it easier for students who move to a new school to keep up, whether it's in the same city or a different part of the country. Common Core aims to provide students with the skills and knowledge they need to succeed, while allowing teachers to decide *how* the information will be taught. You can see how these national efforts, because of a long history of local control of schools, are controversial with students, parents, and administrators.

SECOND LISTENING Page 97

See First Listening B, above.

THIRD LISTENING Page 97

Charter schools are a type of public school. So funding for charter schools comes from taxes. They compete with regular public schools for students. These schools operate under a charter, or contract, from a state, a local school board, or another public organization. Charter schools generally have greater autonomy—more independence, in selecting teachers, curriculum, resources, and so on—than regular public schools.

The first charter schools opened toward the end of the 1980s. From the academic year 1999–2000 to academic year 2009–2010, the number of students enrolled in charter schools grew from 0.3 million to 1.6 million, over a fourfold increase. In 2009–2010, about 5 percent of all public schools were charter schools.

Studies of the effectiveness of charter schools are mixed. Also, some critics fear that these schools will be managed by private companies more interested in profit than education.

ACCURACY CHECK Page 98

1. About how old is an American student when he or she completes K through 12?
2. What two things about the American educational system often surprise people from other countries?
3. What are the three levels of control of education found in each state?
4. What is one type of decision that the state department of education might make?
5. How are the people on a school board chosen?
6. From what three sources does the money come to pay for American public schools, and what percentage of that money comes from each of these three sources?
7. How does the way public schools are funded often cause inequality of education?
8. What is the main difference between a charter school and a voucher school?
9. What is the main objection people have to the No Child Left Behind education bill?
10. What is the name of the national effort made by the states to prepare students to succeed after high school?

CHAPTER 11

The College Admissions Process

VOCABULARY PREVIEW Page 102

1. Most colleges are accredited, which means the schools meet certain standards set by outside evaluators.
2. Over three-quarters of all students—76 percent—are enrolled in public colleges and universities.
3. The average cost in 2012 for tuition and room and board at a four-year college for a student living on campus in a dormitory varies a lot.
4. With such a wide variety of schools of different sizes, types, and locations, it probably won't surprise you to find out that admissions requirements at these colleges and universities can vary, too.
5. Four-year colleges and universities will all require an application and a high school transcript, which is a record of the applicant's grades and rank in their high school class.
6. Very often applicants for an undergraduate program must also include an essay and recommendations from high school teachers

7. Some people say standardized exams don't fairly evaluate a student's readiness for college.
8. Even the most prestigious and most highly competitive colleges and universities will consider other factors.
9. Admissions standards at community colleges are usually more lenient than those at four-year colleges and universities.
10. Many community college programs are vocational in nature, that is, they train students to become medical technicians, office assistants, cooks, airline mechanics, or other skilled workers needed by the community.
11. Students in the United States have many options in pursuing higher education.

NOTETAKING PREPARATION Page 103

Most colleges also ask for test results from one of the standardized tests regularly offered to high school students, the SAT and ACT. Students who are applying to graduate school are usually asked to take other, more specific standardized exams, depending on which college they are applying to. For example, some students are required to take the GRE. Students applying for an MBA program, that is, a Master's in Business Administration, will probably have to take the GMAT, and students applying to law school will have to take the LSAT. You probably know about the TOEFL and IELTS exams, either of which foreign students have to take before being admitted to an American college or university. All of these exams, including the TOEFL and IELTS, are prepared by organizations that are independent of the schools.

FIRST LISTENING Page 104

In this lecture, I'm going to talk to you about postsecondary education in the United States, that is, education that students pursue after high school. Today I'll give you some facts and figures about colleges and universities in the United States and some general information about admissions policies. I will finish up with a few remarks about community colleges.

In this lecture, I'm going to talk to you about postsecondary education in the United States, that is, education that students pursue after high school. Today I'll give you some facts and figures about colleges and universities in the United States and some general information about admissions policies. I will finish up with a few remarks about community colleges.

Let's begin with some facts and figures. The most recent figures I have, from 2010, reveal there were approximately 5,000 public and private four-year and two-year colleges in the United States. These include universities with diverse programs as well as smaller four-year colleges and two-year community colleges. Most of them are accredited, which means the schools meet certain standards set by outside evaluators. Now, when applying to a school, you would probably want to make sure it is accredited. Oh, I should probably point out that in North American English, the word *school* can refer to education in any year from kindergarten to graduate school. And any postsecondary student is "in college" or simply "in school."

There are more private U.S. colleges than public ones, yet over three-quarters of all students—76 percent—are enrolled in public colleges and universities. Some of the smaller, private colleges have fewer than 1,000 students, whereas some of the large, public universities have 50,000 or more students. Almost all of these schools teach both women and men, but there is a small number that accept only men or only women. Some schools may offer only one program of study and others have a great variety of programs. These colleges and universities are located all over the country—in industrial areas, agricultural areas, large cities, and small towns in every state.

College costs can be very high. The average cost in 2012 for tuition and room and board at a four-year college for a student living on campus in a dormitory varies from about $20,000 for an in-state student at a public university to about $40,000 at a private college. Some prestigious universities can cost much more. Most two-year colleges are far less expensive than the four-year schools.

With such a wide variety of schools of different sizes, types, and locations, it probably won't surprise you to find out that admissions requirements at these colleges and universities can vary, too. Two-year colleges usually have few admissions requirements. However, four-year colleges and universities will all require an application and a high school transcript, which is a record of the applicant's grades and rank in their high school class. Very often applicants for an undergraduate program must also include an essay and recommendations from high school teachers with their application. Most colleges also ask for test results from one of the standardized tests regularly offered to high school students, the SAT and ACT.

Students who are applying to graduate school are usually asked to take other, more specific standardized exams, depending on which college they are applying to. For example, some students are required to take the GRE. Students applying for an MBA program, that is, a Master's in Business Administration, will probably have to take the GMAT, and students applying to law school will have to take the LSAT. You probably know about the TOEFL and IELTS exams, either of which foreign students have to take before being admitted to an American college or university. All of these exams, including the TOEFL and IELTS, are prepared by organizations that are independent of the schools.

Standardized admissions exams are sometimes criticized. Some people say standardized exams don't fairly evaluate a student's readiness for college. Others argue these exams favor students from a particular socioeconomic background who have certain cultural and educational experiences. However, the exams are still widely used by colleges and universities as one way to determine who will be admitted. At the same time, most schools try to look at the whole student and consider factors other than simply grades and test scores. Some of these factors can be the level of difficulty of courses taken in high school, participation in extracurricular activities like clubs and sports teams, and work experience. Some schools will have personal interviews with students they are considering for admission.

Many schools, private as well as public, try very hard to have a student population with a wide variety of backgrounds and ages. Even the most prestigious and most highly competitive colleges and universities, which largely admit only those students with the highest grades and standardized test scores, will consider these other factors. Nevertheless, schools of this type, such as Stanford and Harvard, have so many more people applying than they can possibly admit that students who want to get into these schools take grades and exam scores very seriously. This is true for both undergraduate and graduate programs. In general, medical and law schools, both private and public, are very difficult to get into, and, once again, test scores on standardized exams can be extremely important to those applying to these schools.

However, for students who want to attend a public college or university in their own state, it may be enough to graduate from high school in the upper third or even upper half of their high school class. This may surprise some of you who come from an educational system that is highly competitive, a system in which only a small percentage of students who pass a very difficult nationwide, standardized, examination can enter a university. You may be even more surprised by what I have to tell you about community colleges.

An interesting feature of education in the United States is the two-year community college. Community colleges are public colleges that offer somewhat different educational opportunities than those offered by a four-year college or university. First, admissions standards at community colleges are usually more lenient than those at four-year colleges and universities. It's often enough to have completed high school to be admitted. Second, it is cheaper to attend a community college. The tuition and fees are a lot lower. Students attending community colleges also often live at home and so they have lower living expenses. Community colleges allow many people who are unable to go to a four-year college or university an opportunity to take classes for college credit. The two-year programs offered by community colleges usually lead to an associate's degree or a certificate. Many of these programs, but not all of them, are vocational in nature, that is, they train students to become medical technicians, office assistants, cooks, airline mechanics, or other skilled workers needed by the community.

Now, I need to point out that people attend community colleges for many different purposes. Some people may be taking only a course or two in some subject that particularly interests them and may not be planning on getting a degree. Other people may be going to community college full-time and planning to transfer to a four-year college or university after successfully completing two years at a community college. Community colleges are not unique to the United States, but the diversity of programs offered and of students who attend may be. Well, so that's community colleges.

In brief, you can see that educational opportunities and admissions standards at postsecondary schools vary greatly in the United States. Students in the United States have many options in pursuing higher education.

SECOND LISTENING Page 105

See First Listening B, above.

THIRD LISTENING Page 105

With such a wide variety of schools of different sizes, types, and locations, it probably won't surprise you to find out that admissions requirements at these colleges and universities can vary, too. Two-year colleges usually have few admissions requirements. However, four-year colleges and universities will all require an application and a high school transcript, which is a record of the applicant's grades and rank in their high school class. Very often applicants for an undergraduate program must also include an essay and recommendations from high school teachers with their application. Most colleges also ask for test results from one of the standardized tests regularly offered to high school students, the SAT and ACT.

Students who are applying to graduate school are usually asked to take other, more specific standardized exams, depending on which college they are applying to. For example, some students are required to take the GRE. Students applying for an MBA program, that is, a

Master's in Business Administration, will probably have to take the GMAT, and students applying to law school will have to take the LSAT. You probably know about the TOEFL and IELTS exams, either of which foreign students have to take before being admitted to an American college or university. All of these exams, including the TOEFL and IELTS, are prepared by organizations that are independent of the schools.

ACCURACY CHECK Page 106

1. How many public and private four-year and two-year colleges are there in the United States?
2. Are there more private or public colleges and universities in the States?
3. What percentage of all students are enrolled in public colleges and universities?
4. What was the range of the average cost for tuition and room and board at a four-year college?
5. What two items are applicants to all four-year colleges required to submit?
6. In an effort to look at the whole student, what factors besides grades and test scores might a school look at when considering an applicant?
7. Are factors such as the age of the student or their background important or unimportant to most colleges?
8. What are two examples of standardized tests that graduate students may have to take before being admitted to a graduate program?
9. What are three ways that community colleges are generally different from four-year colleges and universities?
10. What kind of a degree can a student get from a community college?

CHAPTER 12

International Students

VOCABULARY PREVIEW Page 110

1. The number of international students studying in the United States has risen quite steadily over the last 50 to 60 years, with an occasional small dip due to political or economic reasons.
2. In number of students, China only recently surged ahead of India, which had been number one for most of the previous decade.
3. Social sciences include such disciplines as sociology, psychology, and political science.
4. Building "bridges," or relationships, between the United States and other countries, and bringing global ways of looking at things are the types of benefits virtually everyone mentions when talking about students going to different countries to study.
5. As one benefit, NAFSA, an association of international educators, cites the contribution international students make with their local spending on shopping, housing, and so forth.
6. In the academic year of 2010–2011, international students and their families made a net contribution to the U.S. economy of about 20 billion dollars.
7. Some criticisms have been raised about policies that encourage not only the admission of so many international students, especially to graduate schools, but also ones that encourage some of these students to remain after completing their degrees.
8. According to NAFSA, international students have only increased the size of Ph.D. programs, not taken away places from U.S. students.
9. Employers do not have to pay some taxes for certain foreign employees that they would have to pay for American employees, which critics believe is an unfair economic incentive to hire foreign graduates.

NOTETAKING PREPARATION Page 111

The text below is the lecture on distance education from which the classmate's notes were written.

Students interested in pursuing distance education degrees need to consider the following six points:

Number 1. Many distance education programs have a residency requirement. The students may be required to take two courses on campus, that is, six hours of credit, or students may be required to spend several days on campus several times during the program.

Number 2. Distance education courses generally have time limits. Courses and programs must be completed within a certain time limit. Assignments must be submitted on time.

Number 3. Admissions requirements are the same as those of an on-campus education.

Number 4. Distance education can save students money in terms of not having to travel to campus for classes, and the like, but the academic fees are about the same as for traditional education. Fulfilling the residency requirements may be quite costly in terms of travel and lodging for students who live far from the campus.

Number 5. Online study requires students to have access to a computer that meets minimum requirements such as the latest version of Windows, a microphone, sound card and speakers, adequate hard drive and RAM, a modem, browser (Internet Explorer or Netscape), and

Internet connection. Connection speed is very important, and many schools recommend having high-speed Internet access like a cable modem or DSL.

And finally Number 6. Distance learning requires that students be disciplined and independent learners. Distance education is not easier than traditional education. Not everyone is temperamentally suited for distance education. The dropout rate from distance education courses and programs is higher than for traditional courses and programs.

FIRST LISTENING Page 113

In your last lecture about education you heard about student admission to various types of postsecondary institutions in the United States. Today I'd like to spend some time discussing international students—in this case, students from other countries studying at U.S. colleges and universities. First, I'll give you some facts and figures about these students, then discuss some of the benefits these students bring to the States, and finally I'll explore three current criticisms related to international students.

OK, let's begin with the number of international students studying in the United States. This number has risen quite steadily over the last 50 to 60 years, with an occasional small dip due to political or economic reasons. Let's take a look at just the first decade of this century. In the academic year of 2011–2012, there were more than 600,000 international students. This was an increase of 39 percent over the academic year of 2001–2002.

Now let's look at where these international students came from. In the academic year 2011–2012, over half of all international students came from just five countries: China, India, South Korea, Saudi Arabia, and Canada. Let me give you some numbers to go with these countries. China sends about 25.5 percent of the international students studying in the States; India, about 13 percent; South Korea, 9.5 percent; Saudi Arabia, 4.5 percent; and Canada, 3.5 percent. China had only recently surged ahead of India, which had been number one for most of the previous decade.

It might surprise you to learn that number four on the list is Saudi Arabia. Although students from Saudi Arabia made up only 4.5 percent of all international students in 2011–2012, the total number of students from Saudi Arabia studying in the States had increased over 77 percent in just five years. The number of students from Japan, which is number seven on the 2011–2012 list with close to 3 percent, decreased by about 44 percent over the same period.

Now that we know their home countries, let's take a look at what these international students are studying. Their top five areas of study are business and management, engineering, math and computer science, physical and life sciences, and social sciences. I think most of you are pretty familiar with the first three areas, but maybe less so with the last two, so let me expand a little on what these include. Physical sciences includes such fields as physics, chemistry, and astronomy. Life sciences on the other hand, involves the study of living organisms and includes biology, microbiology, and biochemistry. Social sciences includes such disciplines as sociology, psychology, and political science, in other words the study of individual and social human behavior.

Finally, let's look at *where* these international students study. The top three states where international students study are California, New York, and Texas. These three states have been the most popular ones for many years. From the list of the top 20 institutions hosting international students in the year 2011–2012, California has two: USC and UCLA; New York has three: NYU, Columbia, and SUNY Buffalo; and Texas has one: UT Austin.

Next I would like to discuss the benefits these students bring to the States. The Association of International Educators, known by the acronym NAFSA, identified five benefits international students bring. The first two are building "bridges," or relationships, between the United States and other countries, and bringing global ways of looking at things into U.S. classrooms. These two are the types of benefits virtually everyone mentions when talking about students going to different countries to study. The next three benefits NAFSA identifies are not always as well-known to the general public. For one, NAFSA notes that the number of international students increases demands for courses in the sciences and engineering, which, in turn, makes these courses more available to U.S. students. For another, NAFSA points out that the out-of-state tuition international students pay at state universities helps pay for programming and services that are available for all students, and these tuition funds come largely from sources outside the United States. Finally, NAFSA cites the contribution international students make with their local spending on shopping, housing, and so forth. For example, in the academic year of 2010–2011, international students and their families made a net contribution to the U.S. economy of about 20 billion dollars.

NAFSA also addresses some of the criticisms that have been raised about policies that encourage not only the admission of so many international students, especially to graduate schools, but also policies that encourage some of these students to remain after completing their degrees—most frequently those who graduate in fields known by the acronym STEM, which stands for science, technology, engineering, and mathematics.

The first criticism is that international students directly compete with U.S. students who want to go to college. Well, although international student enrollment did increase over the past few decades, the enrollment of U.S. citizens and permanent residents also increased at the same rate. And, while the number of U.S. citizens going on to PhD programs did not change much during those years at the same time the number of international students admitted to U.S. PhD programs increased quite a bit, according to NAFSA, international students have only increased the size of these programs, not taken away places from U.S. students. The second criticism is that foreign students remain in the United States and take jobs from Americans. The U.S. government has extended the amount of time that some foreign students can stay in the country after they graduate. Now foreign graduates in STEM fields can extend from 12 months to 29 months their participation in a program known as optional practical training, or OPT, working for American employers. These employers do not have to pay certain taxes for these employees that they would have to pay for American employees, which critics believe is an unfair economic incentive to hire foreign graduates. This 29 months also gives these graduates time to try to find an employer willing to sponsor them for a visa that will allow them to work and live in the States. Some Americans feel this causes unfair competition for U.S. graduates, especially in difficult economic times, and will discourage Americans from even going into STEM fields. However, NAFSA points out these foreign graduates hired to work in the United States make up only 0.07 percent of the total U.S. workforce, and that U.S. students don't hesitate to go into other very competitive fields such as finance and law. NAFSA also notes that a lack of interest in math and science among American high school students is nothing new and not likely related to concern over foreign graduates taking jobs they would have pursued otherwise. And most importantly, the foreign graduates help the United States maintain leadership in technology fields, which is likely to increase employment opportunities for Americans.

The third criticism is a more philosophical or moral one: that is, the United States should not act in ways that encourage a brain drain from less-developed countries. However, NAFSA argues that students who do not want to return to their native countries will likely take their education and talents to another country anyhow, and that if they remain in the United States and become successful they will likely maintain close ties with their home country, perhaps investing in a business there or sending money home to support family members.

Well, we've covered a lot today. I hope I've at least given you some food for thought about the impact that international students have when they pursue postsecondary education in the United States and the likely benefits that they bring to the country both during their studies and after graduation.

SECOND LISTENING Page 114

See First Listening, above.

THIRD LISTENING Page 114

Now that we know their home countries, let's take a look at what these international students are studying. Their top five areas of study are business and management, engineering, math and computer science, physical and life sciences, and social sciences. I think most of you are pretty familiar with the first three areas, but maybe less so with the last two, so let me expand a little on what these include. Physical sciences includes such fields as physics, chemistry, and astronomy. Life sciences on the other hand, involves the study of living organisms and includes biology, microbiology, and biochemistry. Social sciences includes such disciplines as sociology, psychology, and political science, in other words the study of individual and social human behavior.

ACCURACY CHECK Page 115

1. How many international students were there in the United States in the academic year 2011–2012?
2. Before China surged ahead in recent years, which country had sent the most students to the United States?
3. What are the three most popular areas of study of international students?
4. What disciplines do students interested in the social sciences study?
5. Which state in the top 20 list has the most schools hosting international students?
6. Do foreign students make courses in the sciences and engineering more available or less available to American students?
7. What was the net contribution of foreign students to the U.S. economy in the academic year 2010–2011?
8. What four disciplines does the term STEM include?
9. What percentage of the total U.S. workforce do foreign graduates make up?
10. Does NAFSA feel the United States is hurting foreign students' home countries by offering the students employment in the United States?

UNIT 5

The Official Side

CHAPTER 13

The Role of Government in the Economy

VOCABULARY PREVIEW Page 123

1. One of the important characteristics of American-style capitalism is individual ownership of property.
2. Another important characteristic is free enterprise: This means the freedom to produce, buy, and sell goods and labor without government intervention.
3. The idea in a pure capitalist system is for the government to take a laissez-faire attitude toward business.
4. Because the costs of polluting the environment can affect all members of society, the government uses various legal means to try to protect the environment and make companies comply with certain government regulations.
5. You may remember the BP oil spill in the Gulf of Mexico in 2010, which resulted in the worst environmental disaster in U.S. history.
6. The company was charged with violating safety and environmental regulations in building and managing the well that spilled the oil.
7. The government intervenes to see that businesses remain competitive; antitrust laws were passed to prevent companies from joining together to unfairly control prices, what we call price-fixing.
8. The second method government uses to maintain stability in the economy is expenditure, the money that the government spends.
9. The government can raise taxes to take money out of the economy and lower the inflation rate.
10. When the president and Congress do not work together, or when the two parties do not work together, a political gridlock can occur.

FIRST LISTENING Page 126

Let me begin today by saying that the American economy is basically a capitalist economy. One of the important characteristics of American-style capitalism is individual ownership of property. Property includes such things as houses and land, businesses, and intellectual property such as songs, poems, books, and inventions. Another important characteristic is free enterprise: This means the freedom to produce, buy, and sell goods and labor without government intervention. A third characteristic is free, competitive markets. That is, businesses that succeed stay in the market, and those that fail must leave the market. In this type of economy, not everyone will be able to find a job at every moment and not all businesses will be successful, but in a pure capitalist system, the government is not expected to interfere with the natural economic forces.

The idea in a pure capitalist system is for the government to take a laissez-faire attitude toward business, that is, the government's role should be very limited. For example, in a pure capitalist system, the government might provide national defense. It could also make laws protecting ownership and use of private property. And finally, in a pure capitalist state, the government might provide those things that private businesses could not or would not normally provide, such as roads and schools. But otherwise, the government would allow businesses to operate without intervening.

In truth, the United States is *not* a pure capitalist system. The U.S. government today does not maintain a completely laissez-faire attitude toward business. The government's role in business grew throughout the twentieth century, beginning especially in the 1930s. This expanded role of government is a complicated subject, and I'm going to discuss only a few of the issues today, just to give you some idea of why and how the government regulates the economy. We'll be discussing four basic reasons why the government intervenes in the economy.

Let me begin today by saying that the American economy is basically a capitalist economy. One of the important characteristics of American-style capitalism is individual ownership of property. Property includes such things as houses and land, businesses, and intellectual property such as songs, poems, books, and inventions. Another important characteristic is free enterprise: This means the freedom to produce, buy, and sell goods and labor without government intervention. A third characteristic is free, competitive markets. That is, businesses that succeed stay in the market, and those that fail must leave the market. In this type of economy, not everyone will be able to find a job at every moment and not all businesses will be successful, but in a pure capitalist system, the government is not expected to interfere with the natural economic forces.

The idea in a pure capitalist system is for the government to take a laissez-faire attitude toward business, that is, the government's role should be very limited. For example, in a pure capitalist system, the government might provide national defense. It could also make laws protecting ownership and use of private property. And finally, in a pure capitalist state, the government might provide those things that private businesses could not or would not normally provide, such as roads and schools. But otherwise, the government would allow businesses to operate without intervening.

In truth, the United States is *not* a pure capitalist system. The U.S. government today does not maintain a completely laissez-faire attitude toward business. The government's role in business grew throughout the twentieth century, beginning especially in the 1930s. This expanded role of government is a complicated subject, and I'm going to discuss only a few of the issues today, just to give you some idea of why and how the government regulates the economy. We'll be discussing four basic reasons why the government intervenes in the economy.

An important reason that the government tries to regulate the economy is to protect the environment. Because the costs of polluting the environment can affect all members of society, the government uses various legal means to try to regulate businesses and to protect the environment. Companies must comply with certain government regulations. For example, companies may be required to install pollution-control equipment. The government also has regulations about how and where toxic waste can be dumped and imposes fines on companies that do not follow these regulations. You may remember the BP oil spill in the Gulf of Mexico in 2010, which resulted in the worst environmental disaster in U.S. history. It affected the states of Louisiana, Mississippi, Alabama, and Florida. BP and some of its partners were charged for violations of U.S. environmental laws, especially the Clean Water Act and the Oil Pollution Act. In addition, they were charged with violating safety and environmental regulations in building and managing the well that spilled the oil. I should add that BP accepted financial responsibility for cleaning up the spill and also agreed to a court settlement to pay for individual losses people in the area suffered.

Another reason the government intervenes in the economy is to help people who, for some reason beyond their control, earn little or no income. These people may be too young or too old or too ill or otherwise unable to support themselves. The government has various public assistance, or welfare, programs that are paid for with tax money to help these people.

The third reason the government intervenes in the economy is to try to see that businesses remain competitive. Early in the twentieth century, the government passed antitrust and monopoly regulation laws. Antitrust laws were passed to prevent companies from joining together to unfairly control prices, what we call price-fixing. Monopoly regulation laws were designed to prevent any one company from growing to become the only company of its type, without any competition for business. The government believed that it was better to intervene in the economy to be sure that competition was protected. A somewhat related situation, the financial crisis of 2008, showed there may be a possible role for increasing government regulation of banks. In short, many banks were taking risks with others' money, risks that were invisible to the public and to the government. In 2012, Congress was still debating the government's responsibility to avoid financial crisis by preventing banks from taking risks of this sort.

The last reason for the government's intervention in the economy is to maintain economic stability. How the government does this is complicated, but basically, the government uses three methods to achieve stability. The first method the government uses to promote stability is taxation, the means by which the government collects money from people and businesses. The second method government uses to keep the economy stable is expenditure, the money that the government spends. And the third method the government uses to maintain stability is controlling the interest rate on money it lends to businesses. Let's look at each of these methods in more detail.

First, let's look at how the government uses taxation to stabilize the economy. If the economy is growing too fast, inflation becomes a problem. The government can raise taxes to take money out of the economy and lower the inflation rate. But raising taxes can lead to increased unemployment. Therefore, the government has to be very careful to regulate taxes to keep unemployment and inflation in balance.

The second way the government promotes economic stability is through its own expenditures, as I just mentioned. The government has a huge amount of money to spend every year. Some of its decisions about how to spend the money are based on economic conditions in different industries or in different parts of the country. For example, the government may try to help the economy of a certain state by buying goods and services from businesses inside that state.

And a third way the government promotes stability is by controlling the interest rate on the money the government lends to business. If the economy is growing too slowly, the government lowers the interest rate to encourage people to borrow more money—money to start new businesses or expand old businesses. If the economy is growing too fast, the government raises the interest rate. Raising the interest rate will discourage investment in new businesses and in expanding old businesses.

So, these three methods—taxation, expenditure, and setting the interest rate—are the government's main means of maintaining the economy's stability.

Generally speaking, the two major political parties in the United States differ on how big a role they think the government should play in the economy. Members of the Republican Party, the more conservative party, tend to favor fewer taxes, less assistance to the poor, and conditions that help business grow. Members of the Democratic Party, on the other hand, are often more protective of the environment and more understanding of the needs of the old, poor, and sick. Democrats are, consequently, more often in favor of using taxes to pay for social programs and of regulating businesses more closely. The U.S. government's role in the economy can vary because the composition of the government can change every few years. So, the extent to which the government intervenes in the economy changes depending on which party the president is from, which party has a majority in Congress, and how well the president and Congress work together. When the president and Congress do not work together, or when the two parties do not work together, a political gridlock can occur. When this happens, economic growth is affected because businesses are uncertain about interest rates, government regulation, and future sales. But I am getting close to the topic of your next lecture, so I'll stop here.

SECOND LISTENING Page 128

See First Listening B, above.

THIRD LISTENING Page 128

First, let's look at how the government uses taxation to stabilize the economy. If the economy is growing too fast, inflation becomes a problem. The government can raise taxes to take money out of the economy and lower the inflation rate. But raising taxes can lead to increased unemployment. Therefore, the government has to be very careful to regulate taxes to keep unemployment and inflation in balance.

The second way the government promotes economic stability is through its own expenditures, as I just mentioned. The government has a huge amount of money to spend every year. Some of its decisions about how to spend the money are based on economic conditions in different industries or in different parts of the country. For example, the government may try to help the economy of a certain state by buying goods and services from businesses inside that state.

ACCURACY CHECK Page 129

1. What are two examples of intellectual property?
2. What does *free enterprise* mean?
3. What are two examples of the kinds of things the government would be responsible for in a pure capitalist system?
4. Does the lecturer suggest that the role of the government in the economy is greater or less in this century than it was in the last century?
5. What is the government's role in relation to the environment?
6. For what kinds of reasons are some people not able to earn enough money to take care of themselves?
7. Does the lecturer suggest that the government thinks competition is a good or bad thing?
8. Why does the lecturer think the government should regulate banks?
9. What are the three methods that the government uses to maintain economic stability?
10. When the economy is growing too fast, does the government raise or lower the interest rate on money it lends to business?

CHAPTER 14

Government by Constitution

VOCABULARY PREVIEW Page 133

1. Before we begin our discussion of the two important principles of the U.S. government, let's take a look at the three branches that make up the U.S. government.
2. The Congress is primarily responsible for enacting, or making, new laws that are to be followed by the 50 states of the country.
3. The executive branch executes the laws that originate in the legislature.
4. After the president has signed a new law, the executive branch of the government is responsible for seeing that the new law is enforced, or carried out.
5. The judicial branch decides any kind of legal issue that falls under federal jurisdiction.
6. A president who feels very strongly that a new law is wrong may refuse to sign it. Congress can override a presidential veto, but it is a very difficult thing to do.
7. If an investigation shows that illegal activities probably did take place, Congress has the power to impeach, or charge, the person. This did not happen to President Nixon, who resigned before Congress could act.

8. The U.S. Supreme Court, the highest court in the judicial branch, hears cases involving the constitutionality of federal laws enacted by Congress.
9. In 2012, the Court heard arguments that challenged parts of a controversial health-care bill that was narrowly passed by the legislature.
10. The president can check the power of the judicial branch because he is the person who nominates candidates to be federal judges, including those on the Supreme Court.

FIRST LISTENING Page 136

The year 1987 marked the 200th anniversary of the U.S. Constitution. For over 225 years, it has provided the basis for a stable government and has remained basically unchanged. We all know that the United States is a relatively young country. The interesting thing to note, however, is that the U.S. Constitution is actually the oldest written constitution in continuous use in the world. Today we will try to understand the U.S. government better by looking at two important principles provided by the Constitution. These two principles, so important to understanding the U.S. government, were written into the Constitution over 225 years ago and are still in effect today. These two principles are (1) the separation, or division, of powers; and (2) a system of checks and balances. Before we begin our discussion of these two principles, let's first take a look at the three branches that make up the U.S. government.

The year 1987 marked the 200th anniversary of the U.S. Constitution. For over 225 years, it has provided the basis for a stable government and has remained basically unchanged. We all know that the United States is a relatively young country. The interesting thing to note, however, is that the U.S. Constitution is actually the oldest written constitution in continuous use in the world. Today we will try to understand the U.S. government better by looking at two important principles provided by the Constitution. These two principles, so important to understanding the U.S. government, were written into the Constitution over 225 years ago and are still in effect today. These two principles are (1) the separation, or division, of powers; and (2) a system of checks and balances. Before we begin our discussion of these two principles, let's first take a look at the three branches that make up the U.S. government.

To start, the Constitution provides for three branches of government. These three branches are: one, the legislative; two, the executive; and three, the judicial. First, the legislative branch, which is the Congress of the United States: The Congress is primarily responsible for enacting, or making, new laws that are to be followed by the 50 states of the country. Second, the executive branch, which is headed by the president and includes the vice president and the president's cabinet, the members of which he appoints: The executive branch executes the laws that originate in the legislature. By signing the laws, the president actually puts the laws into effect. After the president has signed a new law, the executive branch of the government is responsible for seeing that the new law is enforced, or carried out. Well, these are the first two branches, so we're ready to discuss the third branch. Do you recall what the third branch is? You're right if you said the judicial branch. Well, the judicial branch is responsible for trials and court cases involving individuals or corporations that are accused of breaking a federal law. The judicial branch decides any kind of legal issue that falls under federal jurisdiction. A very important responsibility of the judicial branch is to review cases where someone believes a law may be unconstitutional. In other words, the judicial branch can judge if a particular law is legal, using the Constitution.

From this, you'll already have an idea of what is meant by *separation of powers*. Each branch of the government has its specific role in relation to the country's laws. That is, each branch has its own particular power that is not shared with the other two branches. The writers of the Constitution established this separation of powers to make sure that no single branch of the government could ever have all the power. In addition, to make sure that no single branch could abuse its power or become more powerful than the other two branches, a system of checks and balances was written into the Constitution. This system of checks and balances gives each branch of the government a specific way to check, or limit in some way, the acts of each of the other branches. The best way to understand this system of checks and balances might be to discuss a few examples of how it works.

So first, let's consider how the executive branch can check the power of the legislative branch. The most obvious example is the presidential power of veto. Suppose the president feels that a law enacted by Congress is unwise. A president who feels very strongly that a new law is wrong may refuse to sign it. Now, Congress can override a presidential veto, but it is a very difficult thing to do, so a presidential veto may put an end to this new law forever.

Now let's look at an example of how the legislative branch, or Congress, can check the power of the executive branch. Many of you may have heard of the Watergate scandal, which took place in Washington, D.C., in 1973. In the Watergate affair, President Richard Nixon and his staff were suspected of covering up their involvement with illegal activities. In such a case, where someone in the executive branch is suspected of illegal or unconstitutional activities, the legislative branch is given power by the Constitution to investigate. If the investigation shows that illegal activities probably did take place, Congress has the power to impeach, or charge, the person. A trial could then be held in the Senate to remove that person from office. This, in fact, did not happen to President Nixon because he resigned before the House of Representatives was able to vote on the Articles of Impeachment that were already approved by a House committee.

For another example of checks and balances, let's look at the judicial branch. The U.S. Supreme Court, the highest court in the judicial branch, hears cases involving the constitutionality of federal laws enacted by Congress. For example, in 2012 the Court heard arguments that challenged parts of a controversial health-care bill. This is a bill that was narrowly passed by the legislature, that is, Congress, only after a huge political struggle. It was signed into law by the president, President Obama. In this case, the Court found that most of the provisions of the bill were constitutional.

You might wonder what check the executive or the legislative branch has on the judicial branch. Well, first of all, the president is the person who nominates candidates to be federal judges, including those on the Supreme Court. Because there are only nine Supreme Court justices, the opportunity to nominate even one candidate for the Supreme Court can be an opportunity to change the balance of power on the Court itself. However, once the president nominates a candidate, the Senate must approve the choice. This provides the legislative branch a check on both the executive and judicial branches. Any candidate who is nominated for the Supreme Court by the president can expect to be questioned very closely by members of the Senate. They will ask questions about his or her legal record and opinion on such issues as abortion, gun control, separation of church and state, and so on. Most people who are nominated for the Supreme Court by the president are confirmed, that is, they are approved, by the Senate, but not all.

Under the Constitution, each branch of the government, then, must answer to the other two branches. Therefore, ideally, no one branch can exercise too much power or abuse the power that it has. From time to time, one branch of the government can seem to be more powerful than one or both of the other branches, but this does not usually last a long time. In the long run, each branch carefully guards its own power, and all three branches check and balance one another's power.

SECOND LISTENING Page 137

See First Listening B, above.

THIRD LISTENING Page 137

You might wonder what check the executive or the legislative branch has on the judicial branch. Well, first of all, the president is the person who nominates candidates to be federal judges, including those on the Supreme Court. Because there are only nine Supreme Court justices, the opportunity to nominate even one candidate for the Supreme Court can be an opportunity to change the balance of power on the Court itself. However, once the president nominates a candidate, the Senate must approve the choice. This provides the legislative branch a check on both the executive and judicial branches. Any candidate who is nominated for the Supreme Court by the president can expect to be questioned very closely by members of the Senate. They will ask questions about his or her legal record and opinion on such issues as abortion, gun control, separation of church and state, and so on. Most people who are nominated for the Supreme Court by the president are confirmed, that is, they are approved, by the Senate, but not all.

ACCURACY CHECK Page 138

1. How is the U.S. Constitution different from all other constitutions in the world?
2. What are the three branches of the U.S. government?
3. What is the responsibility of the executive branch of the government?
4. Who is the head of the executive branch of the government?
5. What is meant by "checks and balances"?
6. What is meant by the "veto power" of the president?
7. What normally happens if the president vetoes a law?
8. How can the legislative branch of government—the Congress—check the power of the executive branch?
9. What might have happened to President Nixon had he not resigned?
10. How does the legislative branch have an opportunity to check the power of the judicial branch?

CHAPTER 15

Common Law and the Jury System

VOCABULARY PREVIEW Page 142

1. The basic principle of the U.S. legal system is that an accused person is innocent until proven guilty.
2. In deciding a case, under civil law, the judge consults a code, a complex set of written laws.
3. The judge also decides what sentence the defendant, that is, the person accused of wrongdoing, will be given if guilty.
4. To determine the defendant's guilt under common law, the judge also considers the precedent set by other court decisions.
5. Very often, it is not the judge who gives a verdict, but the jury, a group of six or twelve ordinary citizens, who decide the defendant's guilt or innocence and, in civil cases, how much money should be paid in damages.
6. In either civil or criminal trials, the jury hears testimony from people with information about the case; these people are called *witnesses*.
7. Criminal trials are ones where the government, representing the public, prosecutes individuals accused of committing a crime.
8. The defendant in a criminal case does not have to testify; it is the government's job to prove the person is guilty.
9. The reason that the degree of proof is much higher in a criminal trial is that a person's freedom and even life can be taken away if he or she is convicted, that is, found guilty, of a crime.
10. Michael Jackson's doctor was convicted of involuntary manslaughter, meaning he caused his patient's death without intending to.
11. Often the defendant is allowed to plea-bargain only if he or she also cooperates with the prosecutor in bringing other criminals to justice.

FIRST LISTENING Page 145

To start out today, let me say that the legal system of a country—that is, its system of justice—reflects the history and culture of the country just as much as the other topics we have discussed so far. When we start to discuss law, courts, trials, and concepts of innocence and guilt, there are some important questions that come up. These are questions it might be interesting to think about before talking more about the legal system in the United States. Because people from different cultures might answer these questions differently, let's take a few minutes and see how you would answer these for your country.

Now, the first question: Is it better for a dozen guilty people to go free rather than to punish one innocent person unfairly, or is it sometimes necessary to punish innocent people so that no guilty person escapes justice? Here's another question for you: Is a person guilty until proven innocent, or does it seem more logical to you that a person is innocent until proven guilty? I suspect that the average American would say that it is better to let a dozen guilty people go free rather than to punish one innocent person unfairly. The basic principle of the U.S. legal system is that an accused person is innocent until proven guilty.

Now that you've had a chance to think about these philosophical questions, let's begin by looking at the U.S. legal system in terms of what makes it different from legal systems in many other countries. Um. First, we'll look at common law and how it differs from civil law as practiced in many countries in the world. Then we'll look more closely at the jury system, a system that many foreigners find quite curious. Then I'll make a few concluding remarks about plea bargaining—the way that most cases are settled. I think, then, that you'll have a better understanding of how the United States' approach to law is different from that in your country.

Although different from many legal systems, the U.S. system of justice is not unique. Uh, we have to remember that it is based on a system brought over by the first settlers from England. At that time, there were two basic legal systems in Europe: common law, practiced in Great Britain, and civil law, practiced in other European countries. To simplify greatly, civil law depends on a written code of laws. In deciding a case, under civil law, the judge consults this code, a complex set of written laws, to decide whether the defendant is innocent or guilty and, if guilty, what sentence the defendant, that is, the accused person, will be given. On the other hand, common law, generally practiced in some form in English-speaking countries including the United States, has developed case by case. To determine the defendant's guilt under common law, the judge considers the precedent set by other court decisions as well as considering written law. In deciding a case under common law, then, the judge looks at what other judges have decided in similar cases in the past. So the judge is guided not only by a legal code but also by previous court decisions. And very often, it is not the judge who gives a verdict, but the jury.

The U.S. Constitution guarantees the right to trial by jury. A jury is a group of six or twelve ordinary citizens. The jury hears testimony in either civil or criminal trials and reaches a verdict. A civil trial is one that deals with disputes between private individuals, often involving contracts or property rights. Criminal trials are ones where the government, representing the public, prosecutes individuals accused of committing a crime. In a civil trial, the jury decides which side is right and how much money should be paid in damages. In a criminal trial, the jury decides guilt or innocence.

Now I'd like to discuss two other big differences, in this case between criminal and civil trials. First, the defendant in a criminal case does not have to testify. It is the government's job to prove the person is guilty, not the defendant's job to prove he or she is innocent. In a civil trial, the defendant must testify. Second, for a jury to convict a person in a criminal case, they must believe the person guilty "beyond a reasonable doubt." In other words, the government must present a high degree of proof. The jury in a civil trial decides which side has presented more evidence to support its case. This is a lower degree of proof than "reasonable doubt." The reason that the degree of proof is much higher in a criminal trial is that a person's freedom and even life can be taken away if he or she is convicted, that is, found guilty, of a crime.

The judge at a trial and the jury have very different responsibilities. The judge's main responsibility is to see that the trial is conducted according to the law. Part of this responsibility is to exclude irrelevant remarks and questions by lawyers and witnesses and to decide what kind of evidence the jurors can or can't hear. The jury, on the other hand, decides whether they believe the testimony they hear and whether the evidence presented to them seems true and reasonable.

Most of you know who Michael Jackson was, but you may not know that his doctor was convicted in a criminal trial of "involuntary manslaughter." This means the jury found him guilty of causing Jackson's death without intending to. After the criminal trial, Jackson's family brought civil suits, mainly against the entertainment company that was investing in and promoting a tour Jackson was preparing for at the time of his death. As is often the case, the civil suits may have less to do with gaining money and more to do with a desire to see that justice is done. Because the doctor in the criminal trial received a relatively light sentence, the family may feel there is justice in holding the entertainment company responsible for encouraging Jackson to pursue the tour when the company probably knew he was ill.

Most people in the United States favor the jury system. However, it is also often criticized. Some people criticize the way juries are selected. Some believe that juries make decisions based on emotion rather than facts or that jurors don't always have the education or background to understand complex legal issues. One serious problem is that if the required number of jurors cannot agree on a decision—what is called a "hung jury"—the law requires a new trial with a new jury.

I don't want to leave you with the impression that every legal case is tried in court with a jury in the United States. In fact, only about 20 percent of legal cases actually reach the courts. What happens is that, in civil cases, most often the two sides settle their dispute out of court through their lawyers. And in criminal cases, very often a person accused of a particular crime will plea-bargain. What actually happens in plea bargaining is that the accused person pleads guilty to a less serious crime. Why is this allowed to happen? This is allowed to happen because there is a large number of civil and criminal cases. If all of these cases went to trial, the courts would be very crowded. If an accused person agrees to plead guilty, there will, of course, be no trial in court. This saves the state time and money. Also, often the defendant is allowed to plea-bargain only if he or she also cooperates with the prosecutor in bringing other criminals to justice. For the accused person, the sentence might be less severe than if he or she goes to trial and is found guilty.

My discussion of the U.S. justice system might lead you to believe that not many people end up going to prison in the United States. In fact, the opposite is true. The United States has more people in prison than any other country. You've heard of challenges the culture faces in previous lectures. The high number of people imprisoned is just one more challenge that the country needs to face.

SECOND LISTENING Page 146

See First Listening, above.

THIRD LISTENING Page 146

The U.S. Constitution guarantees the right to trial by jury. A jury is a group of six or twelve ordinary citizens. The jury hears testimony in either civil or criminal trials and reaches a verdict. A civil trial is one that deals with disputes between private individuals, often involving contracts or property rights. Criminal trials are ones where the government, representing the public, prosecutes individuals accused of committing a crime. In a civil trial, the jury decides which side is right and how much money should be paid in damages. In a criminal trial, the jury decides guilt or innocence.

Now I'd like to discuss two other big differences, in this case between criminal and civil trials. First, the defendant in a criminal case does not have to testify. It is the government's job to prove the person is guilty, not the defendant's job to prove he or she is innocent. In a civil trial, the defendant must testify. Second, for a jury to convict a person in a criminal case, they must believe the person guilty "beyond a reasonable doubt."

In other words, the government must present a high degree of proof. The jury in a civil trial decides which side has presented more evidence to support its case. This is a lower degree of proof than "reasonable doubt." The reason that the degree of proof is much higher in a criminal trial is that a person's freedom and even life can be taken away if he or she is convicted, that is, found guilty, of a crime.

ACCURACY CHECK Page 147

1. Under the U.S. legal system, is an accused person guilty until proven innocent or innocent until proven guilty?
2. On which legal system is the U.S. legal system based?
3. How many people are normally on a jury?
4. In a civil case involving property or contracts, who normally decides who is at fault and how much, if any, must be paid in damages?
5. In which kind of trial is the defendant required to testify, civil or criminal?
6. In which kind of trial must the degree of proof be higher, civil or criminal?
7. What is a judge's main responsibility at a trial?
8. What is the jury's main responsibility?
9. What percentage of all legal cases, both civil and criminal, are settled out of court?
10. Why does the state so often allow accused people to plea-bargain?

Videoscripts

UNIT 1 VIDEO

Cowboys in North America

Thank you for having me here tonight and thank all of you for coming. The cowboy basically breaks into four different types: the *vaquero*, which is the traditional roots of the cowboy in North America; and then the *buckaroo* region, which is west of the Rockies; *cowboys* are kind of east of the Rockies; and *cow punchers* are Arizona, New Mexico, Oklahoma, Texas.

You know, I find it amazing I guess in the U.S., that you know, here we live in one of the most high-tech, richest countries in the world, and these people have been able to hold on to their culture, because they love the lifestyle. I mean, a lot of these guys have done other jobs or tried other jobs. Merlin told me that—I asked him if he'd ever worked as anything other than a cowboy and he said yeah, he'd worked at the railroad for one day and he quit; and he worked at a goldmine for one day and he quit.

So, you know, a typical single guy at one of these ranches makes anywhere from eight to twelve hundred dollars a month. They get housing and three meals a day. But they're working seventy to a hundred hours a week. So, when you do the math on it, it's, you know, three to four dollars an hour. And you better love what you're doing. But I find it amazing that there are some cultures that really almost disappear within one or two generations when they're exposed to progress or so-called progress. And these people have for a hundred and fifty years basically continued to do what they've done.

A lot of the gear they use hasn't changed. I mean, what it takes to cowboy is good horse skills, skill with a rope, and a real understanding on how to work cattle on a horse. And you can tell that these guys love the outdoors, I mean, and love being by themselves, love working in these environments even though, you know, some of these guys, uh, Ronnie told me that in the winter, sometimes they've worked when it's fifty below, you know, ten hours, on a horse, fifty below. And you know, he says, it's cold, but you can live in it.

And you don't see a lot of women working as cowboys, and they don't mind being described as cowboys; it's kind of a working title of what they do. You know, generally you see young girls, women that are past child-bearing age because, you know, family's like the most central thing in these people's lives. I mean, that's everything to them.

This is a father and son up in Oregon. And these kids, I mean, kids are very impressive on these ranches, I mean, they give them, the kids have a lot of duties on a ranch, a working ranch. And kids get to see the full life cycle of, you know, spring, summer, fall, and winter.

Since the fencing in of the ranges back in the 1890s, everybody has predicted—called the cowboys, you know, a vanishing breed, last of a breed, dying breed. And I think it's really an evolving breed. It's a business, ranching's a business like any other business, and businesses that are determined to survive evolve, and so they found efficiencies. But still, the cheapest way to raise cattle is by feeding them grass, and you're not going to do that on a four-wheeler on 1.3 million acres. You're going to do it using guys like this. Thank you very much for coming.

UNIT 2 VIDEO

Through the Eyes of a Critic

I brought some things from Galapagos as well. This is a trip where I couldn't bring family. I'm a married man. My wife's name is Monica. We work together to a large extent. We have two children—two boys, Aiden and Anskar, six and nine. On this trip, they couldn't come. And you miss them a lot, obviously. Most trips they can't come.

So, when I got back home, everybody was fast asleep. It was early, early morning. I just opened the door to our house. And I walked in. And I made myself a cup of coffee. And the dog greeted me, Douglas. Everybody else is asleep. And then I felt a little bit sorry for myself. It's like I'm missing out on so much. I see a lot. I experience a lot. But still, I miss maybe the most important thing, and that's my kids! You know.

So I was sitting there, drinking my coffee, you know, doing this with the dog. And then little Anskar, the oldest boy, came out, and he said, "Dad! You're home!" in his pajamas. And he hugged me, and he was sitting in my lap, and then said, "How was your assignment?"

I said, "Good, but never mind that. I'm home now darling. This is so good to see you. How are you?"

"Did you get any good pictures?"

And I said, "Yeah, well," I said.

"Can you show me?"

So I was sitting down with a computer showing him this land iguana with this Galapagos mockingbird, talking about this very interesting sort of collaborative effort, the bird rinsing parasites. The big lizard, that's a vegetarian, is actually walking through the vegetation, scaring up insects that the mockingbird can eat, etc. It's a nice symbiotic relationship. And he was like fascinated by this, Anskar.

And he said, "Well this is wonderful, Dad." And he was really interested. We looked at the sea lions, and we looked at all sorts of things. And he was he was sharing it, and it was so beautiful. It was like the best. You know the frigatebirds they can actually tell me when the orcas come out, come up to breathe because they will be, as you know, they're like scavengers, opportunists. And they will fly over the surface. And when there's a big predator, they will get very close. And they will hover. And the big orca will come up perhaps. And I told him about that, and he was like, "Wow!"

But when we came to this set of photographs, he, especially here, he said, "Dad," this little boy, "These are your best photographs ever."

And I said, "Well, gee, thanks."

And, "Yes, definitely," he said. "Definitely."

And I'm curious, you know, why, what this little boy, "Why do you think these pictures are better than any other pictures?"

And he said, "Well, don't you see? They're... the quality."

"Yeah, well, I do. I've done my best, you know. This is a marine iguana. And, yeah, I was sneaking up to it. And I was illuminating it with a soft box. And it took me ages because they're quite skittish and..."

"Ah, okay. Mmm." Well, but when we came to this picture, he's like, "This is it. This is the best."

And then I hugged him and said, "I love you, you know. Tell me why."

And he said, "Don't you understand?" (You know, like "*idiot*" you know, almost.) "But he's giving you a high five!"

UNIT 3 VIDEO

My Journey in the Muslim World

I was raised in a show-biz family in Manhattan and Malibu, California, and it was an exciting life full of cutting-edge artistic culture and a lot of freedom. So much more. And I left that life to be engaged in what's happening in the world and to travel far and deeply as a photojournalist.

This book is not meant to represent all Muslims everywhere. I'm not an expert on Islam. And it's just what I saw and experienced during my travels in these places. So here I hope to share a wider view of a group of people much misunderstood, especially since 9/11.

Now this is America. This is post 9/11, Muslim America. And it was a great time to kind of for me to revisit America. It was just a very, very classic immigrant experience, I think. I'm not Muslim, I'm not, you know, but they reminded me of my family. You know, a little bit of the old country, a lot of the new country, in this very rich American mix.

This is Dearborn, Michigan. And these are Ryazan dolls, and they're an alternative, Islamic alternative to Barbie.

And this lady fled the civil war in Lebanon. This is Dearborn. And you know Muslim Americans, like all Americans, have fled civil war, dictatorship, economic hardship. I mean, it's just like everybody else. But they were under a certain amount of pressure at that time. And *National Geographic* asked me to go out and see how they were doing and to describe their lives visually.

This is Latif Muhammad, and Florence Muhammad is reflected in the mirror with her granddaughter, Kelly. And they're in a place called New Medinah, Mississippi, which is near Sumrall and it's a Muslim, mostly Muslim village of farmers. And they're mainstream Sunni Muslims.

And this is Zulia Martinez. She is Mexican-American convert to Islam. More and more Hispanic-Americans are converting to Islam. This is in Houston. And this is at a baptism party for one of her Catholic relatives.

This is just the end of the day after a fair in Dearborn. Rainstorm.

And this is Graterford, Pennsylvania, and it's a maximum-security prison. There are about 3,200 prisoners here and 800 of them are Muslim. Most of them are African-American. Most of them are mainstream Muslims, and they were incredibly protective of me.

This is actually a Zoroastrian tradition. This is Los Angeles. This is the beach in Los Angeles where I used to swim, you know, daily as a teenager. These are Persian-Americans, Iranian-Americans, and they jump over fires on their New Year to cast off the bad luck of the previous year, you know, for good luck in the next year.

UNIT 4 VIDEO

The Story of Hiram Bingham

When I was eighteen, I was heading off to college, and for my birthday, my eighteenth birthday, my dad gave me a T-shirt. And on the front of the T-shirt was this, Machu Picchu, the site we're here to talk about and celebrate tonight.

This is an image from 1911. And I had heard of Machu Picchu before, but I didn't recognize the guy on the back. This was a T-shirt my dad had picked up at the Peabody Museum of Yale, which is where Bingham eventually stored a lot of his artifacts. And this was Hiram Bingham. I'd never seen his image before, but he's striking. I mean, he's very tall; he's six foot four. He's handsome. He wears jodhpurs like the best of them.

And so I got into college, I eventually came to understand why it was very exciting to go to Yale University where Bingham himself studied and where he did a lot of his work later on. But I regret to say that I did not end up becoming an archaeologist. I had, as many people do their freshman or sophomore year, a crisis, of sorts and started doing literature and history instead. But it brought me back to Latin America. And my senior year, as I was getting ready to write a senior essay, my advisor said to me, "Well why don't you write on Yale's Indiana Jones?" And, he had me at that.

Hiram Bingham, in a word, was a whirlwind. He was a force of nature. He was smart. He was deeply ambitious. He was a good organizer. He wasn't very good at staying in one place. He went to Phillips Academy in Andover and then on to Yale, where he was able to make a life for himself. He realized that he was very good at teaching his fellow students. He was extremely poor. They were extremely wealthy. He liked to read books. They liked to get notes from people who liked to read books. And he realized that he could be a teacher. However, it was very hard for him to do so because there still was a barrier of both wealth and prestige at Yale that he couldn't quite break through. Much like many of us fear and have in my case moved back to our parents' house after college, he moved back to Honolulu to be with his parents.

However, he had also by then started to think about someone who would change his life and allow him to do many things that he wanted. He'd fallen in love with Alfreda Mitchel. And Alfreda was a kind, warm, and generous person, that Bingham had met in his senior year of college. And with Alfreda they got married soon after. They would have seven sons. They came to live in very large houses in Cambridge where Bingham went to the University of Harvard, Harvard University for his doctorate, and then in New Haven.

Now, his decision to study history at Harvard was actually a fairly radical one for at the time, because he wasn't doing European history, he wasn't doing U.S. history. He was doing Latin American history, and he believed that he was the first person to ever be hired specifically to teach Latin American history in the U.S. Bingham believed that the U.S. had a future in the region that would need experts like himself in politics and economics and history to lead. After a few years of teaching, he found himself getting anxious at being chained to teaching undergraduates, and he instead decided to embark on a new phase of his life and career as an explorer.

UNIT 5 VIDEO

Demon Fish

They can strike out of the darkness without warning. There's something about that that has us hardwired to be terrified. You would never know if a shark is coming. That, I think, both makes them scary and allows people to exaggerate the threat associated with them. Having this perception that sharks are targeting us, of course, makes it much more acceptable to target them.

I'm thrilled to talk to you about this book and I thought to begin I wanted to explain a little about how I decided to really explore this territory to begin with. You know, I've actually, I've spent the vast majority of my reporting career here in Washington covering politicians. Many people said it was obviously a natural transition from politicians to sharks.

So you saw the first recorded shark attack in history in the late 1500s comes from a Portuguese sailor who had the misfortune to fall overboard and couldn't be saved by his companions. And then if you go, you know, if you look forward there are just many tales of sharks circling around different ships and, you know, sailors, either you know basically almost kind of like a wage dispute and like a labor dispute that they complained that the captains couldn't care less if they ended up in the water with sharks and things like that and, you know, time and time again they were seen as this threat.

But sharks were still seen as a fairly abstract threat, and what changed in actually the United States and also a few other countries were when beach goers started interacting with sharks. And so, for example, this is the front page from *the Philadelphia Inquirer* referring to a series of shark strikes off the New Jersey shore in 1916. This in some ways was the inspiration for the movie *Jaws*. Again, people had been familiar with sharks, but they did not know to, you know, to what extent it could be, you know, potentially something that would come up when they went to the beach.

And so when you had four people who were killed within a span of twelve days, that was the moment when you really saw people think of sharks as, you know, a threat at any point. You know, saying "Government to aid fight to stamp out the shark horror," is that, in fact, Woodrow Wilson, who was president at the time and started his political career in New Jersey, actually came under attack for the fact that he did nothing to halt these shark strikes. And that's one thing that you see time and time again: that people somehow think that this is something that you could hold politicians accountable for.

There are actually a couple of academics, including one at Princeton, who recently found that he in fact suffered a political penalty in New Jersey, and particularly the three counties that were most affected by the drop in tourism. And so it was just interesting to see how voters really did punish Woodrow Wilson and thought that, you know, there was something he could do to ensure that they could be safe at sea.

Sources

8: "Crowding our Planet," by Thomas Hayden, NationalGeographic.com, **18:** "Climate Change Creating Millions of 'Eco Refugees,' UN Warns," by Stefan Lovgren, National Geographic News, November 18, 2005, **28:** "Boomtowns: China's Instant Cities," by Peter Hessler, *National Geographic*, June 2007, **40:** "Machisma: Brazil's Girl Power," by Cynthia Gorney, *National Geographic*, September 2011, **50:** "The Geography of Religion," by Shelley Sperry, NationalGeographic.com, **58:** *African Ceremonies*, Vol. 1, Vol. 2, by Carol Beckwith and Angela Fisher, **70:** "Marseille's Melting Pot," by Christopher Dickey, *National Geographic*, March 2012, **78:** "The Singapore Solution," by Mark Jacobson, *National Geographic*, January 2010, **86:** "Green China: Can China Go Green?" by Bill McKibben, *National Geographic*, June 2011, **99:** "China's Middle Class: Gilded Age, Gilded Cage," by Leslie T. Chang, *National Geographic*, May 2008, **107:** "U21 Ranking of National Higher Education Systems," Universitas 21, University of Melbourne, May 2012, **130:** "Bhutan's Enlightened Experiment," by Brook Larmer, *National Geographic*, March 2008, **139:** "The World According to Rome," by T. R. Reid, *National Geographic*, August 1997.

Images

Inside front cover: Robb Kendrick/National Geographic Stock, Monika Klum/National Geographic Stock, Christopher Heaney, Michael Lionstar, **1:** Aaron Mccoy/Photolibrary Collection/Getty Images, **2–3:** Ira Block/National Geographic Stock, **8:** Julio Lopez Saguar/Photographer's Choice Library/Getty Images, **9:** Steve Raymer/National Geographic Stock, **10:** FPG/Archive Photos/Getty Images, **18:** Jonathan Irish/National Geographic Stock, **19:** Jim Simmen/Photographer's Choice/Getty Images, **20–21:** Lynn Johnson/National Geographic Stock, **29:** TAO Images/Getty Images, **30–31:** Chris Johns/National Geographic Stock, **31:** Paul Chesley/National Geographic Stock, **33:** Charles D'Emery/National Geographic Stock, **34–35:** Rich Reid/National Geographic Stock, **41:** Michael Poehlman/Photographer's Choice/Getty Images, **42–43:** Pete Mcbride/National Geographic Stock, **50:** Thomas J. Abercrombie/National Geographic Stock, **52–53:** Melissa Farlow/National Geographic Stock, **58:** Abdelhak Senna/AFP/Getty Images, **59:** Frances Linzee Gordon/Lonely Planet Images/Getty Images, **59:** Martin Harvey/Peter Arnold Collection/Getty Images, **60–61:** Mattias Klum, **61:** Joel Sartore/National Geographic Stock, **63:** NASA's Earth Observatory/NOAA/DOD, **64–65:** Wu Kaixiang/Xinhua/Photoshot/Newscom, **71:** Franco Origlia/Contributor/Getty Images, **72–73:** TEK IMAGE/Science Photo Library/TEK IMAGE, **78:** David Mclain/National Geographic Stock, **79:** Scott S. Warren/National Geographic Stock, **80–81:** China Photos/Stringer/Getty Images, **86:** Greg Girard/National Geographic Stock, **87:** Greg Girard/National Geographic Stock, **88–89:** Spencer Platt/Getty Images, **89:** Bill Pugliano/Stringer/Getty Images, **91:** Grant Faint/Photographer's Choice/Getty Images, **92–93:** Joel Sartore/National Geographic Stock, **99:** Randy Olson/National Geographic Stock, **100:** Justin Guariglia/National Geographic Stock, **101:** kristian sekulic/Vetta/Getty Images, **109:** Jade/Blend Images Collection/Getty Images, **117:** Annie Griffiths/National Geographic Stock, **118–119:** Mike Theiss/National Geographic Stock, **119:** Apic/Hulton Archive/Getty Images, **121:** Hisham Ibrahim/Photographer's Choice/Getty Images, **122:** Randy Olson/National Geographic Stock, **130:** Pete Ryan/National Geographic Stock, **131:** Paul Chesley/National Geographic Stock, **132–133:** National Geographic/Getty Images, **139:** De Agostini/Getty Images, **140:** Taylor S. Kennedy/National Geographic Stock, **141:** Steve Hamblin/Alamy, **148:** Getty Images, **150–151:** Gerard Soury/Oxford Scientific/Getty Images, **151:** Topical Press Agency/Stringer/Getty Images